T0073137

Big Data for Big Decisions

Building a data-driven organization (DDO) is an enterprise-wide initiative that may consume and lock up resources for the long term. Understandably, any organization considering such an initiative would insist on a roadmap and business case to be prepared and evaluated prior to approval. This book presents a step-by-step methodology in order to create a roadmap and business case, and provides a narration of the constraints and experiences of managers who have attempted the setting up of DDOs. The emphasis is on the big decisions – the key decisions that influence 90% of business outcomes – starting from decision first and reengineering the data to the decisions process-chain and data governance, so as to ensure the right data are available at the right time, every time.

Investing in artificial intelligence and data-driven decision making are now being considered a survival necessity for organizations to stay competitive. While every enterprise aspires to become 100% data-driven and every Chief Information Officer (CIO) has a budget, Gartner estimates over 80% of all analytics projects fail to deliver intended value.

Most CIOs think a data-driven organization is a distant dream, especially while they are still struggling to explain the value from analytics. They know a few isolated successes, or a one-time leveraging of big data for decision making does not make an organization data-driven. As of now, there is no precise definition for data-driven organization or what qualifies an organization to call itself data-driven. Given the hype in the market for big data, analytics and AI, every CIO has a budget for analytics, but very little clarity on where to begin or how to choose and prioritize the analytics projects. Most end up investing in a visualization platform like Tableau or QlikView, which in essence is an improved version of their BI dashboard that the organization had invested into not too long ago. The most important stakeholders, the decision-makers, are rarely kept in the loop while choosing analytics projects.

This book provides a fail-safe methodology for assured success in deriving intended value from investments into analytics. It is a practitioners' handbook for creating a step-by-step transformational roadmap prioritizing the big data for the big decisions, the 10% of decisions that influence 90% of business outcomes, and delivering material improvements in the quality of decisions, as well as measurable value from analytics investments.

The acid test for a data-driven organization is when all the big decisions, especially top-level strategic decisions, are taken based on data and not on the collective gut feeling of the decision makers in the organization.

Big Data for Big Decisions

Building a Data-Driven Organization

Krishna Pera

CRC Press
Taylor & Francis Group
Boca Raton London New York

CRC Press is an imprint of the
Taylor & Francis Group, an **informa** business

AN AUERBACH BOOK

Cover image: Shutterstock.com

First edition published 2023
by CRC Press
6000 Broken Sound Parkway NW, Suite 300, Boca Raton, FL 33487-2742

and by CRC Press
4 Park Square, Milton Park, Abingdon, Oxon, OX14 4RN

CRC Press is an imprint of Taylor & Francis Group, LLC

ISBN: 978-1-032-34281-8 (hbk)
ISBN: 978-1-032-01724-2 (pbk)
ISBN: 978-1-003-32134-7 (ebk)

DOI: 10.1201/9781003321347

Typeset in Garamond
by SPi Technologies India Pvt Ltd (Straive)

Contents

Acknowledgments

This book may not have been possible without the support, encouragement, inputs, and advice from a number of highly accomplished professionals.

I would like to acknowledge the debt I owe to the following people in the USA:

- James Taylor (Author, and the leading authority on digital decisioning)
- My fellow alumni from the Indian Institute of Management (IIM), Bangalore; Sonal Singh (Principal Product Manager – SS&C Intralinks at SAS), and Huzura Singh Siviya (SVP – Strategy, Digital and Innovation at Wells Fargo)
- Scott Sobel (Senior Data Scientist at Voyageworks)

…and to the following people in India

- Rajiv Gupta (Managing Director & Senior Partner at Boston Consulting Group)
- Sridhar Ganesh (Author, executive coach, former MD of Adrenalin eSystems Ltd. & former Director HR of Murugappa Group)
- My fellow alumni from the Indian Institute of Management (IIM), Bangalore: Abhilash Lal (Finance Consultant and Independent Director), Amardeep Lakhtakia (AI & Data Science Leader and Influencer), Dinesh Tiwari (Managing Director at Broad Peak Capital Advisors LLP), Rajbir Singh (CEO, i4 Mentors Foundation), Vasan Subramanian (Author and former CTO of Accel Partners), Vikrant Pande (Popular author & Partner at Semco Style Institute India)
- Srikanth Srinivasan (VP and Head of Membership at NASSCOM)

I would like to thank the following accomplished women-in-tech, for their inputs and first review of some of the chapters:

- Sirisha Pera (TCS), Vanipriya (Exotel), Harika T (L&T)

I would like to thank my editor at Taylor & Francis, John Wyzalek, for his guidance and patience, and the consulting editor, Nigel Wyatt.

Some of the chapters in this book are based on a series of articles published by the author in Data-Science-Central between 2016 and 2019; I would like to thank Kurt Cagle, and the editorial team at Data Science Central for their support, and more importantly for reprint permission.

And finally, I would like to thank my family for their support and for tolerating me for over 12 months while I worked on this book.

Author

With over three decades of experience in IT and business transformation consulting, **Krishna Pera** has worked across industry verticals. He has been Head of Global Business Services for a Singapore-listed $34bn commodity trading company, and prior to that he was the Chief Operating Officer of a knowledge-process outsourcing company specializing in digital content solutions for global information media companies. During his career he has set up and scaled several businesses from scratch, and successfully turned around a mid-size services company by operationally integrating acquired companies. He currently runs a consulting firm specializing in data-driven organization and analytics strategy, in addition to mentoring and investing in tech startups.

Krishna Pera has pioneering experience in setting-up and scaling Shared Services Centers, Captives, and Offshore Development Centers for Fortune-500 companies, including the first ever in a validated environment. Decades of experience managing implementations and global roll outs of various enterprise technologies has provided him with a unique understanding of strategic information lifecycle management in transnational firms, as well as every conceivable issue faced by managers in making informed decisions.

Krishna Pera has a postgraduate degree in business management from IIM, Bangalore, and graduate degrees in law and engineering.

Introduction

Topics Covered in this Chapter

1. Inception	Context for the book
2. Data-driven organization: The stakeholders expectations	A view of the Data-driven organization as seen from stakeholders" eyes.
3. Setting up a data-driven organization: Constraints & experiences	Constraints & the need for a step-by-step methodology to create a roadmap and business-case.
4. What this book covers	Broad outline of what this book covers.

I.1 Inception

A decade back, I attended a series of shared services conferences. Almost every speaker and every delegate I met mentioned that they were either setting up, or planning to set up, a center of excellence (CoE) for analytics. There were at least a couple of mentions of the phrase "data-driven organization" (DDO) in every panel discussion. Considering the conference was supposed to be on a completely different and unrelated subject, the popularity and the hype around data-driven organization was quite an eye-opener.

During these conferences, I spoke to several people running technology shared services; a number of them had a mandate and a budget to set up the CoE, while the rest were internally discussing the feasibility. As I came to understand, while an analytics CoE was relatively better understood, building a data-driven organization was just a distant dream. No one, including those who came from consulting companies, had any idea how they were going to go about doing it.

I tried asking: what exactly would a data-driven organization mean? Would 100% of all decisions across the organization be completely data-driven? Were they

DOI: 10.1201/9781003321347-1

planning to focus on CEO level decisions? Most people had no idea; a few mentioned they were working with Big 3, Big 4 consultants; so, the response to my question, if any, had to come from them.

In the meantime, I was also asked to explore setting up a CoE for analytics and to make a business case for a DDO at my own place of work. While I did have some prior experience setting up a center of excellence for business intelligence and business performance analytics, a DDO was not something I ever worked on. The phrase itself was brand new; and to my mind, a DDO had to be a lot more than just another analytics CoE. So, over the next few months, I read every book and every article written on the subject. I also spoke to several senior consultants from the industry and to a few from the new breed of specialized analytics services companies. I had three specific questions:

1. If you were to build a data-driven organization, what would be its structure?
   a. How would you define it? How would you describe its functions and processes?
   b. What makes it unique and more efficient?
2. How does one transform a regular, everyday organization into a DDO?
   a. What will be the roadmap?
   b. How does one build a business case for such an exercise?
3. How do you make sure the DDO prioritizes and supports the big ticket decisions; the decisions which influence the core business outcomes?

None of them, not one, could provide a roadmap for building a DDO, let alone a method to create a business case. Instead, I ended up with 101 diverse definitions for a DDO: each fancier than the last. Also noticeable was undue stress, an overemphasis, on what everyone called a prerequisite for building a DDO; the data-driven culture.

Most articles and white papers listed a series of generic steps: drive analytics from the top, treat data as an asset, hire data scientists, hire a chief data officer (CDO), build data-driven culture, use appropriate technology, democratize, and enable access to data.

While I sincerely believe the authors of such whitepapers mean well, and these generic steps listed above are logical, they are still vague and do not exactly provide an action plan, or a set of tools and templates for building a DDO. In the end, I was even more confused than I was when I started. I made a resolution to keep moving forward, and depend on the one person I trust most: me.

Here is a summary of the conclusions I reached at the end of the exercise:

- There was no book on the market that comprehensively laid down a step-by-step methodology for creating a DDO; a practitioners' handbook. There was no academic paper that laid down a methodology for creating a roadmap for a DDO; a scientific, logical method for transformation in the shortest possible time. So, I might have to create my own path.

- There were no benchmarks as to when exactly an organization could call itself fully, 100% data-driven. There were no prescribed tests, or audits.
- While there was no dearth of maturity models for "analytics as a process", somewhat similar to capability maturity model integration (CMMi) models, none of them were detailed enough. None of them provided measurable parameters that could help organizations clearly determine their level of maturity, or if they had completely mastered the concept of a DDO.
- There was an unspoken understanding in the market: *moderately extensive use of analytics, and a reasonably robust process for analytics, marks a mature to highly-mature DDO.*
- However, there was no measure or a method for understanding "the approximate dollar value" created through use of analytics or data-driven decisions, and I needed this measure for creating a business case.

Most organizations have a small part of the organization extensively using analytics; does this really qualify the enterprise to call itself a DDO?

To my mind, a mature DDO must be adding a *substantial (dollar) value* to the top and bottom-line of the organization, and any maturity model should establish a clear and undeniable co-relationship between the maturity of the DDO and the dollar value created – either through additional profits generated, or by saving direct or indirect costs.

In conclusion, the consolidated wisdom from a variety of sources, including the books and research articles published, and the advice and input from consultants, was not sufficient to help me create a roadmap and a business case for a DDO. I had no choice but create my own path, from scratch.

I.2 Data-Driven Organization: The Stakeholders' Expectations

While there are several diverse definitions for a data-driven organization, I believe the best method would be to clearly lay down who the stakeholders are, and what they expect from the DDO. Most articles I read concur that "stakeholders" includes the executive management, data science team, and the customer-facing team.

However, I believe the stakeholders should be listed based on the people-functions involved through the different stages of a data life cycle, as follows:
I. Those who **consume data** and data-driven insights for decision-making
II. Those who **create and manage data** through the data life cycle:
- Those who design and create data
- Those who distribute data and enable access to data
- Those who are involved in data storage, archiving, and deletion.

I.2.1 Stakeholders' Expectations

So, what do these stakeholders expect? Let us look at this from the perspective of executive management, the key-consumers of data (Table I.1).

Table I.1 The Stakeholders' Wishlist

The Stakeholders' Wishlist (Consumers of Data)	Key Questions
1. **Enterprise data**: Ensure top quality, granular, and relevant data is available in real time	How to ensure - • Enterprise-wide Single Source of Truth? (SSOT) • Multiple Versions of the Truth (MVOT) – customized and personalized, but still based on SSOT?
2. **Big data**: Collect, collate, and report granular data from across the platforms: "Fully integrate" enterprise data with internet, IoT and connected devices etc.	• Data you need vs. data you have • External data vs. internal data. • What data from which platform? • Relevance? Use? • What frequency?
3. Make sure all important data is available and accessible to all consumers of data	• What data is important for whom and why? • Who should access what data and why? • On web? Mobile?
4. Analytics and actionable insights for key managers	• Self-service, on-demand analytics • Customized or personalized data visualization – dashboards • Natural language processing • Cloud-based, accessible on the move, from anywhere in the world
5. Analytics and actionable insights for big decisions; the decisions which influence majority of business outcomes	• How do you identify big decisions? • How do you prioritize big decisions?
6. Early warning systems and alerts	• Key-event driven: What are the key events? • Period-driven: What parameters, what thresholds?

(Continued)

Table I.I (Continued) The Stakeholders' Wishlist

The Stakeholders' Wishlist (Consumers of Data)	Key Questions
7. Automate all processes that can be rule-based and need no managerial intervention or discretion	• Which processes? What rules? • Are there exceptions?
8. All statutory reports to be generated automatically	• Which reports? Do we have all the data necessary in the systems? • What red flags? Exception handling? • Can the reports stand scrutiny and statutory audit?

The stakeholders' wish list above is indicative at best; usually it is aspirational and endless. But for all practical purposes, the above represents the core of what consumers of data usually demand.

I.2.2 The Other Stakeholders' Dilemma

Let us now look at the expectations of other stakeholders; those who create, distribute, and manage data. Usually, these are the people shouldering the responsibility for making the DDO happen, if possible, overnight, like magic; except that they still have no clarity on where to start.

A. Setting Priorities
  • When a newly appointed CDO would like to get started on a transformational journey towards a DDO; what should be the priorities? Should the focus be on every one of the seven items on stakeholders' (consumers of data) wish list? Or should there be prioritization?
  • Is it possible to pick and choose? To prioritize and deliver one or two items on the stakeholders" wish list while ignoring the others in the interim? Or should it be all, or none?
  • Further, where does one start? Should you try and fix your data sourcing and data quality first, or should you focus on delivering "analytics" with the available data? Or try to win a few "brownie-points" first?

B. Creating a Roadmap and a Business Case
  • In most organizations, all investments beyond a threshold value will be subject to scrutiny by an investment-committee prior to approval. The first task of any newly appointed CDO would be to create a "transformational roadmap and business case" for investing in the DDO. So how exactly does one go about doing it?

C. Demonstrating Value from Analytics
- How does the CDO demonstrate measurable dollar value from invest-ments into analytics? How can it be ensured that value is delivered on a continuous basis?

D. Managing the Legacy
- Another issue is that most organizations have a "legacy" ranging from a few years to few decades. The word "legacy" is an umbrella term that includes legacy applications, legacy data, legacy processes and practices, and, most importantly, legacy people – a set of people still living in yester year; and completely opposed to "change".
- The legacy problems can be easily fixable if the organization is relatively small, or relatively young. But, if the organization is a large multi-product conglomerate, covering multiple geographies with multiple subsidiary legal entities, then the complexity of fixing the data quality can be laborious and extremely challenging. Data sourcing, consolidation, and normaliza-tion itself can eat up to 90% of the budget, assuming one can work out a method to do it.

To my mind, exercises such as recruiting a CDO, building a CoE for analytics, or trying to build a data culture across the organization and so forth, will be completely futile unless the data quality is fixed. The other alternative is to compartmentalize and generate "localized analytics" rather than deal with the demon called "data-consolidation and normalization". However, it is highly unlikely that even a small fraction of the stakeholders" (i.e., consumers of data) expectations are going to be met with a set of localized analytics in the name of the data-driven organization.

Finally, bad quality data is usually a result of poor data governance; like a virus, it is bound to spread and infect every part of the organization, rendering even the localized analytics ineffectual before too long.

1.3 Setting Up a Data-Driven Organization; Constraints and Experiences

There is no measure or benchmark for maturity of a DDO, as is the case with a six-sigma organization, or a CMMi organization. A few isolated successes of analytics projects, or a "one-time leveraging of big data for decision-making" does not make an organization 100% data-driven.

If even setting up a pilot for a DDO is complex, scaling it across a large multina-tional organization can be a phenomenally difficult, time-consuming, and expensive exercise; besides it is not easy to quantify what "value" or "return" one can generate out of such an investment in terms of money, manpower, and time.

Given the DDO is an enterprise-wide initiative that is likely to consume and lock up resources for a long period, understandably any organization would insist that a roadmap and a business case be prepared and evaluated prior to approval. The executive management would expect any such DDO initiative to have a clearly defined scope, objectives, and measures of success including a quantified dollar return from data-driven decisions.

While there are several books in the market on related topics; most have been written from the perspective of either organization design, or of handling cultural issues and change management. A few books cover a large number of big data business cases from Fortune 500 and internet companies, and a few others cover case studies specific to one industry vertical.

Ideally, what is required is a step-by-step methodology to create a roadmap and business case, and a narration of the constraints and experiences from someone who has attempted setting up a DDO. This book intends to cover this white space.

1.4 What This Book Covers

Most chief information officers (CIOs) struggle to explain the value from analytics. Given the hype in the market for big data, analytics and AI, every organization has a budget for analytics, but very few make any headway. Most end up investing in a visualization platform like Tableau or QlikView, which in essence is an improved version of the business intelligence (BI) dashboard that the organization had probably invested in, not too long ago. By Gartner's estimate, near 80% of all analytics projects fail to deliver intended value. This book provides a method to ensure "material improvements in quality of decisions, and measurable value from investments into analytics".

Further, there is currently no book on the market that lays emphasis on big decisions; the 10% of organizational decisions that influence 90% of the business outcomes, the key decisions that seriously impact the profitability and growth potential of the company. Qualitative improvement of such key decisions (based on actionable insights) could determine the competitive advantage of the organization in the market.

This book also encompasses a few important topics that have hitherto never been covered in the context of a DDO such as "decision prioritization", the concept of "knowns and unknowns", and "Johari window for organization as a person" among others. Except for a few vague references, there are no books on decision prioritization and identifying the 10% of decisions that influence 90% of business outcomes in an organization.

Every enterprise aspires to becomes 100% data driven, but currently there are no practitioners' handbooks to help in creating a step-by-step roadmap, to set priorities, and to actually deliver value from analytics investments. I sincerely hope this book can provide guidance for such endeavors and encourage organizations to make the journey.

Chapter 1

Quo Vadis

Before the Transformational Journey

Topics Covered in this Chapter

1. Data-driven organization: Refining the meaning & the purpose	From data-driven to insights-driven; it is important to create new operating models based on data-insights.
2. Before the journey: Deconstructing the data to decisions flow a. Data manifest b. Data catalogue c. Data logistics: Information supply & demand d. DDO's & theory of asymmetric information in enterprise context	• The importance of creating a data-manifest. • The logistics backbone for delivering the right data & insights to right person, at right time. • The theory of asymmetric information as applied to enterprise data consumption.
3. The scope, vision & the maturity models	Data-Driven Organization: • Laying down the scope • The vision for the end-state.

DOI: 10.1201/9781003321347-2

INTRODUCTION

Before embarking on a transformational journey toward a data-driven organization (DDO), it is important to understand the true meaning and the purpose of the DDO. It is important to attempt a self-assessment to determine why you have chosen to make the journey, to establish milestones over a time-horizon of at least three–five years, your destination, and a broad definition of the end-state that you are aiming for.

It is also important to understand and document the current operating model of your organization, along with an in-depth analysis of data-to-decisions process-flow; the sources-of-data, the uses-of-data, and the logistics for delivering the data and insights to different end-users.

1.1 Data-Driven Organization: Refining the Meaning and the Purpose

Data by itself may not provide any insights, much less actionable insights. Raw data needs to be sorted, normalized, contextualized, and analyzed before it generates insights; and such insights need to be personalized and delivered to the right decision-maker at the right time to enable them to act based on insights. A data-driven organization, in the context of this book, needs to be understood as an insights-driven organization, where all decisions are taken purely based on data and on insights generated from data.

Further, if nearly all decisions are to be purely based on insights generated from data, then such insights need to reach the right person (decision-maker) at the right time. A true DDO needs to have an enabling infrastructure and protocols to ensure a data manifest is made, updated, and executed.

1.1.1 From Data-Driven, to Insights-Driven

In an April 2018 research report (Marcel et al., 2010), Forrester introduced a new category of companies called insights-driven companies, clocking an annual growth rate of 30% plus and expected to account for over $1.8 trillion in revenues by 2021. The report further elaborated that these "customer-obsessed companies systematically harness insights across their organization and implement them to create competitive advantage through software". SAP hired Forrester in late 2017 to develop thought leadership on how businesses can bridge the gap between being data-driven and truly insight-driven (according to SAP's website). In January 2018, Forrester released a white paper (Taylor, 2018) that highlighted two key findings:

- Importance of moving from "pull" style analytics, to "push" style analytics – prescriptive analytics that proactively make the decision-makers and the executives "act" – tell them "what to do" based on the insights generated.
- New data management technologies, like "data lakes", merely augment the existing ones like "data warehouses", rather than replace them.

Explaining further, the authors of the report lay down "five principles which distinguish how insights-driven companies operate" – among them, two that I have identified as relevant for the context of this book:

- It is important to create operating models based on "data-insights"
- Establishing a strategic focus for insights investments.

In many ways, this research report brings out very important aspects of the meaning and the very purpose of a data-driven organization; to enable data-driven decisions, thus moving the "operating model" away from decisions based on the collective-gut of managers, to the one where the "data" drives every decision within the company, and wherever possible with an "audit-trail" for each decision explaining why and how such a decision was made, with supporting data; a "transparency" in decision-making that hitherto never existed in organizations, ever.

A DDO needs to not just make "data" available to the decision-makers, but also make the "actionable-insights" available to the decision-makers. While the current trend is to promote on-demand analytics and a self-service platform, it is important to go for "push-style" analytics where possible: the prescriptive analytics which alert the decision-maker to an impending-action, and also demand that the decision-maker "acts" on such insights.

1.2 Before the Journey: Deconstructing the Data-to-Decisions Flow

Deconstructing the data-to-decisions workflow as it exists requires an organization-wide due diligence. The first step would be to list all decision-makers and essential decisions. We will be covering this in the chapters ahead.

The next step would be to create a comprehensive data manifest to catalog all data in a data inventory, right from data sources to data end-users. It is also important to capture the volume, variety, and velocity for each of the data elements, and the flow from the source to the end-user. Some of the due diligence tools and the concepts are explained in the following section.

1.2.1 The Data Manifest

In the shipping industry, a "manifest" is a document listing everything that is included in the ship's cargo. Also called a captain's manifest, it is signed by the captain of the ship, and is an acknowledgment of all the goods carried by the ship at a point of time. The "manifest" provides a detailed summary of all the bills-of-lading (shipping receipts), the consignor, consignees, port of origin, port of discharge or port of delivery, along with dates, times, and unique numbers, for each of the listed items on the manifest.

Every organization needs to make a similar document for "data": a detailed listing (inventory) of all the data that organization has at a point of time, along with details like data origin, data destination, data creators and data consumers for each of the unique data elements. Here, the word "data" primarily refers to the "master data" and "meta-data" in the organization.

For example, irrespective of whether an organization has a master data management (MDM) module or not, a "new customer" must be created only at one centralized location and needs to be replicated in different applications that record transactions with that customer. The "data manifest" needs to record details of where all the master data elements called "customer" get created, and where all it gets distributed for replication, reporting and consumption.

Similarly, an organization may allow for raising invoices in any number of different point-of-sale (POS) applications, but each of them need to carry unique serial numbers, the invoicing data needs to be replicated in finance and accounting applications, and the relevant sales and inventory accounts need to be posted for each transaction. The "data manifest" needs to record the details for each of the meta-data elements related to invoices, along with the applications location where they may get created, and where all the data is distributed for replication, reporting and consumption.

The concept of a "manifest" is not new in computer sciences. However, using the concept for capturing the enterprise-wide inventory of data, complete with origin is definitely new, and I have not come across any recorded attempts so far. It is also important to note the data manifest I am proposing here is different from typical ER models (ERMs) and data flow models (DFMs), as both ERM and DFM are usually made for one application at a time, while doing the data design.

The data manifest needs to be one comprehensive list of entities and data elements, across all applications in the enterprise (Figure 1.1). A data manifest is also different from enterprise ontology, and different from data dictionary and data standards, data definitions and so on. A data manifest is the same as an enterprise data catalog.

1.2.2 Data Catalog and Data Dictionary

A data catalog is another popular name for the enterprise data inventory. Many of the new age data quality management solutions, or data governance solutions have a feature for automatically creating a "data catalog". For example, AWS Glue uses a crawler to discover, profile, and automatically create a data catalog, essentially an

DATA MANIFEST
An Example

DATA MANIFEST FOR - ENTERPRISE MASTER DATA

	Entity	Meta-Data-element Id	Meta-Data-Element	Mandatory?	Data Standards (Data Type / Identifiers, Vocabulary, Schema, Format & API)	Data-definition	Data Validation rules	Created in Application	Replicated in Applications Application Id (alpha-Num 4 digit)				Replication Frequency / Protoc
									App-1	App-2	App-3	App-4	
M A S T E R	CUSTOMER	C001	Customer Id	Yes	Numerical, 10 Digit	Customer-identification...		A001	A008	A012	A045	A064	Instantaneously, Event-...

DATA MANIFEST FOR - ENTERPRISE META-DATA

	Entity	Meta-Data-element Id	Meta-Data-Element	Mandatory?	Data Standards (Data Type / Identifiers, Vocabulary, Schema, Format & API)	Data-definition	Data Validation rules	Created in Application	App-1	App-1 Replcn Frq / Prtcl	App-2	App-2 Replcn Frq / Prtcl	App-3	App-3 Replcn Frq / Prtcl	App-4	App-3 Replcn Frq / Prtcl
												Replicated in Applications				
M E T A D A T A	INVOICE	I001	Invoice No.	Yes	Numerical, 12 Digit	Unique Invoice No.		A001	A008	Batch-upload, 24 hours, 12 AM	A091		A012	Instantaneously, Event-driven Trigger	A064	Instantaneously, Event-driven Trigger
		I002	Invoice Date	Yes	Date Format DD-MM-YYYY	Invoice Date		A001	A008	Batch-upload, 24 hours, 12 AM	A091		A012	Instantaneously, Event-driven Trigger	A064	Instantaneously, Event-driven Trigger
		C001	Customer d.													
		M001	Material-id	Yes												
		I005														
		I006														
		I007														
	PURCHASE ORDER	P001	Purchase Order No.	yes	Numerical, 12 Digit	Material identification No.		A001	A008				A012	A045	A064	Instantaneously, Event-driven Trigger

Figure 1.1   Data manifest.

"inventory" of all meta-data elements from the data lake as a separate table that can be edited, to tag and catalog all the data elements. SAP data intelligence has a similar crawler functionality to create a data catalog.

There are several other popular products, like Atlan and Collibra, among others, which help create a data catalog from a data lake. The data catalog can be further tagged and indexed to create a data dictionary.

Data lineage is a record of the data element right from its source through the complete data life cycle.

While an automatic data crawler can help quickly create a data catalog from a complex data lake, it will still take substantial manual intelligence and effort to clean-correct and tag the entire meta-data inventory. Creating a data catalog and data dictionary is an essential part of implementing any "data governance solution".

A data manifest is defined above as a data catalog along with the "from and to addresses" for each of the data elements. A data manifest is a catalog of the data as it flows from origin to destination, through the data life cycle.

1.2.3 Data Logistics: Information Supply and Demand

The phrase "data logistics" was coined in the 1990s, along with "information logistics", essentially as storage, warehousing and transportation models for data and information; a method of managing traffic and content on internet. The "data logistics" (Beck et al., 2019) models are currently being explored in the context of making "data" accessible to large populations of people with widely disparate technological capabilities, storage, and networking infrastructure.

Technically the implementation of data warehouses and data lakes is supposed to make all data centrally accessible and make data logistics easier within an enterprise.

However, we still observe very little improvement on the ground. Managers continue to complain that they cannot access the information they want, when they want to. Further, data warehouses and data lakes by themselves are just places where a large amount of data is stored, ready to be accessed, but quite stationary (Figure 1.2).

Enabling data-driven decisions is possible only when the data and insights are made available to the right decision-makers at the right time. The organization needs to have a suitable data logistics model to extract, transform, and deliver the data and insights from these data lakes to the right decision-makers. The data logistics models can be quite complex given that the "data" needs to flow back and forth into data lakes, as well as from application to application, from person to person, and even from one organization to another organization as required. It is possible to see a complete range of models including inbound, outbound distribution, and reverse logistics.

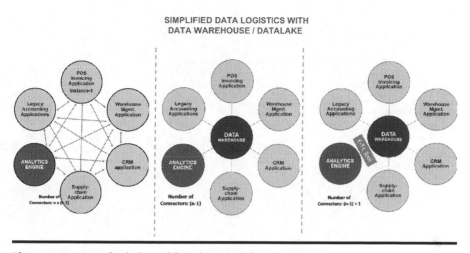

Figure 1.2   Data logistics with a data warehouse/data lake.

The following are the critical components of information logistics design. The word "information" here refers to a combination of data and insights:

- Managing information demand and information supply across the value-chain of the organization.
- Designing the information supply chain – including creation of information, storage, distribution, transformation, consumption, cataloging, archiving, search-retrieval, and repurposing.

Information demand, especially in the context of an enterprise is peculiar; most executives just do not know what information they need to take a decision, let alone the exact specifications for the form and format. So, in the absence of clarity, the decision-makers demand as much information as possible, while the information suppliers (the IT department) just provide what they can, within the constraints. This leaves a permanent imbalance in demand and supply, in not just quantity supplied, but also in the relevance of the "information" supplied (Figure 1.3).

Also, it is important to note that in any typical enterprise, the information supply can never keep pace with information demand. While the information demand continues to increase with each newly recruited executive and with each passing year, the increase in information supply purely depends on the incremental investments in information technology, and can plateau beyond a certain level of investment.

Another noteworthy point is that not all information supplied maybe relevant or useful. The actual relevant information supplied would be a fraction of the total information supplied.

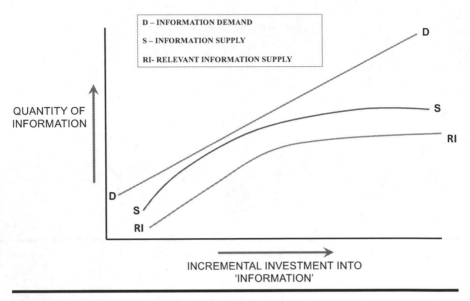

Figure 1.3   Information supply vs. demand.

1.2.3.1 DDO's and the Theory of Asymmetric Information

The theory of asymmetric information as applied to economics was developed in the 1970s by George Akerlof, in his paper titled "The market for 'lemons': Quality uncertainty and market mechanism" (Akerlof, 1978) explains how sellers of used cars have more information than buyers in a market, and how, given the information asymmetry, the buyer may choose to buy poor quality cars (lemons) for the same price, ignoring the good quality cars (peaches) available in the market, eventually leaving only more and more lemons in the market as the uninformed buyer's price leads to what economists call an "*adverse selection problem*". The secondary effects of the phenomenon include possible collapse of the market, if more and more worried buyers withdraw over the fear of being cheated. Akerlof, along with Michael Spence, and Joseph Stiglitz were jointly awarded Nobel Prize for economics in 2001 for their research on asymmetric information.

In the context of an enterprise, the consumers of information (executive managers) are relatively less informed on every new technology being introduced and what "value" it actually delivers on the ground, compared to the suppliers of information" (the IT department). In most cases, the consumers of information also happen the be sponsors of the projects, or people who fund the IT expenditure.

The information imbalance may lead to an "adverse selection problem" – as more and more IT projects do not deliver the promised value, some (if not all) of the consumers of information (sponsors) may withdraw from the market and may refuse to fund the projects altogether.

The theory of asymmetric information is important in the context of a DDO because, in the absence of a common understanding, transparency, and shared goals between the information consumers and information suppliers, no decision ever gets taken based on the "information" provided by the IT department. No manager ever trusts the information (data + insights) supplied. In such an environment, encouraging data-driven culture is unlikely, if not outright impossible.

Data quality is another big concern for the information consumers. If the trust deficit persists, the information consumers will withdraw (due to the adverse selection problem), and this may lead to complete collapse of the organizational operating model, which essentially runs on information.

Further, the suppliers of information (IT department) are likely to know more about the "quality of the information" they produce, than the consumers of information. The information imbalance once again may lead to "trust-deficit" among the consumers of data, which in turn may trigger self-preservation reactions like managing one's own information on Excel sheets, creating a private stash of data, and so forth.

The number of Excel sheets floating around an organization is usually a measure of "trust-deficit" among the executives – resulting from the asymmetric information (Figure 1.4).

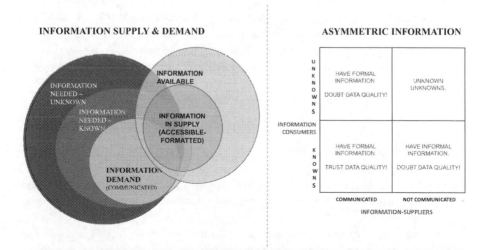

Figure 1.4 The concept of asymmetric information.

1.3 Data-Driven Organization: Defining the Scope, Vision, and Maturity Models

As one embarks on a transformational journey toward a data-driven organization, here are some important questions:

1. If an organization wishes to transform itself into a DDO, what will be the "scope" of such a project? What might be included in the scope and what is explicitly excluded?
2. What business value is one aiming for? How does one estimate the business value to be generated from a data-driven organization?
3. When do we know the DDO has achieved the requisite level of maturity? How do you measure the maturity of the DDO?

Technically, the "scope" of the DDO includes the design, development, and deployment of the complete process chain from data-to-insights, and insight-to-decisions, and continuous improvement from there on.

1.3.1 Maturity Models

There are several big data and analytics maturity models posited by top consulting entities and researchers. The two most popular are as follows:

1. Booz & Company Model (El-Darwiche et al., 2014): The authors of the report at Booz mention that, depending on the maturity of organizational capability, big data can make a significant difference to the top-line and bottom-line of the company. The big data maturity stages are defined based on how widespread or localized the big data implementations are, and more importantly based on potential for generating value. The four stages of maturity are defined as follows:
   • Stage 1: Performance Management: Standard dashboards and performance management by monitoring KPIs.
   • Stage 2: Functional Area Excellence: Function specific big data implementations – from smart-pricing to fraud monitoring, and crime reporting among others.
   • Stage 3: Value Proposition Enhancement: Enhancing the value delivered to customer – from personalization of customer experience, to targeted advertising.
   • Stage 4: Business Model Transformation: Leveraging data to explore new revenue streams, reengineering operating models and so forth.
2. Horton Works Model (Dhanuka, 2016): Horton Works (now merged with Cloudera) has an interesting concept for assessing big data maturity of

organizations. They propose assessing the organizations on four maturity levels as listed below:

- Aware
- Exploring
- Optimizing
- Transforming

The maturity levels are measured based on five capability dimensions:

- Sponsorship
- Data and Analytics
- Technology Infrastructure
- Organization and Skills
- Process and Management

1.3.2 What is Missing?

As I started looking into these models, I realized the words – big data, analytics, and data-driven decisions are often used synonymously. Perhaps they mean almost the same thing in the context of these maturity models.

However, I believe "DDO" is a much larger and all-encompassing concept, which subsumes everything from business intelligence, analytics, and big data to data lakes and data warehouses. For an organization to call itself a DDO, a majority of decisions (if not all) need to be completely data-driven, where possible with an audit trail along with supporting data and analysis providing the context for each of the decisions.

A DDO, by definition, ensures top quality information (data and insights) being supplied to every decision-maker, with information supply nearly matching the existing information demand. A DDO ensures there is very little to no, information asymmetry between information suppliers (CDO, CIO etc.) and the information consumers (executive managers).

The maturity model for a DDO needs to be based on two important parameters:

1. **The need to start from decisions**: What percentage of key organizational decisions are driven by data?
2. **A focus on the value delivered**: What is the dollar value of data-driven decision-making? Does the value exceed investment?

To my mind, any analysis of "DDO" is incomplete without cataloging and analyzing the key organization decisions. Unfortunately, as of now, I have not come across even one maturity model which advocates critically analyzing organizational decisions, and the value being generated by data-driven decisions.

Bibliography

Adam, F. (2019). From Decision Making to Decision Support. In *Oxford Research Encyclopedia of Business and Management*.

Akerlof, G. A. (1978). The market for "lemons": Quality uncertainty and the market mechanism. In *Uncertainty in Economics* (pp. 235–251). Academic Press.

Al-Sai, Z. A., & Abdullah, R. (2019, April). A review on big data maturity models. In *2019 IEEE Jordan International Joint Conference on Electrical Engineering and Information Technology (JEEIT)* (pp. 156–161). IEEE.

Beck, M., Moore, T., French, N.H., Kissel, E. and Swany, M. (2019). Research paper on "Data Logistics: Toolkit and Applications". *GoodTechs'19: Proceedings of the 5th EAI International Conference on Smart Objects and Technologies for Social Good* September 2019: Pages 61–66.

Comuzzi, M., & Patel, A. (2016). *How Organisations Leverage Big Data: A Maturity Model.* Industrial Management & Data Systems.

Dawson, G. S., Watson, R. T., & Boudreau, M. C. (2010). Information asymmetry in information systems consulting: Toward a theory of relationship constraints. *Journal of Management Information Systems*, 27(3), 143–178.

Dhanuka, V. (2016). *Hortonworks Big Data Maturity Model.* Hortonworks, (March).

El-Darwiche, B., Koch, V., Meer, D., Shehadi, R. T., & Tohme, W. (2014). Big data maturity: An action plan for policymakers and executives. *The Global Information Technology Report*, 43, 51.

Haftor, D., & Kajtazi, M. (2009). *What is Information Logistics?: An Explorative Study of the Research Frontiers of Information Logistics.* Linnaeus University

Marcel, B., Orţan, T., & Otgon, C. (2010). Information Asymmetry Theory in Corporate Governance Systems. Annals of the University of Oradea, Economic Science Series, 19(2).

Perales-Manrique, J., Molina-Chirinos, J., & Shiguihara-Juárez, P. (2019, November). A data analytics maturity model for financial sector companies. In *2019 IEEE Sciences and Humanities International Research Conference (SHIRCON)* (pp. 1–4). IEEE.

Retrialisca, F., & Chotijah, U. (2020). The maturity measurement of big data adoption in manufacturing companies using the TDWI maturity model. *Journal of Information Systems Engineering and Business Intelligence*, 6(1), 70–78.

SAS White Paper (2016). Research Study – Assessing Your Business Analytics Maturity: Eight Metrics That Matter. https://www.sas.com/en/whitepapers/accessing-your-business-analytics-maturity-106494.html

Taylor, C. (2018). How to become an insights-driven business. A Forrester Consulting Thought Leadership paper commissioned by SAP Apr 2018.

Winter, R., & Strauch, B. (2003). Demand-driven information requirements analysis in data warehousing. *Journal of Data Warehousing*, 8(1), 38–47.

Chapter 2

Decision-Driven before Data-Driven

Topics Covered in this Chapter

1. The three good decisions	A good manager is one who makes three good decisions out of ten. – Peter Drucker
2. Decision-driven before data-driven	"An organization necessarily needs to be Decision-driven before it is Data-driven, if it has any hopes of ever transforming itself into a Data-driven organization… meaning the organization should know, what decisions it makes".
3. "Big" decisions need to be process-Driven	"But we have noticed the decision-making process across organizations (not just ours) is informal, and more often-than-not is without an audit-trail. No Manager seems to list the decisions that he makes - let alone record the reasons."

INTRODUCTION

An organization needs to be self-aware; it must know itself thoroughly to perform at its optimum and to compete in the market. The purpose of analytics is to help the organization know itself and its business, even more intimately, and even more minutely. An organization should know its core-competencies, strengths, weaknesses, threats, and opportunities. It has to know what products to produce, how to source its raw materials, how to control its inventories and working capital, how to optimize resource consumption while maximizing output, where to market and how to market its products. It has to know its customers, its vendors, and its employees. If *the purpose of data-driven-analytics is to help an organization know itself intimately and take decisions purely based on data and actionable insights,* then those responsible for the analytics investments must know which decisions should be prioritized and need to start from those "vital-few" decisions first.

An organization necessarily needs to be decision-driven before it aspires to become data-driven. A decision-driven organization knows what decisions it takes and how each of those decisions impact business outcomes. A decision-driven organization institutes a formal process and audit trail for what it considers important decisions, if not for all decisions.

2.1 The Three Good Decisions

Some thirty years back, when I started my career as a management trainee with an aerospace company; the 18 months training program included several courses in management.

I still remember the very first classroom session as if it were yesterday. A distinguished-looking retired professor from the Indian Institute of Management, (IIM), Calcutta was introduced by the principal of the staff-college, and as he addressed the class he declared: "I am a Jew! ... Hope none of you have a problem?" (This used to be the time when the Indian Government very strongly identified with the Palestinian cause).

On assuring himself that we had no problems whatsoever, he proceeded to ask the next question.

"Who is a good manager?"

There were a few of us bold enough to try a response. The professor faithfully wrote down everything we said on the board. A wide variety of juvenile definitions ensued, ranging from "someone who always gets work done" to "someone who gets work done more efficiently" as might be expected from a set of green-behind-the-ears freshers.

"How many of you have heard of Peter Drucker?"

Fortunately, a good many of us had. (I came to know much later that Peter Drucker was also of Jewish descent. His ancestors were Jewish, but his parents had converted to Lutheranism).

"Well, glad you have… Peter Drucker defines a good manager as someone who takes three good decisions out of ten".
Not surprisingly, we were all completely lost…
It made no sense… Just 30%? …One fails to clear one's exam at 30%…
The professor then went on to relate how he had asked the very same question when he met Peter Drucker in a seminar. Apparently, Peter Drucker had told him: "A manager must take decisions, even if only three out of ten turn out to be good decisions".

This is one premise that I have kept unchallenged ever since. A manager must take decisions, must take decisions at the right time, and must take as many good decisions as possible.

Over time, I joined a business school to do my MBA, but I guess Peter Drucker was passé by then; I do not remember any professor specifically talking about the importance of taking right decisions at the right time. Since then, I have been through eight different companies in multiple roles, set up and scaled businesses, consulted for several companies across industry sectors for over two decades, set up multiple offshore development centers (ODCs) and shared services for multinationals. But I doubt if I have ever paused to think if I was taking the right decisions at the right time. Ever?

2.2 Decision-Driven before Data-Driven

However, all this changed when I was trying to create a business case for setting up an internal Center of Excellence (CoE) for analytics. After a grueling time trying to take advice and help from different consulting firms and searching through all the published sources, we discovered there was little to nothing available as a process for creating an organization-wide roadmap for analytics. Given the near-complete absence of any published sources, we were forced to come up with an original process of our own.

As the due diligence went on, the most disturbing discovery was that an organization necessarily needs to be decision-driven before it is data-driven, if it has any hopes of ever transforming itself into a data-driven organization. This meant the organization should know what decisions it makes.

Let me explain further: An organization needs to be self-aware and must know itself thoroughly to perform at its optimum, and to compete in the market. The purpose of analytics is to help the organization know itself and its business more intimately. An organization should know its core competencies, strengths, weaknesses, threats, and opportunities. It has to know what products to produce, how to source its raw materials, how to control its inventories and working capital, how to optimize resource consumption while maximizing output, where to market and how to market its products. It has to know its customers, its vendors, and its employees.

If the purpose of data-driven analytics is to help an organization *know itself intimately* and take decisions purely based on data and actionable insights, then those people responsible for analytics investments must know which decisions should be prioritized and need to start from those "vital-few" decisions first.

An organization necessarily needs to know and document what decisions its managers across the functions make every day; how each of those decisions affect the business outcomes; and if those decisions being made by its managers are based on a specific kind of "data". While there are not many, there are a few published sources that emphasize the need for organizations to be "decision-driven before aspiring to become data-driven". While none of them specifically provide a step-by-step roadmap, they do provide the necessary conceptual clarity.

In a brilliant article titled "The decision-driven organization" (Blenko et al., 2010), authors Marcia W. Blenko, Michael Mankins, and Paul Rogers argue that any reorganization of enterprise is most effective, when it starts with a "decision audit". They mention how many CEOs mistakenly think reorganization is a simple exercise of structural change; the CEO believes the job is allocating the right people to the right roles and functions. They mention how most reorganizations fail to deliver the intended value, and quote the example of how Yahoo's failed reorganization of 2006 created 12 layers, resulting in a slowing down of product development as decisions stalled, and overheads ballooned. They contrast Yahoo's experience with that of Xerox, which implemented a decision-driven reorganization in 2001, resulting in a flatter structure, quicker decisions, and a turnaround performance, besides a billion dollar reduction in overheads.

I came across another wonderful article in the December 2020 issue of *MIT Sloan Management Review* (de Langhe & Puntoni, 2020) that validates the central theme of this book. Authors Bart de Langhe and Stefano Puntoni, emphasize the importance of making analytics decision-driven. They argue "data-driven" often means answering the wrong question and reinforcing "existing beliefs". They believe data-driven analytics enable the data scientists, while decision-driven analytics enable the decision-makers. The only dispute I have with them is on their assessment that data-driven analytics addresses the knowns, while decision-driven analytics addresses the unknowns. In my experience, people starting with "data" and trying to recognize patterns, is akin to looking for "unknown answers to unknown questions". More on this in Chapter 3, "Knowns, Unknowns and the Elusive Value from Analytics".

In a 2005 Bain white paper titled "The decision-driven organization – Making good decisions and making them happen", Paul Rogers and Marcia Blenko argue that top-performing organizations make important decisions well, and make them happen, quickly and consistently (Rogers & Blenko, 2005). They also mention "making good decisions means being clear about which decisions matter the most", underscoring the need for identifying the important (big) decisions. Further, the article also emphasizes the importance of "defining clear decision roles and holding people accountable".

2.3 The "Big" Decisions Need to Be Process-Driven

In my view, the only way a manager can exercise deliberate control of the organizational value-chain is through decisions. Good quality decisions are expected to help maximize the throughput of the organization by easing the constraints in the value-chain. A manager is only as good as the quality of his decisions, and a manager delaying the decisions usually results in process bottle-necks within the value-chain. Instituting a formal process for decision-making is expected to help managers be consistent in the quality of the decisions they make. A formal process is expected to help them make "good" decisions nine out of ten times and be accountable for their decisions.

In my experience, the decision-making process across organizations is informal, and more often than not lacks any audit trail. I am yet to come across any organization attempting organization structure based on "clear decision roles" that the Bain white paper recommends. Organizations documenting clear role definitions itself is rare, let alone creating roles based on a documented list of "decisions". While a P-CMM certification compliance mandates documented role definitions, I have never seen the list of decisions being a part of the role definition, ever.

The common exceptions include:

1. **Investment decisions**: Most organizations institute a process for all investment decisions; a formal business case for investments beyond a threshold value; and good number of them have an investment committee specially constituted for clearing large value investments.
2. **Purchasing decisions in public sector or government**: Given the need for public accountability and transparency, most public sector organizations and government departments create a fairly rigid process for all purchasing decisions beyond a threshold value.

It is pertinent to note, there are hundreds of operational decisions that are repetitive in nature, usually made by an everyday manager, and that cumulatively account for a much higher value than all capital expenditure-related decisions taken in the company. For example: the quantum of buffer stock by each stock keeping unit (SKU) may be individually a very small decision, but by annual cumulative value across SKUs, it may be the most important decision that significantly influences the profitability and performance of the company. Given the importance of these "collectively big" operational decisions, it is important to identify and institute a formal process to maintain the quality of decisions, besides creating an audit trail.

If the organization runs on a well implemented ERP like SAP, many of the operational decisions tend to become "configuration settings" or "rules" that you set inside SAP; and the ERP makes those decisions on behalf of the managers. Managers, however, are expected to closely monitor and refine those rules, as often as necessary at least in theory.

In such cases, while the enterprise resource planning (ERP) does enforce a formal process for the decision-making, it is still unlikely for organizations to have a "list of those rule-based decisions" or know which of those "rule-based decisions" qualify as the "big" decisions.

In reality, I am yet to come across any organization which meticulously identifies critical decisions and creates GSOPs (Global Standard Operating Procedures) for each one of them; and that includes Life Sciences companies claiming 100% GxP compliance. The end result of most GSOPs is a report for the sake of process compliance.

2.3.1 Decision Modeling and Limitations

Not all decisions are 100% rule-based and perfectly logical. But many of the sub-steps involved in the decision-making process can be logical and rule-based. So, good practice would be to break down (decomposition) the decision-making process into sub-processes and minutely examine if any of such sub-processes can be rule-based and automatable.

- While rule-based sub-processes can be automated, it is possible to use data analysis to develop a predictive-model for those sub-processes which are not rule-based. However, it is important to use the right model for the right process and understand the limitations of the decision models in predicting the outcomes. A 2014 *McKinsey Quarterly* article (Rosenzweig, 2014) emphasizes the importance of knowing the limitations of decision models and using the right model for the right purpose.
- Where do you start? How does one break down the decision-making process? I strongly recommend decision modeling using a standard notation like Decision Model and Notation (the DMN standard published by the Object Management Group). Many good decision modeling tools are available (such as DecisionsFirst Modeler) and many tools that support process modeling also support decision modeling (such as ARIS, Signavio, or Trisotech). Companies with inhouse modeling teams can use any modeling tool that they have skills and licenses for. While working for a software product company, I personally used Prof. Scheer ARIS (now a part of Software Ag.) for mapping hundreds of business processes and can vouch for its effectiveness.
- Most companies do not realize the complexity of their own business models until they get down to modeling their business processes and decisions. I never knew the complexity of business models in global trading companies until I actually worked for one. If identifying a business-critical decision is difficult,

modeling the decision can be even more so, especially if you do not have inhouse DMN specialists. I would recommend engaging outside expertise or getting your internal teams trained by experts. To start with, you could insist on your team reading a practitioners' handbook like this one.

- Given that decision modeling is a tedious, time-consuming, and expensive process, no company can afford to model every decision it makes. So, it is best reserved for the "big" decisions, the "vital-few" decisions which influence majority of business outcomes (please refer to chapters 5 and 6 for more details on the process for identifying "big" decisions).

2.4 Conclusion

A decision-driven organization needs to know what decisions it takes, and which of those decisions are key decisions that impact on business outcomes the most. A decision-driven organization is expected to be process-driven with documented GSOPs for each of the decisions recognized as important – specifically for those 10% of the decisions which influence 90% of the business outcomes. Most importantly, *a decision-driven organization ensures its success is process-driven and consistent, not people-driven.*

Bibliography

Blenko, M. W., Mankins, M. C., & Rogers, P. (2010). The decision-driven organization. *Harvard Business Review*, 88(6), 54–62.

de Langhe, B., & Puntoni, S. (2020). Leading with decision-driven data analytics. *MIT Solan Management Review*, Dec 2020.

Palmer, M. (2021). Be Decision-Driven, Not Data-Driven: Seven points to consider in your collaborative decision-making process. *TowardsDataScience.com*, May 2021.

Rogers, P., & Blenko, M. (2005). *The Decision Driven Organization*. Bain & Company.

Rosenzweig, P. (2014). The benefits—and limits—of decision models. *McKinsey Quarterly*, 1, 106–115.

Taylor, J., & Purchase, J. (2016). *Real-World Decision Modeling with DMN*. Meghan-Kiffer Press.

Vasal, A, Vohra, S., Payan, E., & Seedat, Y. (2019). Closing The Data-value Gap: How to become data-driven and pivot to the new, Accenture.com white paper of 2019.

Chapter 3

Knowns, Unknowns, and the Elusive Value From Analytics

Topics Covered in this Chapter

1. The unknown unknowns	"In theory, there is supposed to be an untold amount of treasure in terms of data & actionable insights just waiting to be unearthed in Unknown-unknowns".
2. The decision you are making & the data that you need	What to do when you do not have all the data that you need, to support the decisions you are taking.
3. Johari window for an organization. a. Customers' perspective b. Employee perspective	Among other things, the Blind area represents "customer's perception of value" from the organizations' products & services vis-à-vis competition that the Organization is blind to. This represents an opportunity for unearthing hidden attributes influencing the customer behavior through Customer Analytics.
4. In search of value from analytics	The moot question is – By focusing on decisions – which perhaps represent "Known-knowns & Known-unknowns", are we foregoing the seemingly much bigger prize being promised in "Unknown-unknowns"?

DOI: 10.1201/9781003321347-4

There are known-knowns. These are things we know that we know. There are known unknowns. That is to say, there are things that we know we don't know. But there are also unknown unknowns. There are things we don't know we don't know.

DONALD RUMSFELD
(Former Secretary of Defense, US Cabinet Position)

You will always do better if you ignore the information you don't understand, than if you try to act based on it

RICHARD SAUL WURMAN
(Author & Creator of TED Conferences)

Figure 3.1   Knowns and unknowns.

INTRODUCTION

Donald Rumsfeld's famous comment about unknown-unknowns in a news briefing of 2002 has become the mantra of the big data world. There are indeed many who believe the future of data science is in unknown-unknowns, and all the true transformational opportunities for quantum improvements in business are to be found only by leveraging big data analytics into exploring the unknown-unknowns.

I felt compelled to write about the unknown-unknowns when I realized that a fair few of those who went through my articles (published on Data Science Central) have complimented me on coming out with a valuable methodology for perfecting the knowns.

As explained in the earlier chapters, any organization setting out to become data-driven and embarking on an analytics journey needs to prioritize its investments by targeting opportunities with the highest return on investment (ROI) first, and then create a priority roadmap for analytics investments based on relative business value (impact on business outcomes) and complexity score. Now, the moot point is: where exactly is the organization likely to find the highest ROI – is it in known-knowns, or in unknown-unknowns?

I remember reading a number of articles on this very subject when I was tasked with creating a roadmap and business case for analytics – Center of Excellence (CoE) earlier, and several more subsequently. There was one, published on the BBC website by Dr. Mike Lynch – CEO and founder of Autonomy (HP) – where he suggests there is an information goldmine in unknown-unknowns; He goes on: "For CEOs, using technology to spot the unknown-unknowns during this time of economic uncertainty will be regarded as a superpower, helping them to make better business decisions and ultimately beat the competition" (Lynch, 2012).

One particular incident is still very fresh in my memory. I was having one of those Friday evening drinks with a set of consultants (from a well-known consulting company) and after downing a third, one of the partners politely inquired as to the progress I had made on my analytics roadmap assignment. I truthfully confessed I was not making much headway, saying "I still do not have clarity on which specific decisions need to be supported with what kind of analytics." He did not actually rise from his seat, but it felt as if he did, as he looked down at me as a ninety-year-old would at a newborn.

"You are doing it all wrong." He did not exactly call me a novice and a nincompoop, but it felt as if he did. "My dear friend, you are barking up the wrong tree," and he was all mysterious as he declared "Analytics is all about unknown-unknowns … there is a goldmine there."

No one can possibly deny the value of big data analytics when it comes to sifting the known-unknowns and unknown-unknowns in areas such as fraud detection, and identity theft, among others, from huge numbers of credit card transactions, or spotting patterns or mavericks from very large datasets such as social media data. There is a SAS article (Taylor, n.d) which describes how big data analytics can help tackling the growing terror threats – the known-unknowns and unknown-unknowns that Donald Rumsfeld mentioned in his speech in 2002.

But when it comes to enterprise analytics, I believe the size of unknown-unknowns is different for different organizations and is determined by the maturity of the organization. One recent article (Andrews, 2014) I found closer to my thinking was by Anita Andrews of RJ Metrics (which was acquired by Magento-Adobe in 2016). She makes a convincing argument as to why organizations aspiring to be great should explore the unknown-unknowns.

So, what exactly are unknown-unknowns and how do they change as organizations mature? For organizations embarking on an analytics journey, what would be a bigger priority? Known-unknowns or unknown-unknowns? Here is my attempt answering this question.

3.1 The Unknown-Unknowns

Donald Rumsfeld is supposed to have coined this phrase for the first time in response to a question in a news briefing (Graham, 2014) in 2002. I also came across an interview stating that astrophysicist and data scientist Dr. Kirk Borne (Borne, 2015) had been using the phrase a few years before it percolated down to Donald Rumsfeld.

In reality, the concept of unknown-unknowns was first introduced by psychologists Joseph Luft and Harrington Ingham in 1955, when they created the Johari window as a technique to help people understand relationships between themselves and others.

Whatever may be the actual origin, in theory, there is supposed to be an untold amount of treasure in terms of data and actionable insights just waiting to be unearthed in unknown-unknowns (Figure 3.2).

Figure 3.2 explains the concept. Theoretically, one could find as much value in unknown-unknowns as Columbus did when he accidentally discovered America. (Though one could argue Columbus was actually asking a question, albeit a wrong one, when he set sail to discover a sea route to India.)

Big data as a concept has tremendous value where we deal with a huge population of statistical data, and where it becomes nearly impossible to take out a representative sample, no matter what the sampling technique is. Real life examples include pharmaco-genomic data and demographic data among others.

However, any organization embarking on an analytics journey needs to prioritize its analytics investments, targeting the highest relative value first (Figure 3.3).

So, here are a few questions that need to be answered:

1. What should be a bigger priority? Known-knowns or unknown-unknowns?
2. Does it make sense to explore unknown-unknowns, even before exhausting all the actionable insights from the data that is captured-available within the organization i.e., known-knowns?
3. What are the odds of finding highly valuable insights from unknown-unknowns?

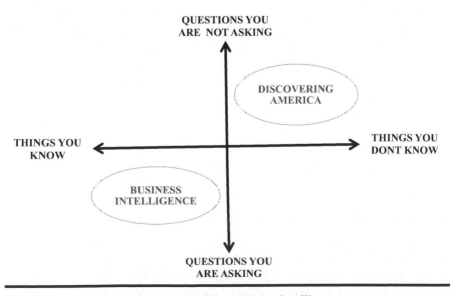

Figure 3.2 Knowns, unknowns, and the business intelligence.

	KNOWNS	UNKNOWNS
UNKNOWN	**UNKNOWN-KNOWNS** We don't know what we know BIG DATA ANALYTICS ON TOP OF "BI"	**UNKNOWN-UNKNOWNS** We don't know what we don't know BIG DATA ANALYTICS (Pattern Recognition, Clustering, Classification etc.)
KNOWN	**KNOWN-KNOWNS** We know what we know BUSINESS INTELLIGENCE	**KNOWN-UNKNOWNS** We know what we don't know BIG DATA ANALYTICS ON TOP OF "BI"

Figure 3.3   Knowns, unknowns, and the big data.

From my experience, a good many organizations are yet to get their business intelligence (BI) strategy right. Most chief information officers (CIOs) would tell you the majority of the BI reports they generate are hardly ever used by their business users.

While a good part of the problem lies in a poorly executed data strategy; we have also noticed that very often the BI initiatives are conceptualized in a way far distant from business reality and requirements, by IT companies which have no understanding of the domain, and as a result poorly address the business problems, and not surprisingly have very poor acceptability among the business users.

3.2 Decisions That You Are Making and the Data That You Need

It is unlikely that an organization will have all the data that it needs within its enterprise applications, or anywhere, in any format within the enterprise. There is always a part of the data that you know you need, but do not have internally, and you need to source it from outside of the enterprise. There will also be data that you need, but you do not actually know you need. The concept of data conundrum will be explained in more detail, in later chapters (Figure 3.4).

However, in the context of the decisions that you are making currently (i.e., the questions that you are asking currently), it is important to understand the concept of the data gap, that is, the delta data that you need but you do not have currently, and what do in such a scenario. Figure 3.4 helps you understand your options.

	You have Data!	You do not have Data!
Decisions You Are Not Making Currently	• Big-data analytics for Pattern Recognition • Trend Analysis • Analysis of Statistical Mavericks	• What opportunities are you missing? • What signals–threats are you overlooking?
Decisions You Are Making Currently	• Focus on 10% of Decisions which influence 90% business outcomes. • Automate all Rule-based Decisions • Prescriptive Analytics for "critical decisions"-Build "push analytics"	• Focus on 10% of Decisions which influence 90% business outcomes. • Source the "data-gap" from internal & external sources • Big-data analytics for Pattern Recognition

Figure 3.4 Decisions you are making and the data gap!

3.3 A Johari Window For an Organization

Last time I created my own Johari window as a part of T-group sessions was close to 30 years back, when I was a fresh management trainee working for an aerospace company.

Those of you who have gone through the exercise would remember the way to self-discovery would be to tell more about yourself (be transparent) and ask for more feedback (Figure 3.5).

Over the last 60 years, the concept of the Johari window has been applied in a wide variety of areas, including a few select attempts for an organization as an entity. As a method to appreciate the source of value from analytics, here is yet another attempt to create Johari window for an organization as an entity interacting with different stakeholders – customers, investors, employees, and society.

3.3.1 Customers' Perspective

Consider the Johari window for an(y) organization from the customer perspective. Among other things, the **blind** area represents customers' perception of value from the organizations' products and services vis-à-vis competition that the organization is blind to. This represents an opportunity for unearthing hidden attributes influencing customer behavior through customer analytics (Figure 3.6).

Similarly, the **unknown** area represents the completely hidden reasons for customer behavior of which neither the customer nor the organization is aware. Technically this area may have opportunities for huge upsides to top-line or bottom-line which can be unearthed through big data analytics.

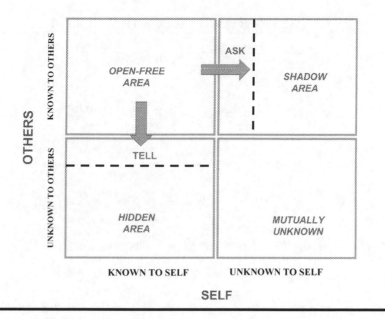

Figure 3.5   Johari window.

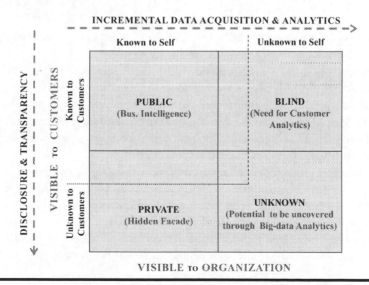

Figure 3.6   Johari window for organization – customer perspective.

3.3.2 Employees' Perspective

The Johari window shown in Figure 3.7 could be redrawn with respect to any of the other organizational stakeholders such as employees, investors, government or even society at large. Consider the picture given here from the perspective of employees.

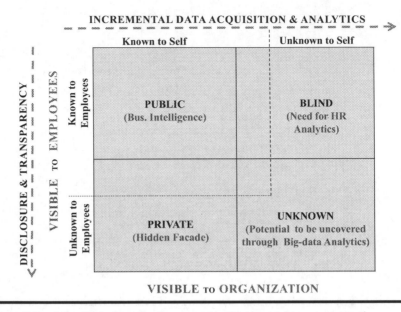

Figure 3.7 Johari window for the organization – employee perspective.

Employee engagement and retention is one of the key issues for global organizations where the primary differentiator is the quality of people.

Large globally spread out organizations at the highest level often lose sight of the intrinsic reasons for higher employee turnover, or lower motivation levels at times: why does one product or geography of the organization do better than the others in terms of employee satisfaction levels? Could the incentives for higher motivation levels in one part of the organization be replicated in different parts of the organization with an equal amount of success? (Figure 3.7)

Organizations often collect a large amount of data though employee engagement surveys like Gallup Q12. The critics of these surveys complain that there is very little correlation between the Q12 score of an organization or a division and the actual business performance. They also quote instances of high Q12 scores coupled with higher employee turnover which turns the traditional logic upside down. HR analytics could help unearth the real reasons behind employee behavior in all such cases.

3.4 In Search of Value From Analytics

Going back to the original question, let's consider this: how does one prioritize analytics investments? Or, how does one create a roadmap of investments for making one's organization data-driven?

Assuming my original hypothesis is still sacrosanct, one must kickstart the exercise by identifying and prioritizing the opportunities where advanced analytics can make a material difference to the quality of decisions. In other words, one must identify 20% of the decisions which influence 80% of the organizational outcomes and prioritize them by decreasing order of relative value. Now, the moot question is: by focusing on decisions – which perhaps represent known-knowns and known-unknowns – are we foregoing the seemingly much bigger prize being promised in unknown-unknowns?

The real answer is – it depends. It really depends on the maturity of the organization and the size of unknown-unknowns.

3.4.1 In Theory

As organizations mature, they tend to expand the region known as known-knowns. They become more process-driven, have more structured relevant data (captured-available with requisite granularity), and, more importantly, have more structured decision-making.

I have also seen a few adaptations of the "four stages of competency" (attributed to Noel Burch of Gordon Training International and also to Abraham Maslow) to the evolution of organization (Figure 3.8).

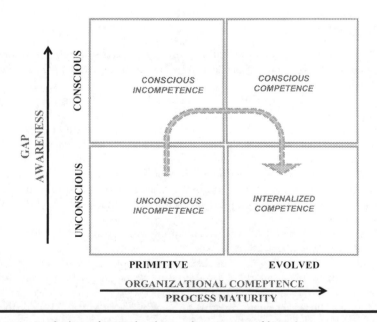

Figure 3.8   Evolution of organization – the process of learning.

3.4.2 In Reality

Organizations do not function in a static environment. Everything from customer requirements to competition, governmental regulations, and compliance requirements are all dynamic in nature and can substantially change overnight. This is apart from the complexity that gets added from organic and inorganic growth, new products, and new geographies being added every year. As a result, most growing organizations are permanently in a catch-up mode with respect to their process framework and IT system's maturity keeping pace with the organizational growth.

In my experience, most organizations growing faster than market struggle with the legacy of multiple IT applications functioning as islands of information, multiple accounting systems, and multiple data definitions, with little or no data governance in place.

Ideally, they should take a pause every few years to consolidate the till-then growth and to integrate operations. The consolidation phase (pause in growth) helps in bringing the process and systems' maturity closer to organizational needs.

A few years ago, when my work involved setting up and scaling shared services for multinationals, I used to talk about the need to create a **growth template** – a kind of process-systems combination, which could be used for quickly implementing-replicating the standard process and systems into any new geography or product line that the organization is expanding into. Well, that is a different story for a different time.

Bibliography

Adizes I., Cudanov, M., & Rodic, D. (2017). Timing of proactive organizational consulting: Difference between organizational perception and behaviour. *Amfiteatru Economic*, 19(44), 232.

Andrews, A. (2014). The big opportunities in the unknown unknowns. RJ Metrics Blog of Apr 30, 2014.

Bhuyan, H. K., & Pani, S. K. (2021). Crime predictive model using big data analytics. *Intelligent Data Analytics for Terror Threat Prediction: Architectures, Methodologies, Techniques and Applications*, 57–78.

Borne, K. (2015). The power of data to know the world, to improve the world, and to change the world, *Dataconomy*, Oct 2015. https://dataconomy.com/2015/10/the-power-of-data-to-know-the-world-to-improve-the-world-and-to-change-the-world/ [Accessed Aug 2022].

Graham, D. A. (2014). Rumsfeld's knowns and unknowns: The intellectual history of a quip. *The Atlantic.com*, March 28, 2014.

Lynch, M. (2012). Data wars: Unlocking the information goldmine. *BBC.com* Apr 13, 2012.

Marim, A. (2019). MI5 and the Met ramp up use of analytics to tackle terrorism. *ComputerWeekly.com*, 03 Apr 2019.

Taylor, J. (n.d.) Director of Public Security, SAS "Why big data analytics holds the key to tackling the changing terror threat". *SAS.com*.

Unsigned Blog (2014). Analytics, knowns, and unknowns. *TextOre.net*, October 26, 2014.

Chapter 4

Toward a Data-Driven Organization

A Roadmap For Analytics

Topics Covered in this Chapter

1. The challenge of making analytics work	"While investment into Advanced Analytics is being considered a survival necessity, Gartner mentions only 30–40% of all analytics initiatives deliver some business value…"
2. Decision-oriented analytics: From decisions To data	The importance of starting from the decision and working out data behind the decisions.
3. The importance of beginning from end	"The problem with starting from data: Is there a light at the end of the tunnel? What is the guarantee there will be some valuable insights once you process the raw-data?"
4. Deciphering the "data behind the decisions"	Unlike the traditional approach, this process helps us identify the "data gaps" behind the decision, and create a "data sourcing strategy" for missing data
5. Meet the ad hoc manager	"While the ad-hoc managers thrive, those few who look for permanent and comprehensive solutions lose out, as the optics of 'looking for a permanent enterprise-solution' are not great."

DOI: 10.1201/9781003321347-5

6. Local vs. global solutions	...a compelling argument as to why organizations must consider implementing an enterprise-wide data-to-decisions transformational exercise.
7. Problem vs. opportunity mindset	The concept of point-fixing a solution to "a specific problem" presupposes that the system is otherwise at its peak productivity and hence one need not look for further opportunities to optimize cost and cycle time, or to reach more customers.
8. Roadmap for data-driven organization	What are the big decisions? Those taken by CxOs? Strategic Decisions? Decisions involving large Capital Outlay.

INTRODUCTION

I am one of those fortunate few who have had an opportunity to work on both sides of the table, as a provider and also as a consumer of technology and business services. A few years ago, while I was working on the other side of the table, I was asked to explore setting up an analytics center-of-excellence to support decision-makers in different business units (BUs) and functions. Nobody was using the phrase "data-driven organization" back then; it was essentially an effort to consolidate all analytics and reporting work from across the organization into one centralized offshore location. I was asked to submit a preliminary proposal with a tentative timeline and a budget. I decided to start by talking to some of the stakeholders.

As I mentioned earlier in this book, there are two distinct sets of stakeholders within an organization:

- Set 1: The consumers of information
- Set 2: The providers of information (the IT department) and the sponsors of the project.

Since I knew the project sponsors would insist on a formal due diligence, my first step was to try talking to the IT department (Set 1) to get some informal understanding on: Business Intelligence and Data Warehousing (BI-DW) practices across the locations, data availability, data quality, key analytics requirements, existing practices and protocols etc... Next, I attempted the ever-challenging task of talking to some of the stakeholders (Set 2) about what they might expect from an analytics CoE (center-of-excellence). Their reactions varied from "can-you-first-make-our-IT-systems-work?" to "would-we-ever-get-the-data-we-need-when-we need-it?".

I tried understanding how many reports they asked for, how many they got, and if they actually derived value from those reports. The responses I received were vague; most people said they did not exactly track such information. Few directed me to talk to their assistant's assistants.

How about what they considered important reports; the reports they would send to board, for example?

I received a black and white response this time. "We make those reports ourselves... collate them from multiple sources... yes... on Excel."

When asked about the relative time they would spend on creating a report vs. analyzing a report, the most vocal feedback was:

"Reports are usually made because we are asked to submit them for reviews. We spend 99% of the time chasing the data, and 1% in creating a report, barely managing to submit it before the deadline... so we rarely get the time to review and analyze a report."

I have persisted and pestered a willing few to try and list the specific data analytics requirements to support their decisions. To cut to the chase, I did not have much success. While some drew a blank, many gave me a list of *everything*, telling me:

"After all I don't know what the board is likely to ask me in my review..."

While my experiences with gathering informal inputs for my proposal, be what they may, somewhere along the line, I decided to expand the scope and started actually using the phrase "data-driven organization". From that point forward, it became imperative for me to not only define the nature of what exactly I was proposing, but also to estimate the investment and the value it would be likely to deliver.

Not one to give up easily, I decided to seek help from consulting companies (those already on board – empaneled) to help me understand the way forward. I called the usual suspects and, as expected, they were more than willing to do a due diligence to suggest a way forward:

"We need to start with all BI reports, consolidate the reports based on actual usage statistics, and add analytics on top of them." Somehow, starting from existing BI reports did not sound right to me. It did not take long for me to understand the concept of data-driven organization was not understood too well by the consultants; at least by those few I talked to.

I tried some of the market leading specialized analytics firms next... a fast-growing new breed. The most common response was:

"Tell us the problem you are trying to solve, we will collect and collate the data from your multiple applications, clean and normalize the data, then run analytics on top of them".

This appeared too transactional. I tried telling them I needed help with listing the problems from across the organization that needed to be resolved, explaining:

"I need a master-plan to identify the opportunities for advanced analytics and create a roadmap for transforming the company into a data-driven organization. I also need a business case with the cost benefits if I am to get the management to fund the initiative. I am keen on identifying all the opportunities for data-driven decision-making in the organization."

Sadly, there were no takers. For some of you, this story may sound familiar.

4.1 The Challenge of Making Analytics Work

Investment into advanced analytics is now considered a survival necessity for organizations wanting to compete in an increasingly digitized marketplace. While the value from analytics in areas such as retail, fraud detection and customer acquisition is now unquestionable, Gartner mentions only 30–40% of all analytics initiatives deliver some business value.

However, most CxOs we have spoken with think that the very idea of data-driven organization is far-fetched, and too big a leap from where they are currently. Some told us they are yet to see results from their SAP business objects and business intelligence investments.

Most admit they seldom know **what data** they need prior to an important meeting, and hence ask for **as much data as they can get**. If they do not know what data they need, they are unlikely to tell you what decisions they will take. It would be futile to ask them to list the decisions that they are planning to take based on the data that they are demanding you must supply here and now.

On the other hand, Chief Information Officers (CIOs) complain that the satisfaction of the business is an ever-moving target, and their internal customers seldom know what they want. Some CIOs mentioned that they produce hundreds of customized reports, most of which are rarely used by the business.

So, there lies the challenge of investing in advanced analytics and making it work, support decisions, and deliver value.

4.1.1 Investing in Analytics: The Fear of Being Left Behind

In 2016, Gartner estimated that on average, 60% of all big data projects fail to deliver intended value. A year later, Gartner analyst, Nick Heudecker said his company was "too conservative" with its 60% estimate and put the failure rate at "closer to 85%" (Delen et al., 2018).

This sums up the experience of global companies investing millions into analytics. Thanks to the hype, every company worth its name aspires to becomes 100% data-driven as of yesterday, and every CIO has a sizable budget for analytics. The odd CIO who is cautious, undecided, and yet to invest, is being called a laggard, and is being made answerable for unutilized budgets, and lost opportunities.

However, barring the obvious winners like fraud detection, social media data analysis, customer profiling and so forth., most companies still do not know where to start or what area they should prioritize. Many CIOs seek the easy way out and invest in a visualization platform like Tableau or QlikView. Both Tableau and QlikView, incidentally, are great products provided one knows exactly what data needs to be analyzed for what specific insights, and if such data is available with sufficient granularity in accessible indexed format.

The net result is that such investments in visualization platforms are just another version of the business objects/business intelligence investments made by the very same companies in the recent past. And no one knows what the return on the investments that were made earlier was.

Internet companies are an exception to the above. Given all the transactional and customer data resides in the same application, and, more importantly, given the clarity on the purpose of analytics, the success rate is far higher. The brick-and-mortar companies on the other hand, carry a legacy of hundreds of disparate, unconnected applications with multiple global instances, sometimes with disparate business processes local to each instance and, in the absence of global standard operating procedures (GSOPs), are not so lucky. They usually provide testimony to Gartner's estimate of 85% failure rate.

4.2 Decision-Oriented Analytics: From Decisions to Data

In their 2012 HBR feature on big data (McAfee et al., 2012), Andrew McAfee and Erik Brynjolfsson describe the opportunity and report that "companies in the top third of their industry in the use of data-driven decision-making were, on average, 5% more productive and 6% more profitable than their competitors" even after accounting for several confounding factors. The same article further states, "The evidence is clear: Data-driven decisions tend to be better decisions. Leaders will either embrace this fact or be replaced by others who do" (McAfee et al., 2012).

Wigmore (2016) defines data-driven decision management (DDDM) as: "an approach to business governance that values decisions that can be backed up with data that can be verified. Data-driven decision management is usually undertaken as a means of gaining a competitive advantage."

From my own experience, the key word that is usually not given the importance it deserves is "data". The decision can only be as good as the data that is supporting it. Not the quantity of data, but its quality and relevance.

I have tried to find out if anyone has already thought through this problem. Surprisingly, there are very few references. The one I found closest to my thought-process was from James Taylor of Decision Management Solutions. While I had not read his book (Taylor & Raden, 2007), at that point of time, my attention was drawn to their work when I read a SAS Institute white paper (2018) citing the book on the importance of starting with the "decision in mind." The paper states: "Some decisions are major (e.g., which countries to do business in), and some are minor (e.g., what to offer as a cross-sell to a customer on the phone)." The same SAS white paper also cites another book, *The 7 Habits of Highly Effective People* (Covey, 2013), which apparently advocates: "begin with the end in mind."

These are the two conclusions I have arrived at –

1. While the SAS white paper does not mention this exactly, it reinforces the method I often use for data-design: *Deriving the data definitions from the decision-making criteria (variables/constraints)*. Identifying and prioritizing decisions is the necessary first step for any organization embarking on a journey to become a data-driven organization (Figure 4.1)

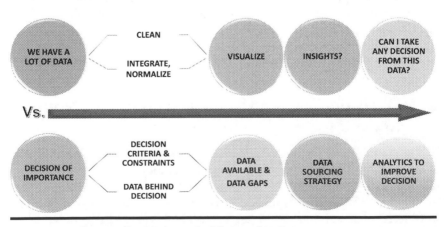

Figure 4.1   Data to decision, or decision to data?

2. The next step is to *identify the data behind each of these shortlisted business critical decisions*, which means identifying the data required for supporting each of the decisions, the data gap, and the data sourcing strategy. Further, for meaningful analytics data needs to be available in the required form, format, and with appropriate level of granularity.

4.3 The Importance of Beginning From the End

So, what is missing with traditional thinking associated with analytics?

Allow me to explain myself further. Consider the traditional analytics process as practiced by most analytics consulting firms. Most of them refer to the analytics process (Figure 4.2) as *the process that goes into making raw-data into interactive analytics* that a decision-maker could potentially use.

Perfectly logical, and almost all analytics companies apply the same logic: "Give me your data, and we will try and bring out some insights out of it."

The missing piece of logic here: Is there a light at the end of the tunnel?

1. What is the guarantee there will be some valuable insights once you process the data?
2. What decisions can I take based on such insights?
3. What will be the "incremental value" generated by such insights?
4. What is the guarantee that such "incremental value" justifies the investment in time, money, and effort involved in "converting raw-data into interactive analytics"?
5. In essence, is there a business case for the analytics project?

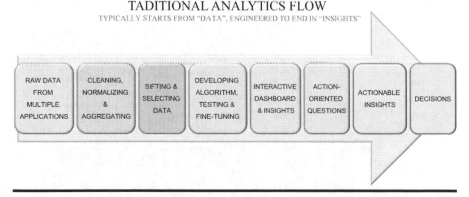

Figure 4.2   Traditional analytics flow.

This is perhaps a perfect example of an exercise for finding unknown answers (insights) to unknown questions (decisions). The success rate improves substantially when we know the question or at least a good part of the question.

In my view, the very idea of starting from data is questionable. While one may still find a few actionable insights by accident, I would expect such insights to be insignificant; and highly unlikely to support the "big" decisions, the vital-few decisions that influence the majority of the business outcomes. The ideal approach would be to reverse the flow.

4.4 Deciphering the Data behind the Decisions

To reverse the flow, one needs to begin with the end in mind, that is, start from a decision (particularly, the 10% of the decisions, that account for 90% of business outcomes); and then work out the data needed to support the decision. It is possible you may have only a part of the data that you need within the enterprise; and an even smaller part in accessible normalized format.

Unlike the traditional approach, this process helps us in identifying the data gaps behind the decision, and in creating a data sourcing strategy for missing data (Figure 4.3).

Here is the gist of the process in seven simple steps.

1. Start from the decision; one of the identified critical decisions.
2. Work out the data behind the decision, meaning, the data that you need, to support the decision.

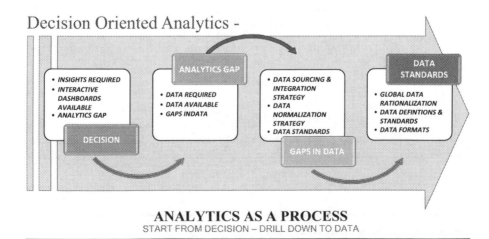

ANALYTICS AS A PROCESS
START FROM DECISION – DRILL DOWN TO DATA

Figure 4.3 Starting from a decision…

3. Initiate a gap analysis: the data-gap, or the portion of the data that you need, and currently not available within the enterprise.
4. Create a data sourcing strategy:
   In the short-term:
   i.   Either source the delta-data, or
   ii. Modify the algorithm, or model to draw insights from available data.
   For the long-term: Need for working out what data with what granularity needs to be captured at transaction level from different transactional IT applications to support the decision.
5. Create an algorithm, or analytics model to draw insights from the data.
6. Institutionalize the data-driven decision-making model, by creating systems, applications, and processes, that can generate all the data you need to support the critical decisions.
7. Conduct a periodic value delivery audit to check if the investment in analytics is actually helping to improve the quality of decisions, thereby generating incremental cashflows.

Starting from a decision and working out the data and the analysis required to support the decision (i.e., the data behind the decision), in essence, means looking for specific answers to specific questions. Which means that business value from analytics is guaranteed, assuming the right data is being analyzed using the right algorithm.

Further, in business, it is usually similar questions that need to be answered time and again. The same decision may have to be taken again and again. Taking a comprehensive look at a decision, along with the variables associated with the decision, and a building a permanent global solution helps in keeping the analytics effort focused, cost-effective and lean, while ensuring a recurring business value from a one-time investment.

Building a permanent global solution requires defining and documenting the processes, systems and standards covering the entire data-to-decisions flow across the enterprise.

WHO EXACTLY IS RESPONSIBLE FOR PROCESS IMPROVEMENT AND INNOVATION?

While organizations have created C-level positions for data and digital transformation, there is often an unresolved confusion as to who exactly owns enterprise-wide process improvement and innovation. Someone is needed with the authority and the mandate to look at the enterprise value-chain in its entirety, identifying and resolving the constraints and bottlenecks for maximizing the enterprise throughput.

4.5 Meet the Ad Hoc Manager!

While we know starting from a decision is ideal, in reality most organizations are run by "ad hoc" managers: people who react to what they believe is a unique one-time problem and look for a unique solution. They are perpetually on the run, resolving one crisis after the other, and hunting for data and analytics to help resolve the crisis, each time. They never get the time to understand if the problem is really unique, or if it is a recurring issue that deserves a permanent fix.

Unfortunately, an overwhelming majority of the stakeholders (information consumers) in most organizations are "ad hoc" managers. The community of "ad hoc" managers is thriving because organizations reward and promote these managers; essentially because they appear to be busy all the time, resolving crisis after crisis. Organizations get conned into believing that activity is effectiveness.

While the ad hoc managers thrive, those few who look for permanent and comprehensive solutions lose out, as the optics of looking for a permanent enterprise solution are not great. To start with, the permanent enterprise-wide solution requires a greater amount of due diligence to prove that the so-called unique ad hoc problem is not only a recurring event, but is, in fact, experienced by fellow-managers across the enterprise, possibly with minor variations. Further, permanent solutions require a greater investment in time, quality of people, and effort, besides budget. Finally, organizations do not accord enough authority to a typical everyday manager to insist on an enterprise-wide solution. An everyday manager is expected to be working within the four walls of his or her division, department, cubicle, and most importantly within his or her brief, and budget.

The result is multiple local applications to cater to the ad hoc requirements, optimized for local conditions and local constraints. The life of a local application may range from a few days to few years, and the number of users may range from one to less than a hundred.

4.6 Local vs. Global Solutions

Here is a compelling argument as to why organizations must prefer implementing an enterprise-wide data-to-decisions transformational exercise, rather than being caught up in helping the ad hoc manager resolve his never-ending crises. Figure 4.4 illustrates how a combination of lack of data governance and multiple disconnected islands of information can lead to complete chaos as the quality of data will be compromised, and any investment in analytics is unlikely to succeed.

Catering to multiple local solutions means multiple data standards, and multiple data definitions which are never in sync., necessitating investments in expensive **data preparation solutions** – such as an extract, transform and load (ETL) solutions on top of a data lake or a data warehouse (Figure 4.4).

The single biggest reason for poor data quality is the inconsistency in the way data is defined and captured in different source IT applications, especially in the

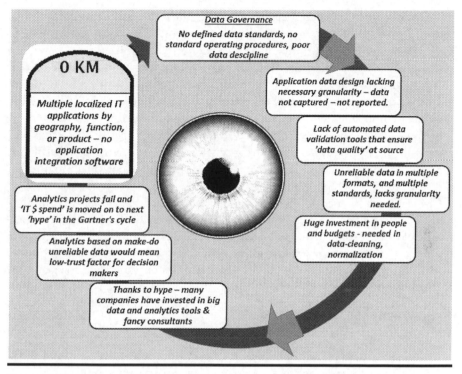

Figure 4.4   How poor governance leads to poor data quality.

absence of a Master Data Management (MDM) module. The inconsistency results in the same data having different granularity, besides different definitions, and different standards in each of the different source systems, making automated integration and normalization extremely difficult.

While there are several reasons why organizations end up getting into this vicious cycle, the following are the most common:

- A poorly implemented best-of-breed strategy and poor integration of localized applications.
- Absence of MDM, data standards, data definitions.
- Most importantly, poor, or non-existent data governance.

Analytics projects are bound to fail if the underlying data quality is poor.

4.7 Problem vs. Opportunity Mindset

Most IT consulting companies, including the new breed of analytics companies, prefer selling resource time; meaning they bill for a set of resources for a period of time, although they do offer fixed bids for developing solutions for specific problems with a defined scope. It is very rare that they attempt to convince their clients to consider an enterprise transformation into a data-driven organization.

And ask any consultant and they will tell you how most of the so-called global multi-national-organizations are notoriously transactional; their focus is almost always on resolving the problems of yesterday, here, and now. None of them have the time to think long-term, to look to the future or at the big picture. Not surprisingly, most analytics projects are centered around resolving a specific problem; hence a one-time fix is acceptable. The enterprise-wide transformational exercises if any, are initiated only when there is a crisis; a crisis serious enough potentially to threaten the very existence of the organization.

Managers in such companies are conditioned to think in the short-term. They may not exactly live one day at a time, but they never propose any initiative that cannot be planned, executed, and validated within 90 days. So, most analytics projects typically start off with an immediate problem that the customer needs to resolve, and consultants usually offer a one-off solution based on static data collated from different sources and normalized. After all, as they know from their collective experience, any big ticket transformational solution will be very difficult to push through (Figure 4.5).

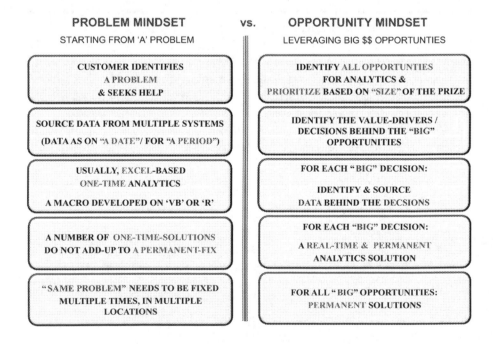

Figure 4.5   Problem mindset vs. opportunity mindset.

The concept of point-fixing a solution to a specific problem presupposes that the system is otherwise at its peak productivity and hence one need not look for further opportunities to optimize cost and cycle time, or to reach more customers.

On the other hand, an opportunity-focused analytics roadmap would involve identifying all the opportunities where analytics can help incrementally improve the efficiency of the process. The process flows are depicted in Figure 4.5. (Note: All internet companies are exceptions. Internet & e-commerce companies have very rich, centralized-standardized data; all data in one application-instance, and hence can invest in advanced machine-learning/AI solutions to offer personalized experiences for each customer).

4.8 A Roadmap for Data-Driven Organization

I have read numerous articles and books on data-driven organizations and how they help organizations function at optimal efficiencies, while keeping them nimble, adaptive, and customer-focused. A number of them talk about the importance of building data culture. However, not one of them tells us what the qualifying criteria are for an organization to call itself 100% data-driven. None of the books or published articles cover or provide a step-by-step method or a roadmap for enterprise-wide transformation into a data-driven organization.

Most consulting companies advocate starting from data, both structured and unstructured. They talk about choosing a few low-hanging fruits or industry-specific business cases based on the experience of others. Most projects are kicked off without clearly laying down success criteria or targeted value, let alone creating an enterprise-wide roadmap and business case.

In my view, in a true data-driven organization nearly 100% of the decisions are made based on data. As most CIOs would agree, a few isolated successes, or a one-time leveraging of big data for decision-making does not make an organization data-driven.

The acid test for a data-driven organization is when the big decisions (meaning all CXO-level strategic decisions) are taken based on data, and where possible, with an audit trail.

The following questions arise at this stage, and we continue to deliberate upon the answers to these questions:

- What are the big decisions? Those taken by CxO's? Strategic decisions? Decisions involving large capital outlay? What exactly would be the process to identify the big decisions?
- How exactly do we quantify the impact on business outcomes?
- What other factors influence decision priority?

What I propose here is a comprehensive methodology for prioritizing organizational decisions based on a holistic set of parameters, which not only considers the dollar value of the decision, but also the cumulative number of times the decision is taken in a year.

For example, a decision on how much buffer-stock to keep in each of the warehouses may be individually a small dollar value decision, but, collectively across locations and cumulative over the year, it could be the most important organizational decision affecting the bottom-line of the company.

Hence, any transformational journey toward a data-driven organization needs to be a two-phase engagement. The first phase exclusively for identifying the 10% of the decisions that influence 90% of the organizational outcomes; and the second phase for working out analytics solutions that could substantially improve the quality of each of the identified decisions.

4.9 Summary

To summarize: if an organization indeed would like to think out-of-the box, and would like to explore all the "big" opportunities where analytics can make a material difference to the quality of decisions, here is the way forward.

1. Identify the **big decisions** – the 10% of decisions that influence 90% of business outcomes.
2. Create a **priority roadmap for** advanced analytics, based on business criticality of the decision and the size of the prize (in dollars).
3. Create a transformational **roadmap** and a **business case** for analytics.
4. Work out the **data behind the decisions** for each of the identified decisions.
5. Identify the **data gap**; i.e., the delta-data, or the data that you need to support the decision, but you do not have currently.
6. Source the **delta-data**; improve the quality of data.
7. Institutionalize **data governance**; introduce data standards and data definitions and others.
8. **Implement analytics** as per the transformational roadmap.
9. Conduct a periodic **value audit**.

Bibliography

Andrew White, Gartner (2019, January 03). Our top data and analytics predicts for 2019. https://blogs.gartner.com/andrew_white/2019/01/03/our-top-data-and-analytics-predicts-for-2019/

Asay, Matt (2017). 85% of big data projects fail, *TechRepublic*, Nov, 2017. https://www.techrepublic.com/article/85-of-big-data-projects-fail-but-your-developers-can-help-yourssucceed/

Barton, D., & Cour, D. (2013). *Three Keys to Building a Data-driven Strategy*. McKinsey Global Institute, (March), 1–4.

Blenko, M. W., Mankins, M. C., & Rogers, P. (2010). The decision-driven organization. *Harvard Business Review*, 88(6), 54–62.

Covey, S. R. (2013). *The 7 Habits of Highly Effective People: Powerful Lessons in Personal Change*. Simon and Schuster.

Delen, D., Moscato, G., & Toma, I. L. (2018, January). The impact of real-time business intelligence and advanced analytics on the behaviour of business decision makers. In *2018 International Conference on Information Management and Processing (ICIMP)* (pp. 49–53). IEEE.

Henrion, M. (2021). Why most big data analytics projects fail. How to succeed by engaging with your clients.

How to build a Data-Driven Organization (n.d.) https://www.tableau.com/learn/articles/how-to-build-a-data-driven-organization [Accessed August 2022].

Introducing Tableau Blueprint (n.d.) https://www.tableau.com/learn/blueprint [Accessed Aug 2022].

McAfee, A., Brynjolfsson, E., Davenport, T. H., Patil, D. J., & Barton, D. (2012). Big data: the management revolution. *Harvard Business Review*, 90(10), 60–68.

Patrizio, A. (2019). 4 reasons big data projects fail—and 4 ways to succeed. *Infoworld.com*, May 16, 2019.

Peregud, I. (2018). Five characteristics of a data-driven company. *tdw*i.org, September 26, 2018.

SAS (2018). Managing the Analytics Life Cycle For Decisions at Scale. *SAS White Paper*, 2018.

Saulles, M. D. (2019). What exactly is a data-driven organization. *cio.com*, 29 Oct 2019.

Taylor, J. & Raden, N. (2007). *Smart Enough Systems: How to Deliver Competitive Advantage by Automating Hidden Decisions*. Pearson Education.

Wigmore, I. (2016). Data-driven decision management. *Whatis.techtarget.com*, Apr 2016.

Chapter 5

Identifying the "Big" Decisions

Topics Covered in this Chapter

1. Taking stock: Existing analytics assets	Setting the Context: Starting with an audit of existing analytics investments & the value-delivered.
2. The lost art of decision making	"Most managers simply did not know what to list as a decision, and they confessed identifying critical decisions was even more difficult. Nearly all of them have listed 'Investment decisions' (which involved purchase of capital goods or capitalizable services) as the most critical decisions that they take."
3. Prioritizing decisions: In search of an objective methodology	"While I expected there would be a mountain of published research on categorization of decisions, and specifically for identifying the critical organizational decisions, I was completely disappointed...There was little-to-no published research on the importance of categorization of decisions, let alone a process for identifying the top 10%."

DOI: 10.1201/9781003321347-6

4. Learning from Bain model	"Winnowing the list: Prioritizing decisions by Value, followed by Degree of Management Attention required."
5. Decision analysis	"While Decision-Management-Solutions recommends evaluating decisions based on the nine different dimensions as shown below, and a proprietary tool called DecisionsFirst for decision modeling; Bain recommends evaluating decisions based on business-value-at-stake, and degree-of-managerial-attention-required."
6. Decision prioritization: Factors to consider	"The criteria for decision prioritization should be based on decision's 'impact-on-business-outcomes'; here the measure "impact-on-business-outcomes" is a consolidated-weighted average score of several different factors"
7. Decision Prioritization: Creating a process framework. • Cross dimensional comparison • Identifying & prioritizing the "big" decisions.	"Our initial approach to decision prioritization was to list decisions sorted by cumulative-annual-value-at-stake for each decision, from highest to lowest. However, we realized once we assign a score against each of the decision-dimensions and do a cross-dimensional comparison, the whole perspective on which-decision-is-relatively-more-important could change, sometimes dramatically..."

INTRODUCTION

Through the preceding chapters, we have established, building a data-driven organization requires identifying and prioritizing the "big" decisions for data-driven actionable insights.

The next question is: how exactly does one go about identifying these "big" decisions? How does one segregate the big decisions from thousands of every day decisions that every manager in the organization makes? We further set out to identify the 10% of decisions which influence 90% of the business outcomes – making the ask even more complicated.

The first time I attempted decision prioritization, we were plainly groping in the dark. We realized the first step would be to list, and categorize all the key decisions in the organization. We told ourselves we would attempt to estimate the business value associated with each of these decisions later. When we began this quest, we did not realize how difficult it was going to be.

5.1 Taking Stock: Existing Analytics Assets

The project sponsors, as they usually do, insisted that we must start with a brief due diligence; an "as-is" analysis to make sure we had a thorough understanding of their existing business intelligence (BI) reports and analytics assets that they had painstakingly built over a long period of time. These project sponsors assured us that the as-is analysis would also shed some light on specific decisions that they take based on data.

The usual mode of an as-is analysis is through a review of earlier BI /analytics projects documentation, followed by interviews with stakeholders. We also proposed an audit – if those projects had ever delivered the intended value mentioned in the design specification.

We picked up a cross section of live analytics projects and asked for the design spec. documents. The agenda was to understand the data-to-decisions process flow, besides conducting a value delivery audit; the underlying assumption being that all live projects must be delivering sizable business value.

As the due diligence progressed, many of our early assumptions proved to be completely false. A few examples are listed below.

5.1.1 Project Trigger

- We assumed analytics projects were usually planned and designed around a set of decisions made by managers. In reality, the word "decision" rarely showed up in the design spec. Most projects were triggered by internal customer requirements.
- We discovered nearly all projects started with data; a huge amount of data that needed to be sorted, normalized, and analyzed to discover patterns, if any, and both clustering and classification algorithms were being used.
- All projects started from collecting data either on a date, or for a defined "period'. The process used for collating data was mostly "Excel"-based, temporary, and meant for one-time use.

5.1.2 Business Value Targeted

- Most project specification documents did not specifically mention the targeted business value from analytics.
- Majority of analytics projects targeted creating visualization of data, interactive dashboards, and self-service analytics. The visualization dashboards were not very different from earlier business intelligence-business objects (BI-BO) dashboards.
- Project design spec. documents did not mention what actionable insights were being targeted, or what kind of decisions were to be taken based on insights.

5.1.3 Ad Hoc-ism

- There was a significant bias toward "pull" analytics, which means just providing whatever the managers (consumers of information) asked for – either by manually servicing each ad hoc request, or through a self-service, interactive analytics platform.
- The number of ad hoc reports asked for, far exceeded the number of standard canned reports they had in their BI application. The ad hoc report requests were just ad hoc, usually communicated through an email, and hence came without any supporting documentation, let alone a justification mentioning why such a report was being asked for and what value the managers expected to derive from such a request.

None of the requests from managers, ad hoc or otherwise, specified what decision(s) they planned to make based on the information they were asking for. While they did have a query-builder to take care of ad hoc reports, the real challenge was that the ad hoc reports often asked for information that they did not have stored anywhere in their data warehouse or data lake; data never captured and hence never reported.

5.2 The Lost Art of Decision-Making

We know it is highly unlikely to find an organization that would list and document decisions. As we know, the usual exceptions are decisions related to large capital outlay or large revenue expenditure. For example, many organizations define protocols for high-value purchase decisions. Most organizations constitute an investment committee to deliberate and decide on large investments beyond a threshold value.

We also know, if listing of decisions itself is uncommon, categorizing decisions is even more rare. It is usually left to the academic researchers to attempt categorizing decisions. A few examples of the usual criteria for categorizing decisions are listed below:

- Programmed and non-programmed decisions
- Major and minor decisions
- Operational and strategic decisions
- Organizational and personal decision
- Individual and group decisions

We quickly discovered there had never been any documented list of decisions in the company. The only available option was to gather the information through stakeholder interviews or by administering a questionnaire for managers.

We tried talking to some of the senior managers in different departments before designing the questionnaire. The idea was to collect some informal inputs useful for designing the questionnaire. The conversations were all similar, if not same. To summarize:

- *All managers believed they took a lot of decisions… though most could not recall which ones.*
- *Everyone agreed that the quality of decisions did make a difference to the quality of business outcomes.*
- *Instinctively, they all knew that some decisions were more important than others, but never paused to think which ones, or to list those important decisions.*
- *When forced to list at least one important decision that they had taken in the preceding 12 months, those who could, invariably mentioned investment decisions involving large capital outlay.*

Some managers asked me the equally disconcerting question in response: "How about you? Do you have a list of important decisions that you take?" The honest answer was that I was equally guilty. I had never made my own list.

While there was no published research on developing a roadmap for a data-driven organization, there were a few well-written articles on the importance of identifying critical organizational decisions. After much discussion, we created a questionnaire that we could distribute among the managers to collect and collate the list of organizational decisions. Bain's case study (Blenko et al., 2011) refers to 33 critical decisions that managers at Nike identified.

However, my initial experience administering the questionnaire was a disaster. Most managers simply did not know what to list as a decision, and they confessed identifying critical decisions was even more difficult. Nearly all of them listed investment decisions (purchase of capital goods or capitalizable services) as the most critical decisions that they took.

We had also included a few questions to understand exactly how each of the decisions listed impacted the organization's top-line and bottom-line, or impacted other strategic objectives. Most managers had difficulty explaining the dollar impact of their decisions on business outcomes.

5.3 Prioritizing Decisions: In Search of an Objective Methodology

While we were collecting the data, I still needed an objective methodology for scoring and prioritizing the decisions based on their impact on business-outcomes. I started my career working for an American multinational called ITW (Illinois Tool Works Inc.), which insisted on applying 80–20 for everything (Pangarkar, 2013). While applying 80–20 to the list of decisions was always on the cards, I still needed to finalize what specific criteria would be most apt for scoring the decisions. I was also keen to understand if someone else had previously attempted the 80–20 categorization of decisions. So, I tried researching to discover if there was a proven methodology for decision prioritization.

Once again, I expected there would be a mountain of published research on the categorization of decisions, and specifically on identifying critical organizational decisions, and once again, I was completely disappointed. There was little-to-no published research on the importance of categorization of decisions, let alone a process for identifying the top 10%. The notable exceptions are listed below.

The first popular attempt at identifying and categorizing decisions was made by the war hero (and the 34th president of USA) General Eisenhower (Figure 5.1).

The famous Eisenhower principle is that prioritizing tasks by urgency and importance results in four quadrants with different work strategies: What is important is seldom urgent, and what is urgent is seldom important.

The Eisenhower box is a primitive but useful tool for enhancing the personal productivity of individual managers. Prioritization of decisions from across the organization requires each decision to be evaluated on a variety of parameters, apart from impact on business outcomes.

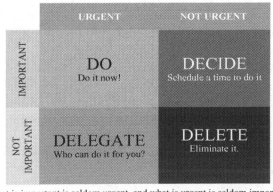

What is important is seldom urgent, and what is urgent is seldom important
-Dwight D. Eisenhower

Figure 5.1　The Eisenhower box.

During my extensive research, I have found only five articles which highlight the importance of categorizing and prioritizing decisions:

1. "What makes strategic decisions different?" (Rosenzweig, 2013)

    While this article does not give any process for categorization of decisions, it does argue that categorization of decisions, and recognizing strategic decisions as different from routine decisions is an important first step before advising people on how to make better strategic decisions.

2. "How to tell which decisions are strategic?" (Shivakumar, 2014)

    Under a chapter titled "A framework for evaluating decisions", this article provides yet another 2 × 2 that has degree of commitment and the scope of firm on its two axes. The degree of commitment is reflected by the extent to which a particular decision is reversible; and the scope of a firm is defined by its choice of products, services, activities, and markets (Figure 5.2).

3. "AI is going to change the 80/20 rule" (Schrage, 2017)

    Michael Schrage (author and research fellow at MIT Sloan School's Digital Center) very convincingly argues that AI is helping analytically aggressive firms shrink Pareto's "vital few" into "vital fewer", and proposes that the 80–20 is more likely to be 90–10.

4. "Focus on key decisions" (Blenko et al., 2010).

    This was the most comprehensive and relevant article for my purpose. I did not get to see this while I was actually working on the project but stumbled upon it a few years later when I was researching for the article I published in

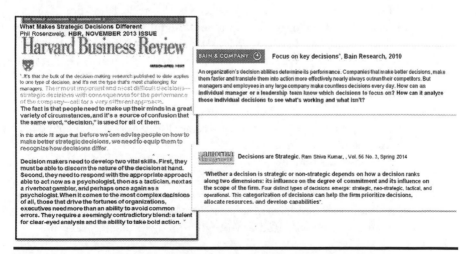

Figure 5.2   Articles on the importance of decision categorization.

Data Science Central. While we still do not get a definitive process for decision prioritization, this article does provide the core steps involved in the process. Excerpts are below:

- Companies that make better decisions perform better and outrun their competitors.
- Managers make countless decisions. How would they know which decisions to focus on? How would they know which specific decisions to focus on?
- Critical decisions are of high value, or of high value over time, and applies the 80–20 rule to identify critical decisions. The process for identifying critical decisions (as per the article) is in two steps –
- Creating a decision architecture: Listing all the organization decisions for each of the business processes in the value-creation flow of the organization; specifically, the decisions critical to success.
  - Winnowing the list: Prioritizing decisions by value, followed by degree of management attention required.
  - Recommends a proprietary decision analysis process – "Decision X-ray Process" (Bain seems to have used this extensively at Nike) which is essentially a diagnosis of *a day in the life of a decision*, what works and what does not, enablers, and so forth.

5 Smart Enough Systems: How to Deliver Competitive Advantage by Automating Hidden Decisions (Taylor & Raden, 2007).

The process presented by Taylor and Raden was closer to my own thinking. They also recommend starting from a decision and analyzing the decisions on nine different dimensions. They have a proprietary decision modeling tool called DecisionsFirst™, which uses the decision model and notation (DMN). I wish I had had more insight into the meaningful work this company does while I was still associated with relevant projects, but I came across their structured approach to decision modeling much later, when I was researching for my articles published in *Data Science Central.* Decision Management Solutions categorizes decisions based on relative score assigned to each decision on nine different dimensions – Repeatability, Measurability, Time to Outcome, Approach, Upside vs. Downside, Regulation, Available Data, Historical Data, & Uncertainty.

In my subsequent advisory work, I have refined my methodology leveraging some of the concepts introduced by James Taylor and Niel Raden in their books; specifically in the area of decision analysis and decision modeling. While I may not have used their DecisionsFirst™ modeler, I pretty much used the same logic and DMN notation for modeling decisions (see Figure 5.3).

DIMENSIONS	CATEGORIES
REPEATABILITY	STRATEGIC DECISIONS
MEASURABILITY (OF OUTCOMES)	PLANNING DECISIONS
TIME TO OUTCOME	KNOWLEDGE WORKER DECISIONS
APPROACH (OF JUDGEMENT)	RESEARCH DECISIONS
UPSIDE vs. DOWNSIDE	FORMULAIC DECISIONS
REGULATION	CONSENSUS DECISIONS
AVAILABLE DATA	OPERATIONAL RISK DECISIONS
HISTORICAL DATA	OPERATIONAL VALUE DECISIONS
UNCERTAINTY	CASE MANAGEMENT DECISIONS

Ref: James Taylor & Niel Raden - "Smart Enough Systems: How to Deliver Competitive Advantage by Automating Hidden Decisions"

Figure 5.3 Dimensions which influence decisions.

5.4 Learning from the Bain Model

While one gets the essence of the ideas Bain conveys through different articles (Blenko et al., 2013; Blenko et al, 2011), I felt it was too simplistic to "winnow the list" just by two factors – (1) the value-at-stake, and (2) management attention required. Here are a few issues immediately noticeable:

- Management attention as a factor is vague and difficult to quantify. Besides, it can mean different things to different people.
- A decision requiring CxO's attention, and another decision requiring the operational manager's attention, cannot be given equal weighting. Further, a decision requiring a single manager's attention, and another decision requiring the collective attention of a number of managers, once again cannot be given equal weighting.
- Given my experiences of applying 80–20 in numerous inventory management assignments, I was clear I must use the cumulative annual value of the decision as the measure for decision prioritization. The Bain study recommends using the value of the decision over time, which perhaps means the same thing.
- Value-at-stake once again is not easy to estimate. Some decisions impact the top-line performance of the company, while some others can influence the bottom-line performance of the company. A 10% reduction in cost not only generates more operating margins than a 10% increase in sales, but also can provide a significant competitive advantage, which in turn can drive sales upward.
- *Data availability and accessibility are very important factors that are completely overlooked in Bain's model.* No matter how important the decision is, if there is no data to support the decision, then it is best left to managerial discretion.

- Technically rule-based automatable decisions cannot be treated on a par with decisions requiring managerial discretion. However, rule-based automatable decisions, are automatable only when there is necessary data being captured and automation infrastructure is in place. In the absence of supporting data, all decisions (without exception) would need managerial discretion.

It is possible Bain's Decision X-ray Process model may be more sophisticated than we understand from the few white papers available in the public domain; we may never know unless we can afford to engage the services of Bain.

Further, we have noticed the decision priority (relative importance) changes when the criteria for assessment change, or the context changes. For example:

- The context does make a difference: The time, place and distance have a bearing on the importance of decision. For example: (1) What percentage to allocate for the advertising budget is a decision that will have a different level of importance when the organization faces a new, fierce competitor and the possibility of a shrinking market share; (2) Most companies fail to understand that the advertising budget needs to be higher for under-addressed market segments where there is a higher potential for growth, than for the mature markets.
- Correlation between the business value generated and the decision: Sometimes it will be difficult to conclude a specific decision alone was responsible for the value generated (established based on the data that the coeff. of correlation = 1). For example, increase in advertising budget can be one of the many different factors responsible for increase in sales.

5.5 Decision Analysis

In my view, there are two distinct varieties of decision analysis:

1. **For Identifying Critical Decisions**: This involves closely analyzing and assigning a score for each of the decisions based on how it may affect the business outcomes.
2. **For Deciphering the Data Behind the Decisions**: This is achieved through decision modeling and by visually depicting how the decision is made in the organization, the actors, the alternative actions, the likely outcomes, and the constraints. (This will be discussed in considerable detail in Chapter 6).

This chapter specifically focuses on decision analysis for the sole-purpose of "identifying the critical decisions".

While Decision Management Solutions (Taylor & Raden, 2007) recommends evaluating decisions based on the nine different dimensions as shown in Figures

5.4 and 5.5, and a proprietary tool called DecisionsFirst™ for decision modeling, Bain recommends evaluating decisions based on business value-at-stake, and degree of managerial attention required. Bain also recommends using the Decision X-ray Process models for analysing the decisions and winnowing for identifying the critical decisions. While the logic is simple and evidently similar to the one that I used earlier, their exact process of winnowing decisions to identify the critical decisions is not provided anywhere in the published material. We may assume we will never find out unless we have the finances to sign up Bain. Two examples follow:

WHICHDECISIONS: **DIMENSIONS WHICH INFLUENCE DECISIONS...**

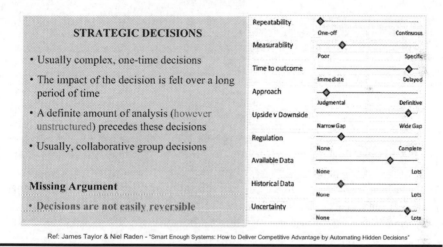

Ref: James Taylor & Niel Raden - "Smart Enough Systems: How to Deliver Competitive Advantage by Automating Hidden Decisions"

Figure 5.4   Dimensions which influence strategic decisions.

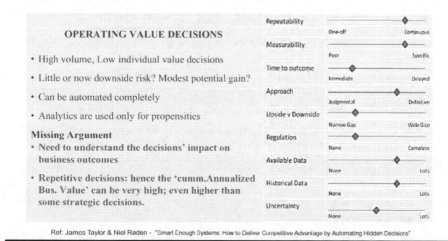

Ref: James Taylor & Niel Raden - "Smart Enough Systems: How to Deliver Competitive Advantage by Automating Hidden Decisions"

Figure 5.5   Dimensions which influence operational decisions.

EXAMPLE 1   STRATEGIC DECISIONS

Figure 5.4 illustrates how strategic decisions typically score on different dimensions as per the process recommended by Decision Management Solutions.

Strategic decisions are usually one-off, impact the organization over a longer time horizon, and carry a higher risk and higher return. However, in my experience, several other dimensions beyond these nine could potentially influence the decisions.

While some strategic decisions are reversible, most are non-reversible. Whether to invest in a new factory closer to the markets is a non-reversible decision once the investment has been made, contract signed, and construction has been kicked off. On the other hand, a policy decision allowing 50% of the employees to work from home is a reversible, editable decision. Both decisions are strategic in nature, may even have similar scores on the nine dimensions shown in Figure 5.4.

EXAMPLE 2   OPERATIONAL DECISIONS

Operating value decisions (see Figure 5.5), tend to be high volume, and each decision individually may not account for a large business value, but annualized business value-at-stake can be substantial and may have a significant impact on the organization's top-line, bottom-line or both. A good number of operational decisions may find a place among the top 10% of the decisions which influence 90% of business outcomes.

5.6 Decision Prioritization: Factors to Consider

My original premise was that the criteria for decision prioritization should be based on the decision's impact on business outcomes; while I knew impact on business outcomes needs to be a consolidated-weighted average score of several different factors, we had limited understanding of what those factors needed to be. We also realized the factors needed to be different for different industries. I worked on a series of alternative models which could possibly be adapted for a diverse set of businesses. Here is a summary of deliberations and conclusions.

The value at stake is composite measure and primarily depends on the following:

- The estimated business value* of each decision (*more on estimating the business value in chapter 6).
- Decision span/or, the scope of business the decision affects (such as the lines of business (LOBs), revenue streams, legal entities, geographies, or markets

covered. Sometimes the scope of the decision is measured by the number of employees, or number of business partners** affected by the decision).
- Number of times the decision is taken in one accounting year.
                    (** "business partners" includes customers, vendors,
                            distributors, and agents, among others.)

We recognized quite early that there would be repetitive decisions which individually are of small value but add up to a much larger value over a period of time. Sometimes, the small-value, high-volume decisions may add up to become the most critical decisions that the company makes.

What Bain calls "managerial attention" is also a composite measure, and very difficult to estimate. Key components include:

- Number of managers involved in the decision-making.
- Time each manager spends on the decision, considering the alternatives.

The issue is, no manager ever keeps a timesheet recording just how long he deliberated on a decision. Further, managerial attention simply overlooks the most important activity every manager engages in every day; the all-important activity of chasing the data. Ask any manager, and they will tell you: "We spend 99% of the time chasing the data, and 1% deliberating the alternatives".

As we started analyzing decisions and discussing with the decision-makers, we were forced to list several other important factors that might significantly affect the impact on business outcomes. We found some decisions are far more complex than others, while some decisions can be rule-based, and routine. While some decisions lead to measurable outcomes, several others do not. Some decisions lead to immediate results and outcomes in the near term, while several other decisions lead to results (outcomes) that can only be felt over a long period of time. Further, some decisions can be reversible, while many others are not. Then there are decisions that need to be taken with very little or no notice, while some decisions can be taken at leisure – after carefully considering all the implications. Unplanned decisions (ad hoc decisions) are usually reactionary and are taken in response to the occurrence of an unplanned, disruptive event. We also felt the planned decisions which emanate from the organization's strategy map and the balanced scorecard needed a higher priority.

In Figure 5.6 there is a comprehensive list of dimensions of decisions, or the factors which influence the relative importance of decisions. In my experience, both *the factors considered* and *the weightings* to be accorded to each of these factors, will have to be different in different companies, in different lines of businesses, and in different countries. So, the exercise of decision prioritization once again becomes even more complicated, especially when dealing with a multinational operating in diverse businesses across continents (Figure 5.6).

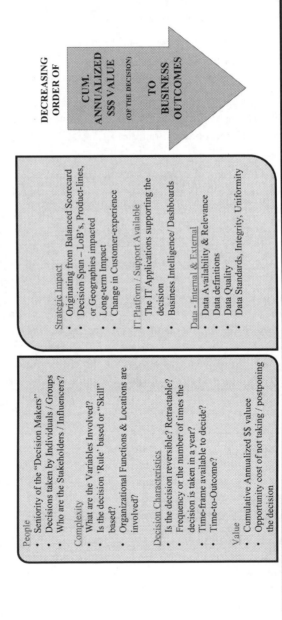

WHICH DECISIONS: THE DIMENSIONS OF DECISIONS -

People
- Seniority of the "Decision Makers"
- Decisions taken by Individuals / Groups
- Who are the Stakeholders / Influencers?

Complexity
- What are the Variables Involved?
- Is the decision 'Rule' based or "Skill" based?
- Organizational Functions & Locations are involved?

Decision Characteristics
- Is the decision reversible? Retractable?
- Frequency or the number of times the decision is taken in a year?
- Time-frame available to decide?
- Time-to-Outcome?

Value
- Cumulative Annualized $$ valuee
- Opportunity cost of not taking / postponing the decision

Strategic Impact
- Originating from Balanced Scorecard
- Decision Span – LoB's, Product-lines, or Geographies impacted
- Long-term Impact
- Change in Customer-experience

IT Platform / Support Available
- The IT Applications supporting the decision
- Business Intelligence/ Dashboards

Data - Internal & External
- Data Availability & Relevance
- Data definitions
- Data Quality
- Data Standards, Integrity, Uniformity

DECREASING ORDER OF

CUM. ANNUALIZED $$$ VALUE (OF THE DECISION) TO BUSINESS OUTCOMES

Figure 5.6   Which decisions?

While I have practically used the phrases "dimensions of the decisions" and the "factors influencing the decision priority" synonymously, there is perhaps a subtle difference between the two. While the "dimensions" of the decision usually refer the nature of the decision – whether it is strategic or operational, how frequently it is made and so on, the "factors" refer to a complete 360 degrees view of the decision, its nature, who makes the decision, how it is made, and all that could potentially influence the decision and its impact on business outcomes.

5.7 Decision Prioritization: Creating a Process Framework

When we started putting together a process for decision prioritization, what became very clear was that we needed to list the decisions in the decreasing order of cumulative-annualized-dollar- value impact on the business.

One needs extra care to understand the words "*cumulative*" and "*annualized*" here. While "cumulative" refers the collective value of repetitive decisions which may have a substantially large impact on the organization's business outcomes; the word "annualized" refers to fact that the dollar impact of the decision may spread across more than one financial year and hence the data needs to be normalized to the value for one financial year. Following Pareto's principle, the actual number of decisions which impact 80–90% of business value is expected to be small, while the actual number and the percentage may differ in different companies.

5.7.1 Cross-Dimensional Comparison

Our initial approach to decision prioritization was to list decisions sorted by cumulative annual value-at-stake for each decision, from highest to lowest. However, we realized once we assigned a score against each of the decision dimensions and did a cross-dimensional comparison, the whole perspective on which decision is relatively more important could change, sometimes dramatically. Figure 5.7 illustrates

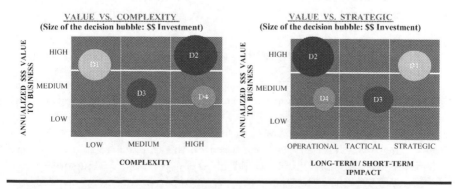

Figure 5.7   Cross-dimensional comparison of decisions.

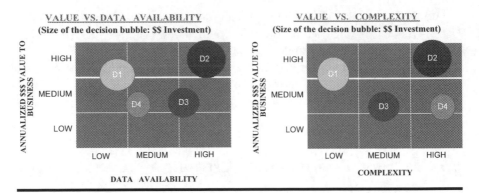

Figure 5.8 Cross-dimensional comparison of decisions.

this: The size of the bubble indicates the dollar value of the investment in each of the decisions.

The operational decision **D2** has the highest cumulative-annualized-$$-value, but is a very complex decision and requires relatively high dollar investment for building analytics. While another operational decision **D1** has a high cumulative-annualized-$$-value, and is relatively less complex, hence a more obvious priority for data-driven decision-making. We may also notice the strategic decision **D4** is highly complex and has a relatively low cumulative-annualized-$$-value-at-stake; not all strategic decisions have a high value-at-stake.

A few decisions which represent the highest cumulative-annualized-value, besides being most complex, may also have little-to-no data available. Hence, such decisions tend to be largely intuitive, purely based on the experience of the managers (see Figure 5.8).

In Figure 5.8, the operational-decision **D1**, has very low data availability which contradicts the earlier conclusion that it could be an obvious priority for data-driven decision-making.

Hence, which decision is a bigger priority for analytics investments is not a bivariate-analysis as Bain recommends, but a fairly complex multivariate analysis.

5.7.2 The Process Framework: Identifying and Prioritizing the "Big" Decisions

Given the need for making the process simple and less complicated, I recommend doing it as a three step process, as follows:

Step 1: Identify and list all decisions, based on their annualized-$$-value impact on business outcomes, and sorted highest to lowest in decreasing order.
  • Care to be taken to ensure majority of important organizational decisions are covered here.

- For repetitive decisions, the value-at-stake needs to be multiplied by the number of times the decision is taken in a financial year, across business units (BUs) and geographies in the organization.
- Total number of decisions need to be counted from across the organization.

Step 2: Identify the "**big**" decisions: The 10–20% of decisions which account for 80–90% of business outcomes.

- Sort decisions based on their potential impact on business outcomes. Some decisions influence top-line, some others impact the cost and the bottom-line, and a few decisions may impact both. Every decision has some influence on the business outcomes of the company; the idea is to assign an approximate dollar number to each of the decisions, albeit based on an empirical formula.
- While the percentage and the number of decisions that account for 90% of business outcomes, will be different for different companies, I would believe it would be no more than 10% of decisions in most organizations.

Step 3: Prioritize the "**big**" decisions for data-driven analytics: Through cross-dimensional comparison of the identified 10–20% decisions.

- Evaluate every decision by assigning a *score* on a variety of dimensions – and a *weighting* to every dimension (the score and the weightings can be different for different organizations, or for different businesses).
- Order the "big" decisions in decreasing order of the weighted average score – from highest score to the lowest.
- Make analytics investments, for each of the "big" decisions, as per the order.

A comprehensive step-by-step methodology for building a roadmap and business case for building a data-driven organization will be covered in the next chapter.

Bibliography

Blenko, M., Mankins, M., Rogers, P., & Bain & Company (2011a). What are your critical decisions?. Forbes.com, April 06, 2011.

Blenko, M. W., Mankins, M. C., & Roger, P. (2010). Focus on key decisions. *Bain.com Insights*, Nov 19, 2010.

Blenko, M., Mankins, M., & Rogers, P. (2013). *Decision Insights: The Five Steps to Better Decisions*. Bain & Company.

Blenko, M., Mankins, M., Rogers, P., & Morrison, A. (2011b). *Decision Insights – Nike's Critical Workout Plan*. Bain Insights, August 08, 2011.

Maddock, M. (2012). What to do when your business sucks too much. Forbes.com, Jul 2012.

Merendino, A., Dibb, S., Meadows, M., Quinn, L., Wilson, D., Simkin, L., & Canhoto, A. (2018). Big data, big decisions: The mpact of big data on board level decision-making. *Journal of Business Research*, 93, 67–78.

Pangarkar, N. (2019). Illinois Tool Works: Making a big impact with small-wins strategy. *Global Business and Organizational Excellence*, 38(3), 18–25.

Rosenzweig, P. (2013). What makes strategic decisions different. *Harvard Business Review*, 91(11), 88–+.

Schrage, M. (2017). AI is going to change the 80/20 rule. HBR.org, Feb 2017.

Shivakumar, R. (2014). How to tell which decisions are strategic. *California Management Review*, 56(3), 78–97.

Stevens, T. (1999). Breaking up is profitable to do. *Industry Week/IW*, 248(12), 28–31.

Taylor, J., & Raden, N. (2007). *Smart Enough Systems: How to Deliver Competitive Advantage by Automating Hidden Decisions*. Pearson Education.

Chapter 6

Decisions to Data

Building a "Big" Decision Roadmap and Business Case

Topics Covered in this Chapter

1. Building a "big" decision roadmap • Identifying & prioritizing the decisions • The roadmap for "data-driven organization"	A detailed process framework for identifying and prioritizing the "big" decisions & for creating a Roadmap for data-driven organization.
2. The data behind the decisions • Decision modeling & analysis • Deciphering the data behind the decision	"A need for decision modeling and analysis before attempting to convert the 'Big-decision-Roadmap' into a full-fledged project-plan, with 'Go-live' events of the analytics-solutions as the mile-stones."
3. Building a business-case • Analytics & the sources of value: The value-drivers • Estimating returns: Comparing kpi's with the industry benchmarks • Estimating the investments	"Every CDO (or CIO as the case may be) will be asked to create a business-case for the 'advanced-analytics-investments' he proposes to make. The incremental value-generated through analytics, necessarily needs to be greater than investment made."

DOI: 10.1201/9781003321347-7

4. From decisions to data: A summary view	"Summarizing the steps involved in creating a Roadmap & building a Business-case for a Data-driven Organization."
5. The data, trust, and the decision maker • What else can potentially go wrong? • Value-promised vs. value-delivered	"Here is a case of everything done right; you have used the right decision, the right analytics model, and the right data, and yet managers resist using analytics... It is important to understand what exactly is influencing this behavior; as it helps us answering the question – what else can 'potentially fail' the analytics projects from delivering the intended value?"

INTRODUCTION

In 2019, as it did for nearly a decade, Gartner (Panetta, 2018) predicted that over 80% of analytics projects would be likely to fail and would not deliver the intended business outcomes through 2022; and over 80% of AI projects would "remain alchemy, run by wizards" through 2020. We may dispute the percentages, but definitely not the predictions. So, before building a roadmap for a data-driven organization, it will be important to understand if there are still any unresolved-unaddressed constraints, and potential opportunities for failure.

Let me summarize our conclusions so far.

We intend to start from a decision and build analytics projects around decisions of importance. We believe the value from analytics is guaranteed since we **do** know the value at stake beforehand, and hence the potential upside for improving the quality of the decision. Further, we intend to identify the "big" decisions; the process of identifying the "big" decisions and prioritization based on impact on business outcomes has been discussed in considerable detail. We recognize the fact that the decision priority can change when we do a cross-factor comparison; when we rate the decisions based on factors other than just the relative value-at-stake and management attention required.

What we are targeting is not success of an isolated analytics project or two, but actually building a data-driven organization, which requires ensuring all key decisions (if not all decisions) are taken based on data, and where possible with an audit trail.

An analytics roadmap essentially is a series of projects sequenced in the decreasing order by the net relative value planned for; meaning, the project that promises the highest relative value is prioritized and scheduled the earliest, followed by the next highest and so on. The relative value at stake here refers to the dollar value of potential upside to the business outcomes that the improvement in the quality of decision would result in. Since we are choosing only those projects with the highest potential for value delivery, in theory, the risk of projects failing is expected to be minimal.

But is it enough to guarantee the success of analytics projects? What other factors determine the relative priority of "big" decisions within the company?

When can we say: Here is an analytics project that actually **delivered** value? What exactly makes analytics projects succeed? More importantly what else can potentially prevent the analytics projects from delivering the intended value?

What kind of due diligence would be required to identify the "big" decisions and create a priority roadmap? How do you estimate the value-at-stake? How does one make a business case for analytics?

6.1 Toward a Data-Driven Organization: Building a "Big" Decision Roadmap

6.1.1 Identifying and Prioritizing the Decisions

We intend to identify and prioritize the "big" decisions for analytics projects, because it will be the most simple and straight forward method for transforming the organization into a data-driven organization. The process framework for identifying and prioritizing the "big" decisions was introduced in Chapter 5 as a three step process:

- Create a master list of decisions.
- Identify the "big" decisions.
- Prioritize decisions for analytics.

As mentioned before, while all "big" decisions have a significant value-at-stake, that alone cannot be the sole criterion for an analytics project to succeed and deliver value. The project may still fail for a number of other reasons, the most important one being the non-availability of the right data to support the decision.

Cross-dimensional analysis of big decisions helps organization to choose the select-few decisions that are most relevant for the organization and meet the other critical to success criteria the organization deems important. A few examples are listed below:

- Can the decision be data-driven?
- Data availability.

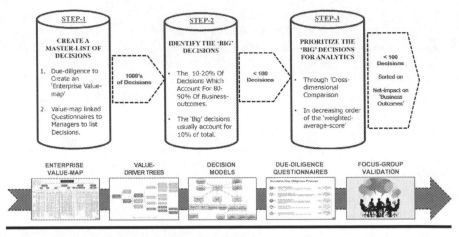

Figure 6.1   Prioritizing the "Big" decisions.

- Seniority of the decision-makers.
- Strategic impact (impact spread over longer horizon).

Figure 6.1 shows a summary of the process framework for identifying and priori-tizing the "big" decisions, and a set of tools that can be used in the due diligence process.

Here follows a complete step-by-step approach for creating the roadmap.

6.1.1.1 Step 1: Create a Master List of the Decisions of the Company

As mentioned before, listing all the decisions in the company may seem easy at the outset but will definitely prove to be the most difficult task in the entire process of building a data-driven organization. The simple reason: most managers will draw a blank when you ask them an open-ended question to list all the decisions that they take. The ideal approach would be a formal due diligence through a carefully drafted questionnaire to unearth the key value-drivers, followed by interviews of key manag-ers and administering a second questionnaire to list the decisions.

Questionnaire-1 is for an enterprise-wide due diligence. The responses to Questionnaire-1 should help design Questionnaire-2 which is a set of customized questionnaires for each department and each role.

6.1.1.1.1 Questionnaire-1: Due Diligence Questionnaire

The purpose of the due diligence is to:
- Create an *enterprise value map* either in Deloitte's format (Lukac et al., 2012), or create *value-driver trees* for different processes across the enterprise.

- Understand and list the key managers, revenue streams, value-chain processes, components of costs, constraints, and dependencies that influence top-line and bottom-line.
- Understand controllable costs and non-controllable costs
- Understand the company's long-term strategy, strategy map, and balanced scorecard
- Understand the rule-based decisions in the company, for example, the configuration specs in the company's enterprise resource planning ((ERP) Software).

6.1.1.1.2 Questionnaire 2: Master List of Decisions

This needs to be customized for different managerial roles. The questionnaire can be administered through a guided discussion either with individual managers, or with a group of managers with a similar role.

The *enterprise value map*, *value-driver trees*, and the *decision models* can be shared with the managers prior to administering the questionnaire. The questionnaire needs to a be a mix of closed and open-ended questions and customized for each set of managers in each department.

a) Questions need to focus on managerial actions that influence either the top-line or bottom-line in each department.
b) Questionnaire must cover complete value-chain processes in each department.
c) For example – an HR Manager in a large services company, where employee cost accounts for more than 60% of cost of goods sold (COGS), could be asked:
   - How do you control workforce costs?
   - How do you plan for workforce requirements? What is your bench-size?
   - How much of revenue do you lose for not having the right resources at the right time?
   - How do you decide how many trainee managers to recruit in each batch?
   - How do you decide between internal promotions vs. external hires?
   - How do you decide between freshers vs. experienced hires?
   - How do you ensure the right workforce is available within your budgets?
d) A marketing manager could be asked:
   - What stops you from selling much, much more?
   - How do you decide on budgets for each territory?
   - How do you decide on advertising spend for each channel?
   - How do you establish correlation between your marketing spend and incremental sales?
e) A finance manager could be asked:
   - How does your financing cost compare with industry benchmarks?
   - What stops you from reducing the financing cost by 50%?

- How do you decide on investing your surplus cash into different asset classes?
- How often do you change your portfolio?

6.1.1.1.3 Validating and Consolidating the List of Decisions

Ideally, this is done in a workshop mode with a focus group comprising the stakeholders, key decision-makers, besides the core team from the CDO's office.

a) List all the decisions from across the departments, business units, geographies, and legal entities.
b) Remove duplicates.
c) Record how many times each decision is being taken, for each manager – Number of times in each year.
d) List unique decisions and total number of times the decision is made in a year:
  - Average number of times the decision in made in a year per manager x number of managers who take such a decision.
e) Categorize the decisions into:
  - Strategic decisions/operational decisions.
  - Group decisions/individual decisions.
  - Programmed decisions/non-programmed decisions.
  - One-time unique decisions/repeat decisions – taken by multiple managers, multiple times, in a year.

6.1.1.1.4 Estimating the Value-at-Stake

To start with, it is important to understand if there is a logical and foolproof method to estimate the value-at-stake. While Bain (Mankins & Davis-Peccoud, 2012) do recommend using value-at-stake as one of the two key factors that influence the decision priority, they do not exactly define a method for estimating the value-at-stake. At the core, the value-at-stake represents a dollar number, the measure for the decision's impact on business outcomes: the revenue that the company earns, or the cost that company incurs for earning such income.

In my opinion, value-at-stake does not represent the absolute numbers of revenue or cost but the positive or negative impact the decision is likely to have on the revenues, resource consumption, or the cost to the company. A good quality decision may substantially enhance the revenue or bring down the cost, while an inferior quality decision may lead to loss of revenue, or incremental cost of operations, or incremental resource cost.

Value-at-stake represents the dollar value of incremental revenue or decrease in the resources consumed or decrease in the cost incurred. It could represent the incremental efficiency of the company, the incremental system throughput that results from easing of the constraints that Eliyahu Goldratt (Goldratt & Cox, 1984) talks about.

For example: Here is how the decisions typically influence the business outcomes:

- Decision 1: Allocating the scarce resources among different functions, or different product lines.
  - o The managers must arrive at optimal allocation of resources that maximizes the revenue and reduces cost; a combination that can maximize the throughput. The value-at-stake essentially needs to be a measure for the potential upside or downside in the projected contribution.

- Decision 2: Right product mix for maximizing the revenue and profitability.
  - o Choosing the right products – the products which are likely to maximize growth and profitability is a critical decision for any company; the value-at-stake can be an estimate of the potential swing in the growth or profitability of the company.

6.1.1.1.5 Value-at-Stake and The Net Annualized Value of Decision

As long as the assumptions are clearly spelled out, value-at-stake *can be an empirical estimate* of the decision's impact on business outcomes. The process of estimation is very similar to projecting the revenue into the future during business planning, or annual budgeting exercise

a) The incremental revenue estimate is usually made either projecting historical data into the future, or by simply based on inputs from a focus group, constituted for the purpose.

b) The other method that I usually prefer is to compare the company's KPIs to internal benchmarks or external benchmarks. A more detailed explanation of this method is provided later in this chapter.

The statistical formulae for calculation of the value-at-stake of the decision can be quite cumbersome. Technically it should be calculated using the formula, $\sum_{k=1}^{k=n} \left(value\ of\ outcome'k' \times probability\ of\ outcome'k' \right)$ where both the value of outcome for each event, and the probability of the event are once again empirical estimates. So, it is just not worth the trouble.

For example: A decision on the product portfolio mix may involve sourcing and analysis of a variety of data including market share, growth prospects, relative positioning, apart from historical sales and profitability of each of the products.

Assuming the range between the uppermost, and lowermost estimates of revenues is being considered for the value-at-stake of the decision, a complicated what-if analysis would be needed to estimate the revenues and profitability that each of the alternatives being considered may result in. Given the exercise needs to be done for hundreds of decisions, it will be far simpler to create an *empirical method* to estimate the value-at-stake.

c) Since we intend to compare and prioritize the decisions based on their value-at-stake, it is important to make sure the value-at-stake as a metric is clearly defined and the data collected is uniform and normalized.

d) It is important to remember the value from a particular decision may accrue over several years; or may accrue several times within one year for repeatable decisions, if the same decision is being taken by multiple managers, multiple times in a year.
  • Annualized value-at-stake of the decision/year = Total life-time $$ value-at-stake of the decision/no. of years through which the decision delivers value.
  • Annualized value-at-stake of the decision = (no. of times decision gets taken in a year × av. value-at-stake of the decision/year).
  • Net annualized value-at-stake of the decision = (annualized value-at-stake of the decision – annualized investment into decision analysis).

Figure 6.2 depicts a typical example. A set of 50 decisions an organization considered important and listed were being examined for relative priority. The value-at-stake as a number was arrived at after a focus group session and the number was an average of high and low estimates. Value-at-stake has been annualized in cases where the impact on business outcomes accrues over a period of several years.

In reference to Figure 6.2:

  • **Column C (number of times a decision is taken in a year)**: this data must be collected during the due diligence, as a product of "Average number of times decision taken/year/manager" × "No. of managers who take the same decision"
  • **Column D (annual value-at-stake)**: Product of "value-at-stake" of the decision, and the "no. of times decision taken/year".
  • **Column E (investment in decision analysis)**: Includes investments in decision-support software, monetized value of time spent by managers deliberating the options, the cost of consultants and so on. Further, the investment value has also been annualized wherever the impact on business outcomes accrues over a period of several years.

(A)	(B)	(C)'	(D) = (B) X (C)'	(E)	(F) = (D) - (E)			
DECISION	Av. VALUE-AT-STAKE	NO. OF TIMES DECISION TAKEN / YEAR	ANN. VALUE-AT-STAKE	INVESTMENT INTO DECISION ANALYSIS	NET. ANN. VALUE-AT-STAKE	CUM. NET. ANN. VALUE-AT-STAKE	PERCENTAGE	
Decision-8	$ 33,500	355	$ 11,892,500	$ 300,000	$ 11,592,500	$ 11,592,500	33.6%	
Decision-5	$ 32,000	185	$ 5,920,000	$ 250,000	$ 5,670,000	$ 17,262,500	50.1%	
Decision-6	$ 6,000	900	$ 5,400,000	$ 250,000	$ 5,150,000	$ 22,412,500	65.0%	
Decision-1	$ 26,000	172	$ 4,472,000	$ 90,000	$ 4,382,000	$ 26,794,500	77.7%	80% cut-off
Decision-11	$ 2,750,000	1	$ 2,750,000	$ 175,000	$ 2,575,000	$ 29,369,500	85.2%	
Decision-21	$ 34,000	23	$ 782,000	$ 40,000	$ 742,000	$ 30,111,500	87.3%	
Decision-7	$ 700,000	1	$ 700,000	$ 55,000	$ 645,000	$ 30,756,500	89.2%	90% cut-off
Decision-2	$ 500,000	1	$ 500,000	$ 10,000	$ 490,000	$ 31,246,500	90.6%	
Decision-4	$ 223,000	2	$ 446,000	$ 12,000	$ 434,000	$ 31,680,500	91.9%	

80% CUT-OFF WAS FOR 4 DECISIONS OUT OF 50 - APPROX 8% OF DECISIONS
90% CUT-OFF WAS FOR 7 DECISIONS OUT OF 50 - APPROX 14% OF DECISIONS

Figure 6.2 Decision Prioritization – A typical example

o "Investment in decision analysis" as a parameter can be ignored, as it is unlikely to be a "relevant cost" in most companies. However, an occasional customer may insist that you include it in the analysis; I did have such an experience.

- **Column F (net Annual value-at-stake):** The value-at-stake after deducting the investment in data analysis.
  o The decisions are to be sorted based on the "net. annualized value-at-stake": highest first, followed by next highest and so on.

6.1.1.2 Step 2: Identifying the "Big" Decisions

- Once the decisions are listed in decreasing order of net annualized value-at-stake, the next step is to cut off and identify the top decisions that account for 80–90% of impact on the business outcomes.
- The "big" decisions typically account for 80–90% of business outcomes. *The cut-off would depend on the count for "big" decisions, and if you can support them with analytics within your budget.*
- In this case, the top two decisions (decision 8 and decision 5) put together account for over 50% of the combined value-at-stake of all the 50 decisions put together. While the top four decisions contribute close to 80%, the top seven decisions put together contribute close to 90% of combined value-at-stake of all the 50 decisions put together.

If these vital-few "big" decisions are taken based on data, it can drive the organization to generate the maximum throughput possible. Prioritizing these "big" decisions for "analytics investments" is the shortest transformational-route to data-driven organization.

With regard to Figure 6.3, Identifying the Big Decisions:

- The first four decisions account for almost 80% of the total value-at-stake.
- The first seven decisions represent the "big" decisions that account for 90% of impact on business outcomes.
- Hence, building analytics for these seven decisions could put the company on the path to becoming a data-driven organization.

6.1.1.3 Step 3: Prioritizing the Decisions for Analytics Investments: Need for Cross-Dimensional Analysis

The example shown in Figure 6.3 refers to a very small and simple organization, and we analyzed a total of 50 decisions, and identified seven decisions accounting for 90% of the business outcomes as the "big" decisions. If it is just seven decisions that need

(A)	(B)	(C)'	(D) = (B) X (C)'	(E)	(F) = (D) - (E)			
DECISION	Av. VALUE-AT-STAKE	NO. OF TIMES DECISION TAKEN / YEAR	ANN. VALUE-AT-STAKE	INVESTMENT INTO DECISION ANALYSIS	NET. ANN. VALUE-AT-STAKE	CUM. NET. ANN. VALUE-AT-STAKE	PERCENTAGE	
Decision-8	$ 33,500	355	$ 11,892,500	$ 300,000	$ 11,592,500	$ 11,592,500	33.6%	
Decision-5	$ 32,000	185	$ 5,920,000	$ 250,000	$ 5,670,000	$ 17,262,500	50.1%	
Decision-6	$ 6,000	900	$ 5,400,000	$ 250,000	$ 5,150,000	$ 22,412,500	65.0%	The "Big" Decisions
Decision-1	$ 26,000	172	$ 4,472,000	$ 90,000	$ 4,382,000	$ 26,794,500	77.7%	
Decision-11	$ 2,750,000	1	$ 2,750,000	$ 175,000	$ 2,575,000	$ 29,369,500	85.2%	
Decision-21	$ 34,000	23	$ 782,000	$ 40,000	$ 742,000	$ 30,111,500	87.3%	
Decision-7	$ 700,000	1	$ 700,000	$ 55,000	$ 645,000	$ 30,756,500	89.2%	
Decision-2	$ 500,000	1	$ 500,000	$ 10,000	$ 490,000	$ 31,246,500	90.6%	
Decision-4	$ 223,000	2	$ 446,000	$ 12,000	$ 434,000	$ 31,680,500	91.9%	

Figure 6.3   Identifying the big decisions.

to be supported with data and analytics, and if the company has sufficient budget, then there will not be any necessity for cross-dimensional analysis of these decisions.

However, in case of larger global organizations where the analysis involves multiple countries, multiple legal entities, and multiple lines of businesses, the total number of decisions to be analyzed could be in thousands and, hence the total number of "big" decisions could be in hundreds. Besides, factors like data availability and complexity can severely impact the success of analytics projects.

A cross-dimensional comparison of the identified "big" decisions can help re-prioritize them based on factors other than just value-at-stake and management attention" (Figure 6.4).

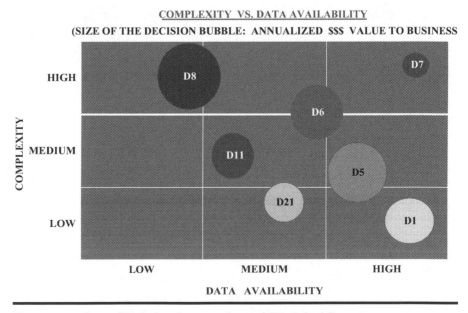

Figure 6.4   Cross-dimensional comparison of "Big" decisions.

Here is an example for cross-dimensional analysis. Each of the decision bubbles represent the "big" decisions. The size of the bubble represents the net annualized value-at-stake.

- We can see that Decision 8 (D8) has the largest annualized value-at-stake, hence the most significant impact on business outcomes. Further, D8 is a highly complex decision and the data availability is low, meaning that attempting analytics projects to support D8 will involve substantial time and effort for resolving the complexity and for sourcing the data required, but not available.
- Decision D1, on the other hand is not a very complex decision, and most of the data required to support D1 is available. So, there is a very high probability of success if one attempts an analytics project to support D1.
- So, the new revised order of priority for the "big" decisions is: D5, D1, D6, D11, D21, D8, D3.

6.1.2 Roadmap for a Data-Driven Organization

If the total number of "big" decisions to be analyzed is a large number, it will be easier to assign a relative score to each of the decisions on each of the dimensions and compute a "consolidated-weighted-average score" that can be the base for reprioritizing the decisions (Figure 6.5).

Once the "big" decisions are identified, and their relative priority has been worked out, building a roadmap is just a sequencing of analytics projects designed to support the identified "big" decisions, arranged by decreasing order of "consolidated-weighted-average-score".

Score Assigned by Focus Group (1-10) , 10 being the Highest Priority The fraction in Red indicates the "relative-weightages" for each of the Factors							
"Big" Decision	Size of Prize($)	Business Criticality	Data-Availability	Managerial-Time	Effect on Customer-Experience	Consolidated Weighted-Average-Score	Revised Priority
Weightages >	0.4	0.2	0.2	0.1	0.1	1.0	
Decision-8	10	10	3	10	8	8.4	3
Decision-5	8	10	9	9	9	8.8	1
Decision-6	8	10	8	9	10	8.7	2
Decision-1	7	7	10	8	8	7.8	4
Decision-11	5	8	5	9	6	6.1	6
Decision-21	4	8	6	10	6	6	7
Decision-7	4	7	10	10	8	6.8	5

Figure 6.5   Reworking priority based on multiple factors.

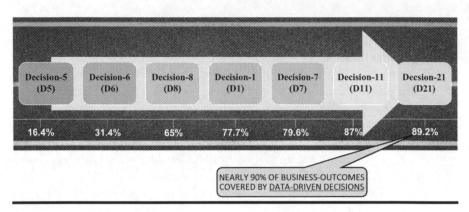

Figure 6.6 Roadmap for a data-driven organization.

Summarizing:

- The focus group believed the relative priority of the "big" decisions would depend on a variety of factors other than just the "size-of-the-prize" ($) and managerial time. So, they identified what they believe are the most important influencing factors and assigned a relative weighting for each of the factors.
- The newly revised priority for the seven "big" decisions: D5, D6, D8, D1, D7, D11, D21 becomes the roadmap (see Figure 6.6).
- The factors considered in the above example include: the size-of-the-prize ($), data availability, business-criticality, managerial time, and effect-on-customer-experience'.

6.1.2.1 Constituting the Focus Groups

While prioritizing decisions, organizations need to choose the factors that they think are most appropriate for their industry and for their specific organization. Hence, the role of focus group becomes extremely critical to get the relative priority right. The focus group must be constituted with the right mix of stakeholders and decision-makers, apart from a carefully chosen team of data modelers, IT solution architects, and data scientists… assuming the decision modeling skills come from an external consultant working with the focus group.

In my experience, *focus groups cannot be relied on to produce data on a blank sheet of paper; they cannot ideate too well in the absence of a framework and an external consultant guiding them.* It is always better to do some pre-work and get the focus group to validate and correct the assumptions, choose the best among the options presented to them, or just to rate each of the options and assign a relative score.

6.2 The Data behind the Decisions

While a roadmap has been prepared, we still do not know what kind of analytics solutions would need to be built for each of the "big" decisions; what insights and what data would be needed to support the decisions, what resources would be needed, or how long each project would run.

Hence, there is a need for decision modeling and analysis, before attempting to convert the "big" decision roadmap into a fully-fledged project plan, with "Go-live" events for the analytics solutions as the milestones.

6.2.1 Decision Modeling and Analysis

The first-step is understanding the decision-making process. It is important to understand if the organization has an existing formal process for taking the "big" decisions: if there is an existing process, all one must do is depict the process using the Decision Model and Notation (DMN).

In my experience, there could be operational decisions that thousands of managers make every day within the organization, and yet the organization may be completely unaware that such an everyday decision could be one of those famed "big" decisions that needs to be a top priority for data-driven decision-making.

If the "big" decision identified does not have any existing formal process within the organization, then it will be imperative to create a suitable decision-making model and a formal process. While there are several popular decision-making models, let us confine our discussion here to the standard Rational Decision-Making Model… usually a six step process, but I have added two additional steps:

1. Problem identification.
2. Identify the criteria for assessing the solutions.
3. Assign weightings for criteria.
4. Generate a list of alternatives.
5. Evaluate alternatives.
6. Choose the best solution.
7. *Test the solution.*
8. *Deploy.*

In my view, The decision-making approach is best depicted using the DMN standard published by Object Management Group (Figure 6.7). The example in Figure 6.7, sourced from Decision Management Solutions (Taylor & Purchase, 2016) shows the decision model for "Hold or Sell a Distressed Mortgage?" with all its variables, constraints, and dependencies.

The pictorial description of the decision model is helpful for discussing the constraints and evaluating the alternatives with the focus group; besides providing clarity on the information needed to make the decision.

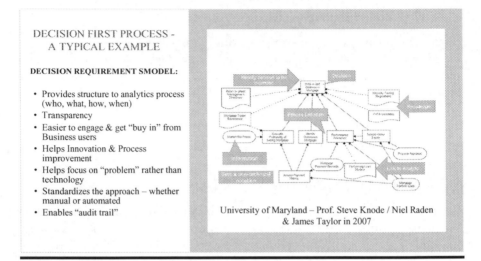

DECISION FIRST PROCESS -
A TYPICAL EXAMPLE

DECISION REQUIREMENT SMODEL:

• Provides structure to analytics process
 (who, what, how, when)
• Transparency
• Easier to engage & get "buy in" from
 Business users
• Helps Innovation & Process
 improvement
• Helps focus on "problem" rather than
 technology
• Standardizes the approach – whether
 manual or automated
• Enables "audit trail"

University of Maryland – Prof. Steve Knode / Niel Raden
& James Taylor in 2007

Figure 6.7   Decision first process – decision modeling using DMN notation.

6.2.2 *Deciphering the Data behind the Decision*

While the decision model provides a generic direction on the kind of questions that need to be answered for making the decision, what I propose is to dig deep and try unearthing the complete requirements of data that can potentially support the decision (Figure 6.8).

The focus of the decision analysis here is to find out *the data* that is required for supporting the decision. So, with the decision model in place, the focus group needs to dig further on the following:

1. What specific questions need to be answered to make this decision?
2. What kind of analysis and insights will help the decision-making process?
3. What kind of data is needed to support the decision?
4. How much of such data is available within the enterprise? What is the data gap?
5. What should be the data sourcing strategy? How can we source and normalize the data?
6. Assuming this is a recurring decision, how does one set up a system to ensure all the data that is required for making this decision is permanently made available?

Once all the required data is available, building an analytics solution is a fairly simple and straightforward process. Given the analytics project is specifically addressing

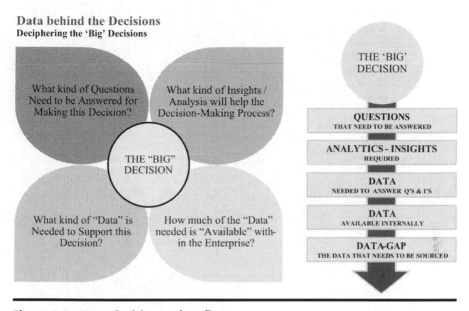

Figure 6.8   From decision to data flow.

a "big" decision and given all the required data is available; the value from data-driven decision-making, meaning making a material difference to the quality of the decision, is guaranteed.

Note: It is quite possible to plan an integrated analytics project to potentially address more than one "big" decision at a time, assuming all the data that is needed to support such decisions is integrated, normalized, and available. Further, most organizations invest in an advanced analytics platform that sits on top of a data lake or a data warehouse. In such a case, it will be possible consolidate and build a set of solutions that address all the "big" decisions at one go (Figure 6.9).

6.3 Building a Business Case

Every CDO (or CIO as the case may be) will be asked to create a business case for proposed advanced analytics investments. The purpose of a business case is for evaluating the return on investment, understanding the risk and reward. The CDO needs to conclusively prove that the incremental value generated through analytics necessarily needs to be greater than investment made. So, for building a business case, we need a credible method to estimate the incremental value generated, and the investments required.

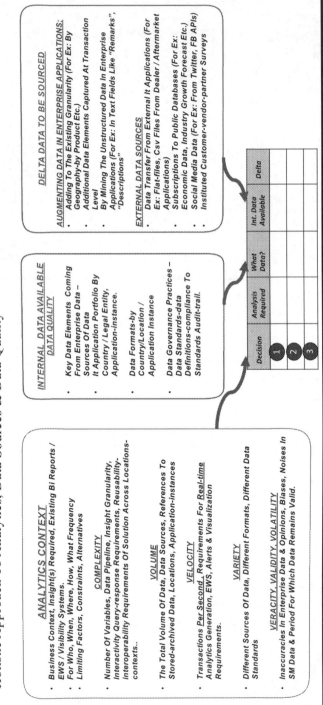

DATA-DRIVEN DECISION MAKING – A SUMMARY VIEW
Holistic Approach To Analytics, Data Sources & Data Quality

ANALYTICS CONTEXT
- Business Context, Insight(s) Required, Existing Bi Reports / EWS / Visibility Systems.
- For Who, When, Where, How, What Frequency
- Limiting Factors, Constraints, Alternatives

COMPLEXITY
- Number Of Variables, Data Pipeline, Insight Granularity, Interactivity Query-response Requirements, Reusability-interoperability Requirements Of Solution Across Locations-contexts..

VOLUME
- The Total Volume Of Data, Data Sources, References To Stored-archived Data, Locations, Application-instances

VELOCITY
- Transactions Per Second, Requirements For Real-time Analytics Generation, EWS, Alerts & Visualization Requirements.

VARIETY
- Different Sources Of Data, Different Formats, Different Data Standards

VERACITY, VALIDITY, VOLATILITY
- Inaccuracies In Enterprise Data & Opinions, Biases, Noises In SM Data & Period For Which Data Remains Valid.

INTERNAL DATA AVAILABLE –
DATA QUALITY
- Key Data Elements Coming From Enterprise Data – Sources Of Data
- It Application Portfolio By Country / Legal Entity, Application-instance.
- Data Formats-by Country/Location / Application Instance
- Data Governance Practices – Data Standards-data Definitions-compliance To Standards Audit-trail.

DELTA DATA TO BE SOURCED

AUGMENTING DATA IN ENTERPRISE APPLICATIONS:
- Adding To The Existing Granularity (For Ex: By Geography-by Product Etc.)
- Additional Data Elements Captured At Transaction Level
- By Mining The Unstructured Data In Enterprise Applications (For Ex: In Text Fields Like "Remarks", "Descriptions"

EXTERNAL DATA SOURCES
- Data Transfer From External It Applications (For Ex: Flat-files, Csv Files From Dealer / Aftermarket Applications)
- Subscriptions To Public Databases (For Ex: Economic Data, Industry Growth Forecast Etc.)
- Social Media Data (For Ex: From Twitter, FB APIs)
- Instituted Customer-vendor-partner Surveys

Decision	Analysis Required	What Data?	Int. Data Available	Delta
1				
2				
3				

Figure 6.9   Data-driven decision-making – a summary view.

6.3.1 Analytics and the Sources of Value: The Value-Drivers

So far, we have been working on the assumption that the potential upside to revenues/and profitability is the measure of value from analytics. But in reality, the value may accrue from a variety of sources, such as:

1. Operating efficiencies
2. Managerial time arbitrage
3. Time to market arbitrage
4. Forecasting effectiveness arbitrage
5. Customer retention arbitrage
6. Time to information arbitrage… and others.

There can be many more sources of incremental efficiencies, and value-drivers that advanced analytics can potentially power the organizations with.

The core argument of this book (and my articles) has been that all decisions are not equally important, and a vital-few "big" decisions account for over 90% of business outcomes. While researching for this book, I came across an interesting argument in an L.E.K. Consulting white paper (L.E.K. Consulting, 2017). The core message of the paper is paraphrased below:

• Improvement in operating-performance drives shareholder value creation
• Three categories of value-drivers: growth drivers, efficiency drivers, and financial drivers
• Most organizations manage their business as if all operating factors (KPIs) are equally important. Not all of them have an equal impact on the shareholder value creation.
• Managers are usually aware of the variables that drive the operating efficiencies and pursue each of them aggressively. However, the list of variables is often too long, and managers may end up spending more time and energy on KPIs which are comparatively less important; and *organizations may even unintentionally reward such managers.*
• It is important to identify key drivers of value; the factors that most influence the value and are controllable. L.E.K calls these "value-drivers".
• L.E.K argues that identifying and focusing the management attention on the key value-drivers (those few with significant influence on shareholder value creation and which are controllable) is the key to effectively managing shareholder value creation.

In my view **a decision is, essentially, the manager exercising control over the process: changing the process variables so as to maximize the throughput**. The "big" decisions, the 10% of decisions that "control" 90% of business outcomes, essentially refer to the very same key value drivers that L.E.K talks about in its white paper.

(L.E.K. Consulting, 2017)

While L.E.K proposes focusing on value-drivers which are controllable, I have mentioned that organizations must prioritize the "big" decisions that are not just controllable, but also can be data-driven. The concept of data-driven big decisions can bring in a paradigm shift in the way organizations manage the shareholder value creation **from people-driven success, to process-driven-successes**. We may note that what L.E.K discusses in this paper is still people-driven-success.

However, I believe L.E.K's method for value-driver analysis; specifically developing a value-driver map of the organization, can be a very useful tool for identifying the "big" decisions, besides the key value-drivers. I have personally used both value maps and value-driver trees.

Recently, SAP has introduced what it calls an "ultimate what-if analysis" (Nguyen, 2020) as a part of its SAP Analytics on Cloud; a new functionality for creating interactive value-driver trees. Technically one can create a value-driver tree simulating the complete enterprise value-chain and evaluate how changes in each value-driver affects different parts of the business, apart from the overall enterprise performance. (Note: value tree analysis is a proven and age-old technique, said to be based on the Dupont Model of the 1920s).

6.3.2 Estimating Returns: Comparing KPIs with Industry Benchmarks

Another equally important method to estimate the potential for incremental value generation, would be to analyze the key performance indicators and compare them with internal benchmarks and industry benchmarks. In my experience, key performance indicators within an organization itself can vary widely, from location to location, and from manufacturing plant to manufacturing plant. For example: Inventory turns within the organizations can widely vary between different plants indicating managerial slack and the scope for improvement and, more importantly the potential upside we are after, meaning if the inventories in all the manufacturing plants within the organization were to be managed equally efficiently, at least to the level of the internal benchmark, a substantial number of hidden efficiencies would be released (Figure 6.10).

Industry benchmarks apart, there are function-specific benchmarks available. For example, WERC, the professional association for logistics and supply-chain management, provides a comprehensive list of metrics and benchmarks for logistics (in-bound and out-bound).

Figure 6.11 shows a company with four plants: the total turnover is around $ 800 million, and the total inventory is about $ 60 Million (Figure 6.11).

Data that we gather from Figure 6.11: The inventory number of days varies from eight days for Plant 1 to 45 days for Plant 2, and the overall organizational average is 24.75 days. Hence, the internal benchmark is eight days, while the industry benchmark is four days.

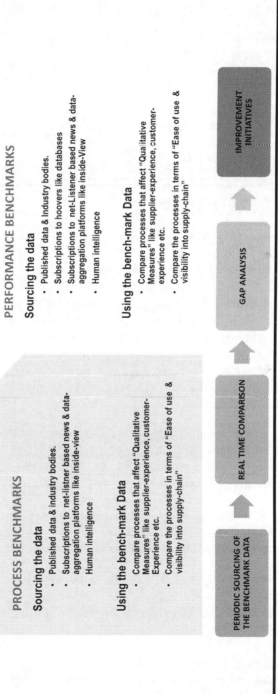

BENCHMARKING
in a nutshell!

PROCESS BENCHMARKS

Sourcing the data

- Published data & industry bodies.
- Subscriptions to net-listner based news & data-aggregation platforms like inside-view
- Human intelligence

Using the bench-mark Data

- Compare processes that affect "Qualitative Measures" like supplier-experience, customer-Experience etc.
- Compare the processes in terms of "Ease of use & visibility into supply-chain"

PERFORMANCE BENCHMARKS

Sourcing the data

- Published data & Industry bodies.
- Subscriptions to hoovers like databases
- Subscriptions to net-Listener based news & data-aggregation platforms like inside-View
- Human intelligence

Using the bench-mark Data

- Compare processes that affect "Qualitative Measures" like supplier-experience, customer-experience etc.
- Compare the processes in terms of "Ease of use & visibility into supply-chain"

PERIODIC SOURCING OF THE BENCHMARK DATA → REAL TIME COMPARISON → GAP ANALYSIS → IMPROVEMENT INITIATIVES

Figure 6.10   Using benchmarking data.

#	KEY-PERFORMANCE INDICATOR	PLANT -1	PLANT -2	PLANT -3	PLANT -4	ORG. AVERAGE	INTL. BENCH-MARK	COMPARING ORG.AV WITH INT. BENCH-MK	INDUSTRY BENCH-MARK	COMPARING ORG.AV WITH IND. BENCH-MK
1	INVENTORY (NO. OF DAYS)	8	45	32	14	24.75	8	-16.75	4	-20.75
2	ASSET-TURNS	1.75	0.95	1.05	1.6	1.3375	1.75	0.4125	2.1	0.7625
3	MFG. OVERHEADS / UNIT PRODUCED	xxx	xxx	xxx	xxx	xxx	xxx	xxx	xxx	xxx
4	REVENUE / EMPLOYEE	xxx	xxx	xxx	xxx	xxx	xxx	xxx	xxx	xxx
5	PROFIT / EMPLOYEE	xxx	xxx	xxx	xxx	xxx	xxx	xxx	xxx	xxx
6	Y-O-Y GROWTH IN REVENUE	xxx	xxx	xxx	xxx	xxx	xxx	xxx	xxx	xxx

Figure 6.11 Estimating the value.

So, if all plants were to operate at the same inventory-levels as Plant 1, the overall Org. inventory would come down by 16.75 days, or in other words, the inventory of the organization can be brought down from $ 60 million to around $ 20 million, meaning a reduction of $ 40 million in inventory. If all plants were to operate at the industry benchmark of four days of inventory, then the overall inventory of the organization could be brought down to around $ 10 million, meaning a reduction of $ 50 million in inventory. As any saving on inventory carrying cost directly adds to the bottom-line, the potential upside to the profitability can be easily calculated.

Now the difficult part is to assign that value to specific decisions. For example: there are three "big" decisions that can help bring down the inventory of all plants closer to industry benchmarks.

1. To invest in analytics solutions that can improve forecasting accuracy.
2. To invest in supply chain visibility solutions.
3. To increase the number of MRP runs in the enterprise resource planning (ERP) software.

While the third decision may incrementally cost nothing (assuming all plants run on the same ERP), decisions 1 and 2, would require additional investments. Allocating the potential upside to specific decision can be done either by:

• Running a pilot experiment and working out sensitivity of inventory levels to interventions in supply chain visibility, or forecasting accuracy.
• Arrive at an empirical number with the help of focus group and allocate the potential upside to decisions 1 and 2.

Building a business case, per se, is like forecasting; looking into the future and projecting the estimated revenues and anticipated costs associated with a project, over a period of five to seven years, and then working out an internal rate of return (IRR) and net present value (NPV), based on a set of assumptions. So, no organization expects 100% accuracy in value estimates if they agree with the direction and the overall logic presented in the business case; an empirical estimate for incremental value generated is usually acceptable. However, I always prefer the pilot approach if sufficient time is available. The sensitivity analysis helps organizations identify the specific value-drivers and the specific constraints, affecting the throughput of the organization. The L.E.K white paper also endorses this view.

6.3.3 Estimating the Investments

While I have provided a couple of methods above to estimate the incremental value generation, the investments proposed need to be worked out based on the roadmap that was created.

The roadmap sequences the proposed investment into analytics projects; each project addressing one or more "big" decisions. The prioritization of the projects is based on a variety of factors besides value-at-stake.

With reference to the example shown in Figure 6.12, a series of four projects have been planned based on the roadmap created to support the identified seven "big" decisions. The first project (P1) is essentially implementation of an on premises advanced analytics platform that sits on top of an earlier implemented, currently live instance of a data lake that stores all the enterprise data, both structured and unstructured. Project P1 is budgeted to last 60 days, and involves an investment of $ 2 million, that includes the first year's software license costs.

Projects P2, P3, and P4 are all analytics projects addressing the seven "big" decisions, sequenced as per the roadmap, and which are planned to be built on the newly implemented advanced analytics platform (Figure 6.12).

The investments required for P2, P3 and P4 and the expected duration of the projects are all provided in the schematic above. The schematic indicates, by day180, technically all the seven "big" decisions will be data-driven. However, analytics models would require continuous fine tuning and there will be a period of stabilization during which the models are perfected. If it is a machine learning algorithm, incremental changes in the training data will keep initiating changes in the algorithm; the algorithmic stability comes in over a period time. So, there must be a budget for application management services for the advanced analytics platform and for the analytics solutions built on top of the platform.

In conclusion, the investments are most likely to be recurring costs, and the benefits from data-driven decision-making are expected to be visible only after the period of stabilization. The business case needs to reflect this reality.

6.4 From Decisions to Data: A Summary View

The following are the steps involved in creating a roadmap and building a business case for a data-driven organization.

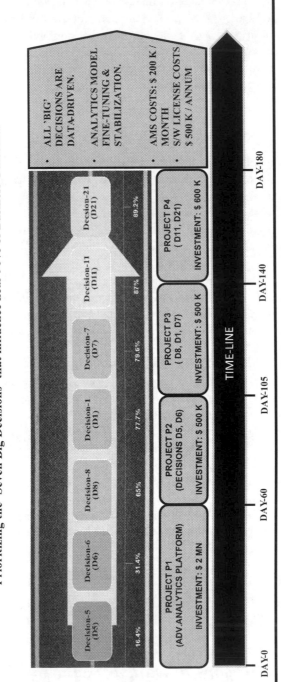

Figure 6.12   Roadmap and project plan for data-driven organization.

List and Categorize Decisions

1. List all the decisions in the organization, ideally with the help of a focus group specifically created for the purpose (Figure 6.13).
2. Categorize the decisions; based on a variety of criteria including strategic impact, data availability, complexity, retractability, group decisions among others.
   - Since not all the decisions can be data-driven, identify and discard the decisions that will have to be taken purely based on instincts of the managers.
   - Not all decisions are important. Discard the decisions that are of little value, one-off and unimportant.

Estimate Value-at-Stake and Prioritize Decisions

3. Conduct a due diligence to analyze the nature and the relative importance of each of the decisions. Gather data on factors like value-at-stake, managerial time, complexity, number of times the decision is made in a year.
4. List the decisions by decreasing order of value-at-stake; The value-at-stake represents the dollar value of the impact the decision may have on the business outcomes.
5. Identify the 10–20% of the decisions that account for 80–90% of business outcomes; the "big" decisions.
6. Re-prioritize the "big" decisions based on a set of factors your organization considers important.

Create an Analytics Roadmap

7. Create a roadmap for data-driven organization, sequencing the analytics investments targeted at the "big" decisions, exactly as per the order of priority.
8. The roadmap must cover all the "big" decisions that influence 90% of business outcomes. So technically, if all the listed "big" decisions are supported with data and analytics, the organization can call itself a data-driven organization.

Data Behind the Decisions and Estimated Investments

9. For each of the identified "big" decisions, initiate a thorough decision analysis aimed at understanding the insights and data required for supporting the decision.
10. Cross-check how much of the data needed to support the decision is internally available within the enterprise.
11. Estimate the time and effort required for sourcing the delta data to create and implement a process model for capturing the missing data on a continuous basis.
12. Create a timeline for the roadmap, complete with detailed project plans for each of the analytics projects. Estimate the investments required over a period of five to seven years (Figure 6.14).

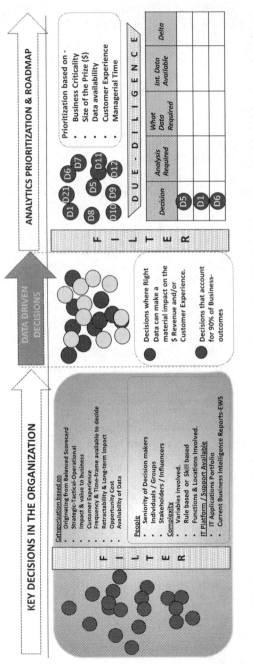

Figure 6.13 **The process for identifying the "Big" decisions.**

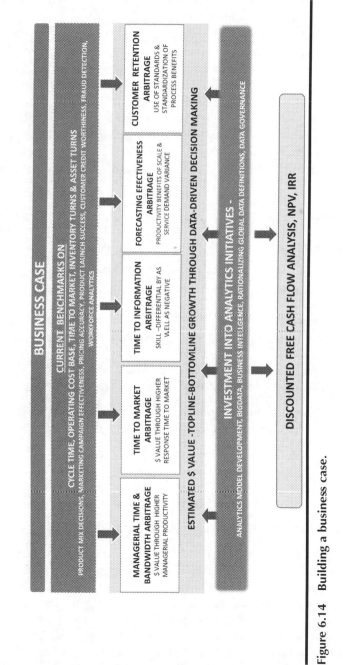

ROADMAP TO DATA-DRIVEN ORGANIZATION
BUILDING A BUSINESS CASE

Figure 6.14 Building a business case.

Create a Business Case

13. Estimate the returns from data-driven decision-making.
    - There are multiple sources of dollar benefits that can be generated through data-driven decision-making.
    - The benefits may start accruing only after the analytics algorithms are stabilized. Typically, the benefits start accruing from the second ear onwards.
    - Estimate a high and a low dollar number for overall returns.
14. Project the investments required and the estimated benefits over a period of five years.
15. Create discounted cash-flow statements and estimate the IRR and NPV.
16. Create sensitivity analysis around the high and low estimates of dollar returns.
17. List all the assumptions.
18. Indicate the high and low IRR from data-driven decision-making.

6.5 The Data, Trust, and the Decision-Maker

6.5.1 What Else Can Potentially Go Wrong?

Many analytics projects do generate great insights and interactive visualization, and yet most managers continue to resort to ad hoc and intuitive decision-making. Why? There are a couple of possible explanations:

- They have little trust in the *data* available in the company, hence little faith in the analytics.
- The analytics do not specifically generate the actionable insights required for improving the quality of a specific business decision.

Here is a case of everything done right: you have used the right decisions, the right analytics model, and the right data, and yet managers still resist using analytics.

It is important to understand what exactly is influencing this behavior as it helps us answering the question: *What else can potentially prevent analytics projects from delivering the intended value?*

6.5.2 Value Promised vs. Value Delivered

Often, the value delivered is far lower than value promised; there are three post-implementation challenges that may prevent analytics projects delivering value.

1. **Resistance to Change**: The biggest challenge is *managing the change and making the managers move away from gut-based decisions to data-driven decisions*. No matter how well the analytics projects are designed, developed, and implemented, no matter how precise and timely the insights being generated

are, it is the actual utilization of such analytics, and the insights by the decision makers, that determines the actual on-the-ground value generated by analytics.

The utilization rate of analytics is a composite measure of the following:

- Average percentage of time a manager makes data-driven decisions utilizing the insights generated by the analytics.
- Average percentage of managers using analytics to make data-driven decisions.

2. **Maintaining Data Quality**: The other big challenge is ensuring the data quality and availability on a continuous basis. We have witnessed in multiple assignments, while it is common for people building extract, transform and load (ETL) solutions and process controls to ensure the data quality and availability is fixed before the "go-live", it soon deteriorates because either the ETL solutions failed to keep up, or, as happens more often, the process controls fail. Unfortunately, there are no measures for data quality and availability, but low utilization level is often a result of lack of trust in the data being analyzed as managers stop valuing the insights being generated.

3. **Functional Change Management**: Business situations are anything but static. The underlying conditions and the assumptions keep changing continuously. Hence, any analytics solution developed needs to accurately reflect the reality, meaning the underlying analytics model must be configurable, and ideally, configurable by the business managers, without the necessity of any additional coding. If the functionality of analytics applications does not keep up with changing business functionality or conditions, once again managers will stop using the application, resulting in low utilization levels.

Bibliography

Angara, R. (2017). How to create a value-driver tree in SAP analytics cloud. Step-by-step. *SAP.com Blogs*, Nov 2017.

Burrows, A. (2018). How to define value-drivers. *SuperchargedFinance.com*, Sep 2018.

Courtney, H., Lovallo, D., & Clarke, C. (2013). Deciding how to decide. *Harvard Business Review*, 91(11), 62–70.

Craft, R.C., & Leake, C. (2002). The Pareto principle in organizational decision-making. *Management Decision*, 40(8), 729–733.

Decosmo, J. (2018). Why you should take a decision-first approach to analytics. *Forbes.com*, (Forbes Technology Council). Oct 17.

Goldratt, E. M., and Cox, J. (1984). *The Goal: Excellence in Manufacturing*. North River Press.

Goldratt, E. M., and Cox, J. (2016). *The Goal: A Process of Ongoing Improvement*. Routledge.

Hilgefort, I. (2020). Using SAP analytics cloud and a value driver tree for visual planning and simulation. *LinkedIn.com/Pulse*, April 2020.

L.E.K. Consulting (2017). *Identifying and Managing Key Value Drivers*. L.E.K. Consulting *Executive Insights*, XIX, 36, 2017.

Lukac, E. G. and Frazier, D., & Deloitte Consulting (2012). Linking strategy to value. *Journal of Business Strategy*, 33, 4, 49–57.

Mankins, C. M., & Davis-Peccoud, J. (2011). Decision insights: How organizations make great decisions. Bain white paper 2011.

Nguyen, J. (2020). Creating the ultimate what-if analysis. *Blogs.sap.com* March 18, 2020.

Panetta, K. (2018) Gartner top strategic predictions for 2019 and beyond, *Gartner.com* https://www.gartner.com/smarterwithgartner/gartner-top-strategic-predictions-for-2019-and-beyond Oct. 16, 2018

Schmitz, C., Tschiesner, A., Jansen, C., Hallerstede, S., & Garms, F. (2019). *Industry 4.0: Capturing Value at Scale in Discrete Manufacturing*. McKinsey & Company.

Taylor, J., Fish, A., Vanthienen, J., & Vincent, P. (2013). Emerging standards in decision modeling.

Taylor, J., & Purchase, J. (2016). *Real-world Decision Modeling with DMN*. Tampa: Meghan-Kiffer Press.

von Halle, B. & Goldberg, L. (n.d.). The OMG decision model and notation spec (DMN) and the decision model (TDM). modernanalyst.com.

Chapter 7

Unchartered

A Brief History of Data

Topics Covered in this Chapter

1. The history of data
2. Growth of enterprise data
3. Enterprise applications & the rise of ERP
4. The need for "one version of truth"
5. Evolution of databases
6. The evolution of enterprise data
7. Y2K and the aftermath
8. Enterprise application integration
9. Life before Internet: Electronic data interchange
10. Master data management
11. The "unstructured data"
12. The era of Internet

DOI: 10.1201/9781003321347-8

INTRODUCTION

We keep hearing stories about how data (or the lack of it) failed an organization. In my opinion, it is actually a case of organizations failing their data. The data that you don't plan for, don't capture, and don't report never comes to your rescue when the sky is finally falling on your head.

So, for those companies serious about transforming themselves into data-driven organizations, it is important to understand data, its history, and the evolution of enterprise data management practices over the last few decades.

7.1 The History of Data

While the concept of observing and measuring the characteristics of a process, person or thing is as old as the oldest civilization, the word data (plural for "datum", meaning single value) is about 400 years old. As international trading picked up in the early 17th century, hundreds of new joint stock companies were registered in England, and a need arose for keeping records of the performance of the companies. Given the locked-in capital and limited liability, the joint stock companies had a duty to record and report data (both qualitative and quantitative information) representing their current and projected profitability, before paying dividends and taxes, or as a necessary precondition before they raised more funds from the shareholders. The Industrial Revolution and mass production introduced further complexity; accounting data pertaining to the companies had to be diligently recorded in books and reported to the shareholders. The process became more formal after Britain passed the Joint Stock Companies Act in 1844, which introduced the concept of auditing the books. With the advent of computers after the Second World War, every institution which could afford a computer – including governments, universities, scientists, and companies – started collecting and distributing huge amounts of "data", the term which began to be widely used to represent the information stored on computers.

7.2 Growth of Enterprise Data

Before the early 1980s computers meant mainframe computers, and they were prohibitively expensive; hence only a few large companies, governments, state funded universities and R&D (research and development) institutions could afford them. The rest of the companies continued to rely on good old manual bookkeeping, and the public at large lived in blissful ignorance. The programming languages were cumbersome, and so were the tapes on which the data had to be stored. All that suddenly changed with the introduction of personal computers (PCs), when the whole process of data gathering, and reporting become more affordable and more companies started moving their data on to computers. The floodgates were literally thrown open with the introduction of the internet. Most of us know the story so far.

7.3 Enterprise Applications: Rise of ERP

The introduction of word processors, spreadsheets, and affordable personal computers meant the data could be stored and managed by individual functions like marketing and finance; hence the monopoly hitherto enjoyed by a centralized computer department was somewhat dented. However, larger companies needed to process large amounts of data, specifically in complex data-intensive activities like running monthly payroll for thousands of employees, or for running the then popular MRP-II program involving thousands of part numbers. A good majority of enterprise transactions, like receiving reports and issue vouchers for materials, salary advances and attendance data for employees were completely off-line, and continued to be recorded on paper: printed forms, usually filed in quadruplicate, in multiple colors with a carbon paper in between them. This transactional data had to be painstakingly entered into the mainframes by the ubiquitous data entry operators before the running of any MRP-II or monthly payroll. Data entry backlogs ranging from a few days to few months were not unknown.

7.4 Need for "One Version of Truth"

As mentioned, before the 1980s, computers usually meant mainframes, if one ignores the short-lived phenomenon of mini-computers such as the DEC PDP series. The use of computers was usually limited to recurring and massive data-crunching exercises, like payroll for thousands of employees or doing an MRP run in a large manufacturing company with thousands of part numbers in the inventory. The complexity in some industries such as manufacturing, or defense, was too massive for manual calculations, for example, a single car has well over 30,000 parts. A typical aircraft manufacturing company may have well over a million part numbers in its inventory, including specific parts for different variants of the same aircraft that they must continue to overhaul while the aircraft models remain in service. Then there is the further complexity of some components needing mandatory replacement based on the number of hours of use, while other components such as rubber items are "lifed", meaning they have an expiry date and hence they must be replaced by a specific date, irrespective of the flying hours of aircraft. The MRP run in aircraft industry used to be an 8–16 hour exercise, meaning the mainframe computers could not be used for anything else during this period.

However, all this changed by the late 1980s. As PCs became more common, many individual departments such as finance, HR, and materials control started developing their own small applications using simpler to use software like dbase-III and Lotus 123. This meant all the paper-based data from purchase requests and invoices had to be entered into different applications, both on local PC based and on the centralized mainframes. As applications grew within a company, so did the *versions of truth*. Each of the applications were being fed a different kind of data from a different instant, and each had its own data structure. Over a period of time, no two applications carried the same kind of data, or the same *version of truth*.

The advent of client-server applications further changed the landscape. While the mainframes were being replaced by client-servers, the mainframe applications grew wings and spread out, but unfortunately each application went to a different server, with its own database, and with its own unique data structure. By the end of the 1990s most Fortune-2000 companies had thousands of applications, sometimes each replicating the same data in a different format, sometimes each carrying a different set of data with no common table column that could help connect two applications. The islands of data, same, similar, disparate, with people newly designated as chief information officers (CIOs) totally clueless, and most business users resorting to the only option left open to them: *Rely on Excel*.

The core business applications were mostly homegrown till about the 1980s, important exceptions being operating systems like Unix, DOS, and CAD/CAM software. The software usually came bundled with hardware, preinstalled. Packaged software as a business picked up in the late 1980s and early 1990s. Technically, packaged software was supposed to bring in much-needed consistency. In reality, the data layer in the three tier architecture being customizable, data structures and data definitions continued to be as different as there are number of applications in a company. The net result was that no two applications could talk to each other.

By the early 1990s most large multinational companies had hundreds of applications sitting on different servers, each of them with a unique data structure, and sometimes with multiple instances of the same application in each of the geographies they operated in. Monthly record-to-report transactions and accounts consolidation were always a nightmare. Most companies had a time lag between the books of accounts and reality on the ground, ranging from a few weeks to few months; meaning the accounting books reflected the financial picture of the company as of a date a few weeks or months earlier.

7.5 Evolution of Databases

As data within the enterprise grew, programmers started to realize the need for an effective method to organize, store, search and retrieve data. Charles W. Bachman was credited with creating the first-ever database in the 1960s, followed by IBM. The database management systems were initially quite cumbersome, but with the introduction of relational database management systems (RDBMSs), and indexing and so forth (based on Codd's 12 rules), there was substantial increase to the speed of data query and retrieval. the introduction of structured query language (SQL) by

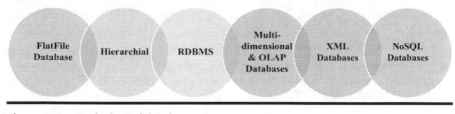

Figure 7.1   Evolution of databases.

Relational Software Inc. (now Oracle Corp.), and subsequently stored procedures further eased up both programming effort and data query and retrieval.

While Edgar F. Codd proposed a relational model for databases in 1970, it took more than a decade for relational databases to become popular on the market. The ease of query, the speed of search and retrieval of information, easy-to-understand English like SQL, and most importantly faster access to data using indexing all contributed to the popularity of relational databases. Oracle was officially launched in 1979.

In a way, the IBM PC, client-server architecture, and RDBMSs all contributed to one another's increasing acceptance and popularity in the market. The popularity of RDBMSs remained high and unchallenged right through the 1990s and early 2000s. However, the rise of the internet and the need for managing vast amounts of unstructured data opened up a quest for launching new databases that could manage unstructured content as well as structured relational databases. An overview of the evolution of databases is shown in Figure 7.1.

7.6 Evolution of Enterprise Data

With the launch of SAP R/3 in the early 1990s, it suddenly looked like a single application replacing the disparate applications sitting on vastly different databases might finally become a reality. R/3 in many ways was the best-engineered and the most comprehensive software ever; it covered almost every aspect of a manufacturing business, was completely customizable, and could potentially bring in the much-needed standardization. If implemented right, R/3 could mandate that all transactions should happen on-line; with each financially relevant transaction automatically creating entries for debit and credit in a relevant account. If implemented right, R/3 could ensure, and a company could close its books on any day to takeout a balance sheet and profit and loss (P&L) exactly representing the true picture of the financial position of the company. Technically, the ERP implementation was supposed to consolidate data from multiple applications, spreadsheets, and manual registers among others, all brought into a single application, a unified database, and a companywide single version of truth. When SAP R/3 was launched on the market in the 1990s, most CEOs believed implementing SAP would not only fix the "millennium bug", but also would mean adopting the industry best practices and standardizing internal processes across the value-chain, and across the geographies. SAP R/3 was as perfect a solution as there could be, specifically for manufacturing companies.

SAP was also the most comprehensive software package to hit the market ever, and if *implemented well*, could truly transform the processes across the organization, while financial accounts would be updated in real time. Here are some pointers as to what "*implemented well*" means:

- All business processes from across geographies are covered within SAP.
- All transactions are run within SAP, online in real time. No off-line business processes.
- Organization structure, charts of accounts, bills of materials and so on are defined at the most granular level.
- No consolidated entries into books of accounts ever. All accounting entries only through running transactions at the most granular level.
- Books of accounts can be closed, P&L and balance sheets can be produced at any instant of time. Books of accounts represent the true financial picture of the company of that instant.

However, in reality a good many R/3 implementations were half-hearted and covered only a part of the enterprise economic activity. For example, a very large pharma company based in New Jersey kept their entire sales and distribution activity outside of SAP, in what they called "proven" legacy client-server applications – meaning multiple legacy applications running in different points-of-sale. So, a battery of programmers was hired to run BDCs (bulk upload of flat files) for porting the transactional data (invoices, stock transfers etc.) from legacy sales applications into SAP, so that relevant financial accounts would be posted and SAP reflects the true picture of actual sales and stocks in each storage location.

The whole job was a nightmare given any data validation error pertaining to a specific row in the flat file, needed to be pulled out, investigated, corrected and reuploaded as a separate flat file. Any corrections to the master data, such as new products added, or new customers needed to be carried out in each of the legacy applications in each point-of-sale. Compounding the issue was the cost of the licenses and cost of connectivity. SAP sold named-user licenses; hence they needed as many additional licenses as there were points-of-sale to do the transactions (raise the invoices and delivery challans) within the same instance of SAP. A prohibitively expensive affair! The other issue was with the cost of connectivity: while locations within continental USA were well connected, the overseas locations had to be connected via VSATs (very small aperture terminals) which were very expensive.

While companies did invest in SAP or equivalent, they still had a whole bunch of upstream and downstream applications running the transactions in different departments, geographies, and locations. A few good companies were replicating individual transactions into SAP using BDCs. Most others were simply passing monthly consolidated accounting entries to reflect the incremental sales revenue and reduction in inventories. So, in the absence of transaction-wise entries, the reports generated within SAP can at best provide a financial overview of the performance of the company. Then there were a set of new applications which focused on white spaces that a traditional ERP did not cover, such as customer relationship management (CRM), or supplier relationship management (SRM) among others. Companies such as Siebel, and i2 Technologies quickly created a market of their own. Net-net nothing really changed; now there is an ERP (usually SAP) plus a variety of commercial off-the-shelf (COTS) and homegrown applications with each having its own database, data definitions, data formats and data standards.

7.7 Y2K and the Aftermath

The information technology market experienced something akin to a California gold rush towards the end of the millennium. While manufacturing companies quickly migrated their applications from mainframes into a client-server architecture and implemented some ERP, large banks, public services, and insurance companies still relied on mainframes to do their heavy duty number-crunching. Inertia and risk aversion apart, the chief technology officers (CTOs) of banks and insurance companies, did not believe the client-server architecture could handle the huge volume of transactions that they experienced every day. But as the year 2000 approached, they realized most of their legacy mainframe applications had a provision of only two characters for the table column called "year". There was widespread panic, and no one knew what exactly might happen as the year changed from 1999 to 2000. Many feared the computers might crash bringing the operations of banks and public services like trains to a grinding halt.

Amid the panic, information technology budgets and strategy became the focus for every CEO, and every boardroom. IT people were backroom boys no more. IT budgets were enhanced, and every pending IT migration project was cleared, pronto. While some fixed mainframe programs painstakingly, most companies preferred migrating to best available ERP, or a brand new client-server application developed ground up. Thousands of new programmers were hired, and thousands more were imported from India, specifically for handling the "millennium bug".

Y2K was in many ways a wake-up call for technology architects and data modelers alike. The importance of database modeling, data standards, and portability of data was understood firsthand.

7.8 Enterprise Application Integration

As the number of applications grew with in a company, so did the variety of data. It was not uncommon to find multiple isolated instances for each country or each legal entity; Sometimes multiple applications independently developed on different technology stacks, for different divisions or different geographies. Each application used its own data definitions, data types and data standards. No two internal applications could "speak to" each other (a euphemism for data interchange), and there was redundant data all over the enterprise landscape, the time lag between applications stretching from a few weeks to few months. In some cases, such as integration of applications, was not a choice, but a necessity: for example, the localized invoicing applications at points-of-sale needed to be integrated with the centralized accounting application so as to ensure accounts could be closed every month. For a while organizations attempted point-to-point integration of critical applications using batch upload of data on flat files.

Enterprise application integration (EAI) was thought of as a method to connect disparate applications through a middleware technology, so as to ensure data consistency (point-in-time consistency and transaction consistency) between applications. While EAI could effectively keep different applications in sync, it was never meant for controlling data redundancy, or for introducing non-existent data standards. EAI quickly caught the imagination of CIOs everywhere, as the most effective method to connect legacy mainframe applications with the new client-server applications, but by the late 1990s, it was time to integrate the legacy client-server applications with the new phenomenon called the internet. For example, banks, insurance companies, and appliance makers among others needed to sync the data related to the product portfolio from their internal servers with their websites. While there were many middleware products in the market, the most popular included IBM's MQSeries, TIBCO, Vitria, SeeBeyond, and WebMethods.

Middleware technologies were complicated, and each product vendor used a different approach; While MQ used the concept of message queues, TIBCO used a "bus" architecture, WebMethods used a hub and spoke. The message formats ranged from XML, JSON to an IDOC. Both MQ and WebMethods used a Publish-Subscribe model for data interchange (Figure 7.2).

Since middleware needs to connect non-standard legacy applications, the adapters that connect specific applications needed to be custom developed. Building adapters and implementing EAI tools was an extremely long and tedious process. In 2002, I remember bidding for setting up a middleware center of excellence for a Fortune-500 company based at Atlanta. They had thousands of application-specific adapters and were building more, and employed over a hundred people with annual budgets running into millions.

Overtime, the ERP vendors themselves developed an integration module. Initially SAP launched an integration tool called Business Connector (Powered by WebMethods) in 2000. Subsequently they launched a more comprehensive EAI module called SAP XI (SAP Exchange Infrastructure), as a part of their NetWeaver launch in 2004. The name of the EAI module was changed to SAP PI (Process Infrastructure) in 2007. Oracle launched its own EAI tool bundle called Oracle Fusion around 2007.

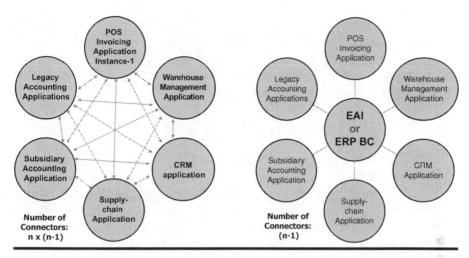

Figure 7.2 Enterprise application integration vs. point-to-point integration.

Middleware implementations still remained complex, long, and tedious. Each time the base applications being integrated were upgraded, the integration components needed to be recoded and retested. Slightest changes to the data structure of the base applications could potentially trigger integration components to crash, and hence necessitated recoding and testing of the middleware components.

A good number of Fortune-2000 companies have invested in EAI, but most have limited localized implementations connecting only a small percentage of their application portfolio. A few attempted implementing B2B Enterprise Integration. Gartner predicted through 2018 that organizations would lack a postmodern application integration strategy; postmodern being a reference to the implementation of new, distributed, loosely coupled cloud-based ERP modules. To conclude: enterprise-wide application integration is a never-ending exercise, and data consistency between applications is a utopian dream. Organizations continue to have islands of information; disconnected and disparate applications; and, as of 2021, data variety is a bigger problem than it ever was.

7.9 Life before the Internet: Electronic Data Interchange

Business entities need to exchange information with other business entities located across the world. Once, this happened through "snail-mail", then through telephone and telex, and subsequently through electronic data exchange (EDI), business to business enterprise application integration, (B2B EAI), and finally through the internet. Before the advent of internet, airline ticketing systems relied on centralized computer systems like *Galileo* (European Consortium) and *Apollo* (United Airlines) that connected travel agents from across the world. *Lloyds List Intelligence* has a 300-year-old history of accurately providing information on the whereabouts of merchant ships. Data collection and interchange was through connected computer terminals where possible, otherwise through a variety of methods including file transfer protocol (FTP), or just by mailing a computer disk or a tape.

DATA CHAOS

In a sense, the number of excel sheets floating around indicates the measure of data chaos an organization is subject to.

Take the case of large multinationals with hundreds of legal entities spread across five continents. The effects of multiple instances of isolated applications – each with its own data types, definitions, and standards, shows most prominently during the accounts consolidation at the corporate headquarters every quarter.

Each of the hundreds of legal entities not only needs to file tax returns for country specific jurisdictions, but also needs to send its accounts for consolidation at corporate headquarters. ERPs like SAP allow each company code to be mapped to multiple charts of accounts – one for local tax reporting, the other for global consolidation. If the organization is on a global single-instance SAP with each legal entity in the group-company mapped to a standardized chart of accounts for global consolidation, then consolidation is an automatic process which requires little intervention. If the organization at least has a standardized chart of accounts in all the legal entities with financial closing software like Oracle Hyperion or SAP BPC (Business Planning and Consolidation), then once again the job is fairly simple, assuming the charts of accounts are completely in sync.

However, the reality is very different in most organizations. Given the unique and different reporting requirements for its country jurisdiction and for corporate headquarters, every three months the accounting teams fight a heroic battle to somehow extract the information required out of Excel spreadsheets, which they alone can understand. The accounts consolidation team at corporate headquarters fights an equally heroic battle to chase the information from every one of the countries to somehow meet the deadlines for reporting the consolidated accounts for the holding company.

If you notice an organization reports its audited financial results a good six to eight weeks after the quarter has closed, you know all is not well within. You can instinctively diagnose the organization has a disease called "data chaos" and is possibly operating at a fraction of the industry benchmark efficiency.

Global trading and commerce required the data from requests for proposals (RFPs), requests for quotes (RFQs), purchase orders, and invoices and so on to be shared between sellers and buyers quickly, if not instantaneously. Health insurance records required the payer, the provider, and the government to exchange data seamlessly. Prior to the era of the internet, electronic data interchange (EDI) enabled such data interchange.

Electronic data interchange represented complete data interchange processes including the standards for electronic document format, the transmission process, exchange protocol, and the software for document interpretation. Between the late 1970s and the 1990s, serious efforts were made to introduce data standards for EDI. Examples include: ASC X12 or Accredited Standards Committee X12 (part of ANSI or the American National Standards Institute); UN/EDIFACT or United Nations Electronic Data Interchange for Administration Commerce and Transport; IATA Cargo-IMP or International Air Transport Association Cargo Interchange Message Procedures; and HL7 or Health Level Seven International and HIPAA or the Health Insurance Portability and Accountability Act (1996) for healthcare and healthcare insurance.

7.10 Master Data Management (MDM)

By the late 1990s, there were two distinct approaches to what CTOs believed was their IT strategy. While a small set of organizations preferred a centralized global single instance ERP, a good many preferred what was then called "best-of-breed" approach. Best-of-breed essentially meant choosing the best available software for each department, and each function. For example, a CTO could choose SAP for manufacturing and logistics, Peoplesoft for HR, a legacy application for payroll, Seibel for CRM, and i2 Technologies for factory planning, demand planning and demand management. In a true spirit of democracy, many multinationals let the local IT directors choose the "best-of-breed" suitable for their country specific needs. For example, a global pharma-major could be running on PeopleSoft for HR function in the USA, while their UK locations could be running SAP HR.

Very soon, the organizations which opted for the best-of-breed approach ended up having huge number of disparate, disconnected applications, and a crippling problem; the necessity for keeping the master data in all the applications in portfolio in complete sync. For example, the number of customers, and the number of stock keeping units in a point of sale invoicing system and the accounting system need to be exactly same; the data needs to be in complete sync. A new customer, or a new material created in a POS invoicing system needs to be replicated instantaneously in the accounting system as well, without which a sales invoice generated at POS cannot be replicated in the accounting system as a finance invoice, which triggers a credit entry in the sales account and a debit entry in the inventory account.

Master data management (MDM) software enables one-time creation of master data which triggers automatic updating of connected master data tables in different applications. For example, SAP NetWeaver, launched in 2003, included an MDM module. Assuming it is implemented well, customer-master or materials-master needs to be updated in the MDM module alone, and then it flows automatically into every connected application, ensuring customer-master and materials-master stay completely in sync across applications.

Unfortunately, the MDM implementations were not many, and of those few organizations which have attempted them, not all have completely succeeded. MDM implementations require that data model, data standards and data definitions are in sync between the applications, which in itself is a massive exercise. For example, the table structures for customer-master and materials-master needs to be in sync between the applications, once again a very difficult and time-consuming exercise.

7.11 Managing the Enterprise Content: Structured & Unstructured

The data within the enterprise is not just what you have on your relational databases. There is perhaps a hundred times more data in different kind of documents, contracts, correspondence, official reports, emails, inter-office memos, maps, images, videos, and photographs and so forth, that lies unexplored in different desktops, tapes, disks, and physical documents across the enterprise (Figure 7.3).

Some of the enterprise content can be structured and tagged. For example, depending on the kind of email software used, almost all of the email data does get automatically tagged and achieved. Most of the email platforms allow users to search and retrieve emails based on a variety of search criteria.

7.11.1 Searching across Documents

As enterprises started realizing the need for archiving, storing, and retrieving documents, an entirely different branch of tools called document management systems were introduced. The purpose was to tag, index, archive, and store the documents in an electronic format, and retrieve them using unique tags or key words. An access control on top of the application restricts the access to different users based on their clearance level to simply create, read, update, or delete (called CRUD). The first few document management systems to be introduced in the 1980s were called electronic data management systems (EDMs) which restricted the file format, but subsequent versions allowed all kinds of document formats from PDF to Word and Txt. The later versions of document management systems (DMS) on the market supported a variety of functions, including accessing the documents from anywhere in the world using the internet, collaborative editing, and versioning of the document by each user.

7.11.2 Searching within a Document: Markup Languages

Then came the next set of requirements – the need for searching for a "key word" or a "string" (a short phrase) within a document, or across several documents. This,

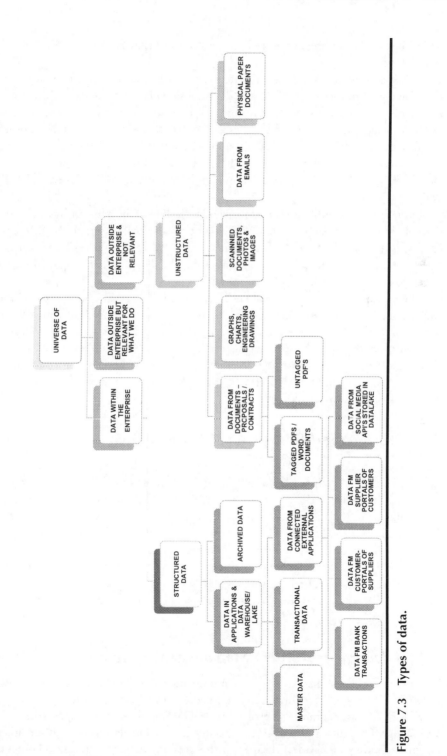

Figure 7.3 Types of data.

practically, is like reading an entire book to note all instances where a "key word" can be found.

This was a difficult ask, but the related requirements have been there ever since the advent of computers, specifically in the publishing industry. It started with adding markup tags for defining formatting (styling) of the text in the document. For example, a tag could define where a paragraph starts and where it ends, another could define the "bold" format for text and yet another for "underlining" text. The markup however had no standard, and it could be as defined by the typesetting services company which might use software like Penta, or Datalogics Pager, or IBM's Script.

In the publishing industry's quest for standardization of the markup tags, the standard general markup language (SGML) was born. The International Organization for Standardization (ISO) created SGML based on IBM's general markup language (GML) which was widely used by the military and defense industry right from the 1960s to share machine readable documents.

The next big development was HTML from Tim Berners Lee, which paved the way for the internet. Tim Berners Lee also helped establish a W3C (World Wide Web Consortium) in 1994, which in turn introduced XML – finally a versatile method to markup/tag the text not just define styles by also to create a Metadata that could help search within the document. There have been multiple advancements ever since including XHTML, XPath, and XQuery – a method to query and retrieve "strings" from the documents.

7.11.3 Structured Data vs. Unstructured Data

As the popularity of XML grew, industries, specifically publishers, realized that once they had a document in XML format, it could be easily converted into any other format (for example ePub, or Mobi). So, they started storing a fairly large number of documents in XML format. In theory, it meant that, not only could they search across the ISBNs (books), but they could also search within an ISBN for a specific "string" or "key word". A promising set of technologies.

The reality has been different, though. Most organizations (including a few publishers) have failed in enforcing a single global standard with respect to DTD (document type definition) and the XML schema making it impossible to search within the document.

7.11.4 Enterprise Content Management Systems

There are multiple terms used here including enterprise content management systems (ECMS), digital asset management systems (DAM) among others.

The ECMS are said to have evolved from DMS, a method to manage the content along with digital rights and user-specific access controls and so on. One other important variety of CMS evolved from the need for managing the web content.

Specifically in large publishing houses such as CNN, and *Time* with in the initial days, the most popular included the likes of Vignette, Plumtree, and IBM WebSphere. As of now, there are hundreds of options – specifically for web-content management, the most popular include Open Text, WordPress, and Drupal among others.

7.12 The Era of the Internet: External Data

Before the internet, in the case of business-to-consumer (B2C) mass-marketed consumer products, businesses never got to know their end-customers direct. Since the products became usually sold through a series of channel partners – clearing and forwarding agents, distributors, super-stockists, wholesalers, and retailers – end-consumer sale in most cases was at least a tertiary sale. The more links in the channels, the more distant the businesses became from the end-consumer. Knowing customers and their preferences was usually a statistical approximation arrived at from a sample survey.

The internet fundamentally changed the way organizations operate. For the first time, social media channels have provided a direct connection between the businesses and the end-consumer – an opportunity unheard of before the advent of the internet. Internet advertising has already overtaken television advertising in revenue. Television and print advertisements these days typically carry an enticing invite to visit the website, while print advertisements carry QR codes which mobiles can read and take customers directly to the relevant interactive web-advertisement ... so, all roads lead to the internet.

The internet and social media also churn out huge amounts of useful data on target customer segment, consumers, suppliers, business partners, competitors, and potential employees and so on. Assuming one understands how to sift through and analyze terabytes of external data in conjunction with enterprise data, organizations can now provide precise actionable insights for the decision-makers.

7.13 Conclusion

Before embarking on a journey to create a data-driven organization, one needs to understand the state and nature of the data within the enterprise. This chapter has covered the evolution of enterprise data right from the 1950s to the age of the internet, and various attempts made through the history to structure, standardize and manage data models, databases and data exchange between applications.

Chapter 8

Building a Data-Driven IT Strategy

Topics Covered in this Chapter:

1. Introduction	Setting the context. Why business-aligned IT strategy is as important as an effective data strategy.
2. Information technology strategy: Decoding the problems	What exactly goes wrong with IT in organizations?
3. Should data drive your IT strategy?	A container should define the liquid it holds, or should you choose a container for its contents? Is IT strategy a sub-set of data strategy? Should you define data strategy first and then define IT strategy?

DOI: 10.1201/9781003321347-9

4. Getting "IT" right A. Business aligned information technology B. Benchmarking C. Organizational workflow: Information supply-chain D. Workflow and the speed of the information supply chain E. Enterprise value chain and information supply chain F. Resource optimization G. Value from IT H. Enterprise architecture: Compatibility and cohesiveness	Focus on distinct value-drivers for building an effective IT strategy; an effective IT strategy cannot be built without laying down the foundation with an enterprise-wide business-aligned data strategy.
5. Summary: The making of the holy-grail	Business-aligned IT strategy; the stakeholder's wish-list.
6. Does information technology really matter?	A historical perspective on growth of information-technology in organizations…from an enabler to a differentiator, and then to a distinct competitive advantage.
7. Application portfolio analysis and rationalization.	The exercise of taking a comprehensive look at complete application portfolio to cull the applications that need to be retired, reengineered, or replaced. A necessary first step before developing an IT Strategy.

INTRODUCTION

Until recently, data strategy, if such a thing existed in an organization, had always been a sub-component of IT strategy. It has been said, if data is the blood, the information technology infrastructure is the circulating system that enables organizations. We know a poorly designed IT strategy could mean poor quality, disconnected data, that is delivered with a time lag greater than the useful life of the data. Hence, building a cohesive and business-aligned IT strategy is as critical as building an effective enterprise data strategy.

We keep hearing it is important for organizations to get their IT strategy right before attempting a data strategy. But should a container define its contents, or should the contents define the container? Data strategy first, or IT strategy first?

A strategy essentially is a series of long-term decisions; An IT Strategy is a sub-component of the business strategy – a series of long-term decisions on how to shape information technology so as to support the organization in meeting its long-term business goals. *So, an IT strategy, at the core, is a set of important strategic decisions. The question is: how does one ensure these decisions are data-driven?*

Here is a critical look at what constitutes a data-driven IT strategy.

8.1 Information Technology Strategy: Introduction

About fifteen years ago, we were invited by a well-known generics pharma company to discuss the possibility of setting up an offshore development center. There was no RFP yet, but the global CFO had reached out to me as my sales team sold me as an expert; as someone responsible for setting up the first ever ODC in a validated environment. As it was usual practice then, the IT teams and chief technology officer (CTO) designate reported to the CFO in that company. After a few more meetings and a couple of conference-calls, it was suggested that I should work with his Indian team to broadly define the scope and the terms of reference for the RFP. Since my company will also be bidding, I was supposed to operate at arms-length. So, I fixed up an appointment with their local CTO to understand their IT application portfolio, strategy, and objectives.

The Indian CTO was roughly my age. I was told he had started out as a programmer in one of those SMBs (Small and Medium Businesses), and worked his way up as a project manager, and then as an IT Director for a local Indian pharma company, before he was finally recruited as the Indian CTO for the multinational.

The meeting started pleasantly enough. The CTO spent a substantial amount of time explaining how he had inherited a dysfunctional and almost non-existent IT infrastructure, and how by sheer grit and determination he had transformed the information technology as a function, built an entire data center with state-of-the-art facilities. I was given a quick tour of the place, and as if to prove how advanced their infrastructure was, I was also given a demonstration of the newly installed retina scanner which guarded the door to the data center. Dan Brown's *Angels and Demons* had been published just a few years before, and a retina scanner was indeed considered state-of-the-art then.

I noticed the first signs of strain when I asked him to show me a list of all his applications in the portfolio, and identify/segregate the global and the local (India-specific), with usage statistics – meaning details like the number of users, last recorded date of using the application, and the incremental change in data size by month for the preceding year or so. It turned out they did not have one ready, but they promised to get back to me soon. The CTO got a little restless as I asked him if their SAP was global single instance. Turns out it was not, but he was proud of the fact that the decision-making in the company was quite decentralized and democratic. Every country leadership decided for itself on its IT budgets, IT applications, and yes … IT strategy. I asked him how many countries ran SAP; a fair few I was told, while the rest ran on JDE and a variety of legacy applications. I asked him if his internal customers were happy with him, he sounded modest when he mentioned no one had complained so far.

I was finally shown the "holy grail", their IT strategy document. It was a very colorful deck of slides essentially covering: the big and tall of what they had done in the year before, the most hep-and-happening hardware and software they would like to acquire, and how it was crucial to have as many of them as possible – to stay competitive. There was an undue stress on the word "competitive", and a not-so-well concealed hint that they would lag behind unless they bought the latest in the market. Then there were budgets, and a broad shopping list for the year ahead.

I asked them if there was a separate *data strategy* document. The question was not understood too well, but they brought me the design spec for their data warehouse under implementation. I tried explaining it further… I asked about data governance and master data management. They did have a governing board: a small team consisting of a couple of finance managers, a sales manager, and the CTO himself. Being a pharma company, they also had GSOPs (global standard operating procedures) and a template for requesting changes in the master data elements. Before I could commend them, they also told me the governance board decided only on changes with respect to SAP…. "after all they are all senior people and they have limited time." All decisions related to data-design and any changes to master data of the smaller applications was left to the wisdom of external vendors and the IT department.

By now, the welcome smiles had disappeared; but I was still wearing my sales-hat, so I did my best to humor a prospective customer. I had not ventured to ask questions like "Does the governing board function only on paper?", or "When did the governing board actually meet last?" and so forth. Instead, I sympathized with him as he complained about his internal customers, and how they asked for everything "yesterday". It was a herculean effort to keep a straight face and listen to everything, and nod in agreement as often as I could without throwing up. I will not go into what I had to do to deliver what they asked for, or how that finally ended. The story may sound familiar to some of you.

In my experience, here is what organizations usually cover in the name of information technology strategy:

- Big and tall of achievements
- Technology trends and industry benchmarks
- New projects being proposed
- Budgets

In a few really rare cases:

- Balanced scorecard for IT department
- Key performance indicators
- Internal customer satisfaction survey

In most cases, it is less than adequate. I believe one needs to take a far deeper look to understand if the information technology architecture of the organization is geared up to deliver a distinct competitive advantage.

8.2 Information Technology Strategy: Decoding the Problems

Over the years, whenever I have had to create an IT strategy for clients or for internal consumption, I have referred to hundreds of articles, papers, and books published on the subject. In my experience, the academic papers can either be too esoteric, or just too academic. I found most of the articles on the internet to be very generic, full of motherhood statements, and each one a poor copy of the other. Most white papers from Big 3 and Big 4 provide a series of surveys such as "What percentage of respondents are doing *something*, or not doing *something*". While one thanks them for the interesting piece of information, one is still in the dark as to how exactly a world class IT strategy should be developed step-by-step, especially if one cannot afford to engage them. In my view, IT initiatives fail because, they are planned and executed without sufficient *data*.

So, *what* exactly goes wrong with information technology in organizations? Here is a summary…

1. **Bottlenecks in the information supply chain:** The information architects who conceptualize the IT solutions work in compartments; one small solution at a time, addressing one small part of the value-chain, with each solution optimized only for local throughput. The result is an uneven, unbalanced information supply chain, with in-process inventory build-up, and serious bottlenecks.

   For example: The in-process information bottlenecks are most visible in the build-up of Excel sheets used for downloading (extracting) the data from upstream applications and uploading (transformation & loading) into one or more centralized downstream applications. Global consolidation of accounts from multiple enterprise resource planning (ERP)instances of subsidiary companies every month is a chaotic exercise, and entirely dependent on Excel. The reconciliation of accounts after consolidation is a headache for the finance managers, and an absolute nightmare for the auditors, who try and make sense of the accounts before they certify them.

In a 2012 WSJ article titled "Financial services subledger accounting – Driving the finance function to a lower common denominator" (Shilling et al., 2012), Deloitte highlights how "a cottage industry being brought to life to unravel the spaghetti and patch environment, highlighting aging systems, manual Excel based systems, and control risks." The article further mentions every time data is moved from one financial repository to another, a break point is introduced into the supply chain that necessitates continuous monitoring and reconciliations.

2. **Value-chain Coverage**: Ideally information technology initiatives need to cover the complete value-chain in entirety, in a single centralized application instance – for example, a global single instance SAP. However, when IT initiatives are designed to address only a part of the value-chain, leaving the other part to the mercy of manual / legacy systems, then it results in an imbalanced, uneven information supply chain.

3. **Addressing Business Requirements**: I have noticed, way too often,
   - The IT initiatives get conceptualized far away from business reality and requirements, by freshly minted CTOs and software developers with limited-to-no understanding of the domain; and as a result, poorly address the business problems, and hence, not surprisingly have very poor acceptability among business users. Once again, big data initiatives are no different. I have witnessed organizations investing in data visualization platforms, not because they have a clearly laid out analytics project with specific business benefits, but because they have a budget.
   - Lion's share of IT budgets being allocated to resolving the same business problem, year after year. Solutions built at enormous cost and efforts, being scrapped before they deliver any meaningful business value, year after year! (Kark et al., 2017).
   - In a nutshell, the IT initiatives fail, when they fail to address the core business requirements. Collecting business requirements data as of now is more of an art than a science, largely dependent on the skills of the people handling the project. The purpose of agile methodology, DevOps and others. is to fix this gap.

4. **Business Value**: I believe, every information technology solution conceptualized needs to have a core purpose: To deliver value and to enhance the business performance of the enterprise, with more output from less input: fewer resources, and in shorter cycle times.

   In my experience, few IT initiatives specifically look at enhanced business performance as a key outcome, and even fewer companies actually measure the metric before and after the IT intervention. Big data initiatives are no exception.

The question is: Is it possible to improve the success rate of IT initiatives if they are planned and executed based on sufficient *data*?

8.3 Should Data Drive Your IT Strategy?

As we know, most organizations view IT strategy as an integral part of the business strategy; an enabler for achieving the business goals, and a differentiator driving the competitive advantage. As mentioned, until recently, data strategy was seen as a sub-component of the IT strategy; something to be derived from IT strategy. But over the last decade, the hype around big data has suddenly changed the way organizations look at data. While the data is the "new oil" (The Economist, 2017), the most important asset for the digital age, the IT still remains a cost center. The data is expected to drive the decisions, if not all the decisions, at least the big decisions.

Strategy, at the core, is a series of decisions, a set of long-term decisions. Most strategic decisions (if not all) do qualify as the "big" decisions that we intend to make data-driven. The IT strategy essentially is a is a series of long-term decisions defining the action plan for the information technology department over a horizon of 5–7 years. The question is… should data drive your IT strategy?

In my view, the answer is an emphatic "Yes!" … and if we can identify the "big" decisions, as we do in case of IT strategy, we have a set methodology for deciphering the data behind the decisions (see Chapters 5 and 6).

More importantly, given the core purpose of data-driven IT strategy is to deliver business value, enhance the business performance of the enterprise; it is imperative to discover the key-value-driver

Follow up questions to consider:

1. What are the key value-drivers for the IT strategy? Do they define the "big" decisions of the IT strategy?
2. What kind of data would be needed for supporting the big decisions of the IT strategy?
3. What are the sources of such data?

8.4 Getting IT Right

So how do you get IT right? What are the *key value-drivers* of the IT strategy?

There are several articles on aligning business strategy and IT strategy. The companies which rely on strategy maps and Kaplan's balanced scorecard, usually make the IT strategy a sub-component of the operations strategy. There is a 2013 BCG white paper (Michael et al., 2013) that lays emphasis on being an early adopter of cutting-edge technologies – aptly titled "Ahead of the curve!" The IT Capability Maturity Framework (IT-CMF) (McLaughlin, 2013) developed by Innovation Value Institute (IVI) provides a framework to assess the maturity of technology in an organization; based on four key-strategic areas and 36 critical capabilities.

I have advocated focusing on seven distinct pillars (value-drivers) for building an effective IT Strategy; and it is equally important to lay down the foundation with an enterprise-wide business-aligned data strategy (Figure 8.1).

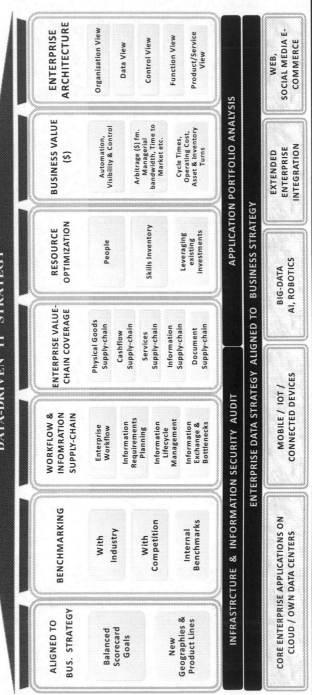

Figure 8.1 Getting IT right!

Table 8.1 Business-Aligned Information Technology

Value-Driver	The "Big" Decision(s)
Aligned to Business Strategy	• What kind of IT initiatives are required for enabling the organization to meet its strategic business goals?
Data to be Sourced: The IT strategy forms an important component of an organization's business strategy as laid down in its strategy map and balanced scorecard: the key sources of data for devising the IT strategy.	

Building a data-driven IT strategy leveraging the analysis of the seven value-drivers shown in the picture is explained in greater detail in Table 8.1.

8.4.1 Business-Aligned Information Technology

The IT strategy must closely follow the business strategy. Ideally every new proposal for business investment needs to cover the IT investments required to support such initiative. An effective IT strategy must cover every new geography, every new product line that the company plans to invest in, and a templatized plan for quickly laying down the essential IT infrastructure for any new adjacency, and the marginal cost of rolling out the enterprise applications into the new adjacency needs to be as optimal as possible (Table 8.1).

8.4.2 Benchmarking

Benchmarking with the competitors', and the industry's best is a must. While what competition "does" matter, one needs to clearly distinguish between a passing fad, and a real breakthrough technology. A passing fad roughly corelates to what Gartner describes as "hype". Please refer to Gartner's hype cycle for emerging technologies (Costello & Rimol, 2020) (Table 8.2).

Table 8.2 Benchmarking

Value-Driver	The "Big" Decision(s)
Benchmarking	• What are the industry benchmarks? What are the internal benchmarks? • What are the competition benchmarks? • What kind of IT initiatives are required to meet or exceed the benchmarks?
Data to be Sourced: Benchmarking with industry and competition is an important source of data for devising the IT strategy. The data behind the "big" decisions (listed above) will be the key for devising an effective IT strategy to drive the *competitive advantage*.	

Table 8.3 Information Supply Chain

Value-Driver	The "Big" Decision(s)
Organizational Workflow and Information Supply Chain	• What kind of IT initiatives are required to better the organizational workflow and to improve its efficiency? • What kind of information bottlenecks are likely to adversely affect the information supply chain and • What kind of IT initiatives will be required to address the information bottlenecks?

Data to be Sourced: Percentage of organizational workflow automated or enabled by IT applications. Information Requirements Planning, Information Exchange Requirements, Document / Information Life Cycle Management Requirements and others, as relevant for automating / enabling the organizational workflow. The process-bottlenecks in the information supply chain affecting the organizational workflow.

A good many of the technologies that may appear to be fancy to invest in, quickly move from a peak of inflated expectations into a trough of disillusionment and may never reach the slope of enlightenment.

8.4.3 Organizational Workflow: Information Supply Chain

The percentage of workflow that is completely automated or enabled by an IT application is a key metric that needs to be targeted and tracked while designing the IT strategy.

The core purpose of information technology in the organization is to automate the workflow or enable the business-transaction workflow. IT applications are expected to enable the information flow across the enterprise – ideally all business transactions (financially relevant or not) – and cover each of the transactions from beginning to the end, "cash-to-cash." For example, while a company-wide, well-implemented single instance ERP can ensure smooth flow of data across the organization; disparate and disconnected applications and manual Excel sheet-based information exchange can create chaos, and bottlenecks in the value-chain, adversely impacting the throughput (Table 8.3).

8.4.4 Workflow and the Speed of Information Supply Chain

The Speed of Enterprise Information Supply Chain is a measure of how fast the information is being made available within the organization. A byproduct of workflow automation, is automated collection and reporting of business metrics, thereby increasing the speed of the information supply chain.

Faster and accurate information can help organizations improve their overall operating efficiency. Other direct benefits include:

- Improved efficiency of the organizational workflow.
- Reduction in the cycle times and resource costs.
- Substantial improvements in the asset turnover and inventory turnover. For example:
  ⇒ Accurate and timely data on *delivery lead time* can help an organization plan its inventories better and help bring down the inventory levels across the organization.
  ⇒ Quality of *forecast data* can affect the quality of demand planning, the material requirements planning (MRP) run, and the in-process inventory levels in each stage of the value-chain.

8.4.5 Enterprise Value-Chain and Information Supply Chain

The value-chain in an organization is an interlinked web of multiple supply chains. Underneath every physical goods supply chain, there is a services supply chain, and an information (data) supply chain. The overall throughput (as defined by the theory of constraints) of the value-chain would be *co-dependent* on throughput of services supply chain and information supply chain. Any constraint in the information supply chain can adversely affect the throughput of the value-chain (Figure 8.2).

The enterprise value-chain and the organizational workflow are not exactly synonymous, especially in case of large multinational companies and global conglomerates. I am trying to make a distinction here, so that it will be easier to understand that the information supply chain extends beyond the borders of individual subsidiary companies, lines of business, plants, and countries.

While the organizational workflow refers to process-automation and information supply chain within one legal entity, one plant, one LOB at a point of time; the enterprise value-chain refers to the combined and integrated value-chain of the conglomerate right up to consolidation of accounts, and managerial information at the global headquarters.

One may include even the *extended enterprise integration* connecting the suppliers and customers into enterprise-applications for information exchange (Table 8.4).

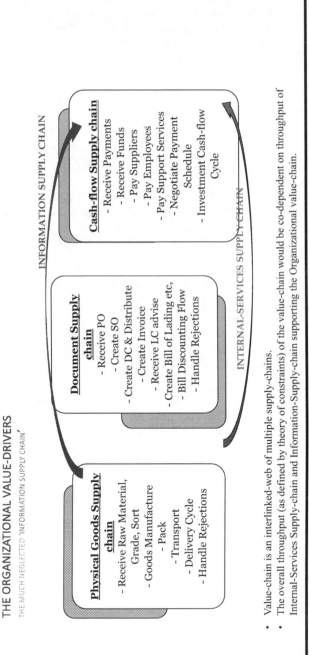

THE ORGANIZATIONAL VALUE-DRIVERS
THE MUCH NEGLECTED 'INFORMATION SUPPLY CHAIN'

INFORMATION SUPPLY CHAIN

Physical Goods Supply chain
- Receive Raw Material, Grade, Sort
- Goods Manufacture
- Pack
- Transport
- Delivery Cycle
- Handle Rejections

Document Supply chain
- Receive PO
- Create SO
- Create DC & Distribute
- Create Invoice
- Receive LC advise
- Create Bill of Lading etc,
- Bill Discounting Flow
- Handle Rejections

Cash-flow Supply chain
- Receive Payments
- Receive Funds
- Pay Suppliers
- Pay Employees
- Pay Support Services
- Negotiate Payment Schedule
- Investment Cash-flow Cycle

INTERNAL-SERVICES SUPPLY CHAIN

- Value-chain is an interlinked-web of multiple supply-chains.
- The overall throughput (as defined by theory of constraints) of the value-chain would be co-dependent on throughput of Internal-Services Supply-chain and Information-Supply-chain supporting the Organizational value-chain.

Figure 8.2   Understanding the information supply chain.

Table 8.4 Enterprise Value-Chain

Value-Driver	The "Big" Decision(s)
Enterprise Value-Chain Coverage	• What kind of IT investments would be required to cover the enterprise value-chain, end-to-end – across the geographies and product lines? How long it is expected to take? • What will be the mechanism to manage the information supply chain in the interim? • What kind of IT investments will be required to manage the gap in interim?

Data to be Sourced: IT application-footprints along the entire enterprise value-chain, and the gaps representing manual / Excel sheet-based data-interchanges.

The enterprise value-chain is a super-set of value-chains of each of the subsidiaries, countries, product-lines; a combined value-chain that represent the entire cash-to-cash processes across the enterprise. An effective IT strategy ensures a fully integrated set of applications covering the complete enterprise value-chain, end-to-end.

I have always recommended a thorough organization-wide due diligence before creating the IT strategy, and the very first step of such due diligence is to capture the entire cash-to-cash value-chain processes and map each sub-process with the respective-application(s) supporting the process. Any manual processes and Excel sheets being emailed are indications of *unresolved bottlenecks* in the information supply chain, as constraints which adversely affect the efficiency of the supply chain and throughput of the organization.

We need to look at transactional data as the throughput of the organizational supply chain. Any constraints in the process would lead to bottlenecks or *in-process queues* of information being passed on from one stage to the next. For example, a proper waybill or excise invoice is a must for the manufactured goods to be dispatched through the factory gate. If, for some reason, raising an excise invoice takes 30 minutes, while the goods can be loaded and dispatched in 15 minutes, there will be an in-process queue of goods ready to be dispatched, but waiting for the invoices to be cut. A typical line balancing problem, constraint not a part of the goods supply chain, but of the underlying information supply chain.

Waiting for data, waiting for documents, or waiting for a decision to be made based on data, are all typical experiences of a day-in-the life of an organization. And the data in the organization is not supposed to be sitting idle in its repository, but actually flow through the supply chain like blood in a circulatory system. The faster it flows, the faster your inventory turns, the faster your assets turn... maximizing the throughput of the organization. No wonder the $800-an-hour erudite consultants keep telling us the data is the new oil, the lifeblood of your business.

From my experience, this is something that most organizations miss out, and miss out by a mile (Figure 8.3).

The case studies below will help explain this concept further.

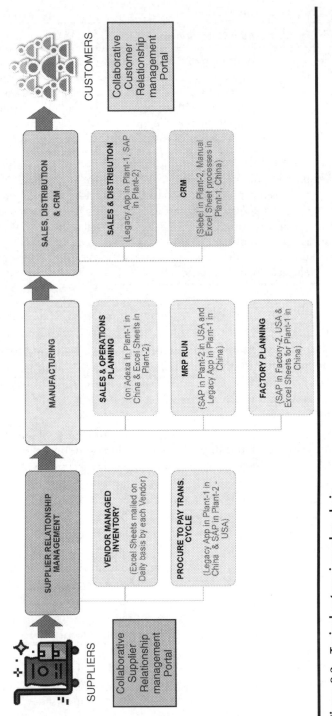

Figure 8.3 Typical enterprise value-chain.

CASE STUDY 1

The IT Director of a global pharma company asked me if there is a method for creating a business case for investing into middleware, for implementing one of the popular EAI (Enterprise Application Integration) solutions. Apparently when they were implementing SAP, their sales leadership insisted that their sales processes were unique, and their legacy sales management system could not be replaced with SAP. So, while their procure-to-pay was completely mapped on to SAP, their order-to-cash process stayed outside on a legacy application. One of their options to close the month was by running a bulk monthly sales-to-inventory transaction directly in financial accounts, which however resulted in SAP missing out all-important granular invoice level transactional data, without which no sales analytics can be generated out of SAP. The other option involved running a batch upload on invoices from legacy applications onto SAP to replicate the transactions – while making sure the invoice numbering, inventory levels and so forth were all in complete sync. between SAP and the legacy application. Given hundreds of thousands of invoices were being generated from 250+ locations, the batch upload literally required a battery of resources to work the night-shift and to do the flat file preparation and error handling.

I was asked to help them create a business case for implementing EAI – for integrating SAP with the legacy sales application. The IT director was very happy when I told them about the annual saving on batch upload resources alone was enough to pay for the investment into EAI and some. However, I warned them that keeping master data on both applications in sync. would still be a monster unless they implemented the master data management (MDM) module of SAP or equivalent. The smile vanished from the man's face as he bitterly commented that there was no winning with people like me.

CASE STUDY 2

A more serious example comes from Global Trading companies. Given the nature of their operations, they tend to be a huge web of multiple legal entities located in multiple countries who buy and sell from each other. A typical cash-to-cash transaction would involve at least three countries and three different legal entities. A typical transaction is depicted in Figure 8.4.

Co. Z has its global headquarters in UK, while it has 100% subsidiaries and separate legal entities in China and Australia. Sourcing metal scrap from Australia and selling it in China is a simple transaction; while the ship bearing metal scrap travels direct from Australia to China, the paper transaction can typically go through at least three different legal entities, depending on differential tax structure in different countries.

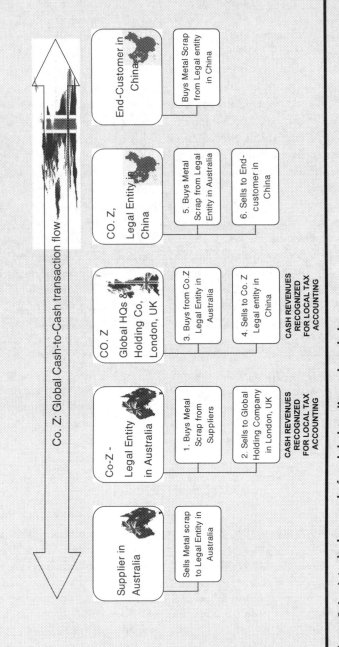

Figure 8.4 A typical example for global trading value-chain.

IFRS compliance requires Lateral, Upstream and Downstream transactions need to be disclosed. The global headquarters in London *cannot recognize revenue from internal sales between subsidiaries*, till the final sale (Transaction No. 6 – Legal Entity in China selling to end-customer in China) is complete, while each of the subsidiaries need to recognize expenses and revenue from each transaction instantaneously, for tax filing in their respective countries. To summarize – the cash-to-cash transactions do not start and terminate within one legal entity, but span across multiple legal entities. The global template and SAP rollout needs to ensure value-chain transactions cash-to-cash are to be mapped in their entirety.

The consulting entity implementing SAP had made two critical mistakes:

1. They had not done any chart-of-accounts rationalization between different countries. The CFO of each country was given freedom to create his own chart-of-accounts; in most cases, they simply replicated the same problem-ridden chart-of-accounts that they had in applications was copied onto SAP. The CFOs in most countries were qualified chartered accountants, and yet it is surprising these most qualified chartered accountants and CPAs do not understand what chart-of-accounts means, and why it is so important to design it right.

2. The other mistake was with respect to the global template and rollout strategy – the consulting entity was used to SAP implementations where the transactions typically terminate within in one legal entity and one company code. So, they created a global template to implement each country's transaction cycle as it terminates within the legal entity (company code) therein. However, as explained above, the transactions in these companies span multiple legal entities and headquarters.

They went ahead and rolled out the SAP in 20 odd countries as they had service level agreements (SLAs) and a deadline as committed. However, soon the CFOs of these countries were a very unhappy lot. Apart from filing returns for tax/legal compliance in their respective country, a bigger share of their work was to send reports on inter-company transactions, asset-class wise risk, budgets and so forth to headquarters. Given the SAP instance was never configured to address these requirements, sending these monthly/ad hoc reports to global headquarters (GHQ) continued to be on Excel sheets. *While the transactional rigor demanded by SAP and poorly configured charts-of-accounts added to their workload, the reports generated by SAP needed substantial makeover in Excel before they were ready for GHQ.* Given there are multiple versions, multiple formats of these Excel sheets received, consolidated, downloaded, and uploaded at GHQ every day, consolidation of accounts and managing a single-version-of-truth at headquarters continued to be a nightmarish exercise.

Excel sheets being used for global accounts consolidation makes keeping a single-version-of-truth and audit trail, a near impossible task, and assisting the external auditors to sift through the maze of transactions every quarter-end is often a thankless job.

By the time the issues with chart-of-accounts and the rollout strategy were flagged to the top management, the flawed global template had been rolled out to 20+ countries, the implementation costs exceeding several tens of millions. Fixing the chart-of-accounts in SAP in each country can be a very complicated and expensive exercise, sometimes as good as a new implementation. The SAP Consulting company continued to be in denial, while the chief information officer (CIO) and the global finance teams ended up blaming each other for the fiasco.

It was pointed out to the CIO's team that the global template needed to be corrected first; SAP can be mapped to multiple charts-of-accounts, one for local legal tax compliance and another for global consolidation. In the interim, point-to-point integrations, automated rule-based data validation within Excel, cloud-based collaborative data sharing and validation models, and finally lookup tables for mapping the charts-of-accounts from each of the countries to chart-of-accounts at global headquarters. I will not go into how it ended.

Note: A global single instance SAP with a group company code, and subsidiary company codes defined could have helped retain *master data integrity* and *transactional integrity*, besides ensuring zero lag in accounts reflecting a real picture of business as of date. A global single instance SAP, consolidated-standardized chart-of-accounts, and rollout strategy covering the value-chain transactions cash-to-cash, with headquarters first, followed by country-specific implementations.

On the other hand, a best-of-breed approach with individual instances of disparate applications in each country could mean a *broken transactional integrity* and *broken master data integrity* between application instances in each country, which in turn imposes a huge and unmaintainable overheads in terms of Excel sheet uploads and downloads for reporting and keeping the application-instances in sync.

In my experience, commodity trading companies can have very complex business models, while the data capturing models and transaction-capturing-mechanism can be quite primitive, specifically when they operate in upcountry locations in third world countries. Buying commodities like cotton or tobacco directly from farmers are often purely cash transactions, captured and formalized as bulk-accounting transactions in the ERP much later, with a lag ranging from weeks to months. Sometimes the lag between the physical transaction and the electronic record of the transaction

Table 8.5 Resource Optimization

Value-Driver	The "Big" Decision(s)
Resource Optimization	• What kind of resources are required to support the new IT initiatives? • What kind of resources are available? • How to optimize resource utilization?
Data to be Sourced: Arbitrage from: Incremental revenue, managerial bandwidth, cycle times, asset turns, inventory turns, operating cost, marginal cost-base, time to market, and customer-retention, among others.	

can be a few weeks to a few months. Inventories of commodities are further subject to other losses like weight losses, and loss due to decay. Over a period of time, the difference between the physical inventory and the inventory on record in ERP can amount to 3–5% of the total inventory, while the typical profit margins in trading companies can be less than 2–3%. The statutory auditors of these companies have their jobs cut out. The complexity in the industry is often matched by the confused global template creation and rollout strategy by consulting companies. I used to hear one of the largest trading companies had set aside the largest ever budget for SAP implementation. I was told they have not made much progress even after years of struggle and a couple of CIOs later.

A good IT strategy must draw up a plan to cover, capture and automate the organization's transactions cash-to-cash right up to final end-customer, as near real-time as practical, while ensuring 100% transactional integrity (Table 8.5).

8.4.6 *Resource Optimization*

When it comes to the IT strategy, organizations need to optimize on the following resources.

i. **Budgets**: The usual logic for annual budget allocations is always based on what you spent last year plus a little something. More often than not, the budgets allocated are barely enough to maintain the applications in the portfolio, let alone plan for a comprehensive overhaul. However, information technology can take center stage when the organizations particularly feel vulnerable; the trigger could be something like a Y2K, or some major data leak that caused considerable damage.

ii. **People**: The availability of right people to implement, develop, and maintain the software.

iii. **Skills/Technology Stack**: I have seen organizations take decisions based on factors like technology stack, and internal skills available, but personally I do not think they are primary factors. Decisions for investing in information technology need to be taken purely based on strategic cost-benefit and long-term impact assessment.

8.4.7 Value from IT

Every information technology solution ever conceptualized needs to have a core purpose: To deliver (dollar) value and to enhance the business performance of the enterprise; to automate processes, more output from less input, with fewer resources, and in shorter cycle times; to inform people and generate actionable insights (Table 8.6).

But, in my experience, few IT initiatives specifically look at enhanced business performance as a key outcome, and even fewer companies actually measure the metric before and after the IT intervention.

I have seen hundreds of so-called IT strategy documents across the world; a select few based on balanced scorecard, but practically none of them precisely quantify the dollar value returns from IT investments. Not too many companies insist on a business case for investments in information technology initiatives, and those few who do, do not insist on a dollar value return and discounted cash flows. An effective IT strategy needs to have mandatory protocols for creating a business case for every large IT investment; a cost-benefit analysis, as a must.

The typical sources of business value from information technology are listed below:

1. **Automation of business processes**: Improving efficiency, productivity, and quality, by reducing manual intervention.
2. **Building visibility into operations**: For the managers at all levels, through reports, alerts, and early warning systems. More visibility could mean more control – and enhanced business performance.
3. **Arbitrage from**: Managerial bandwidth, cycle times, asset turns, inventory turns, operating cost, marginal cost-base, time to market, customer retention.

(A comprehensive model for estimating dollar value from analytics investments is given in Chapter 6 – the model could be adopted for any technology investment.)

Table 8.6 Value from IT

Value-Driver	The "Big" Decision(s)
Value From IT	• What kind of $ business value is being targeted with new IT investments? • What kind of incremental efficiency is being targeted? • What is the incremental throughput being generated?
Data to be Sourced: Arbitrage from: Incremental revenue, managerial bandwidth, cycle times, asset turns, inventory turns, operating cost, marginal cost-base, time to market, and customer retention, among others.	

8.4.8 *Enterprise Architecture: Compatibility and Cohesiveness*

While a data-driven IT strategy can be comprehensive, covering every part of the enterprise value-chain, it still needs a framework for creating a cohesive information architecture compatible with the each of the components of the enterprise.

It is important to take a comprehensive view of the organizational work design as an interaction between people and technology in workplaces (called a sociotechnical systems approach to business engineering). A variety of approaches, standards and certifications have evolved over the last few decades. The most popular include ARIS (Architecture of Integrated Information Systems) (Scheer & Emminghaus, 1994), TOGAF (The Open Group Architecture Framework) (Josey, 2016), and SOM (Semantic Object Model) among others.

I worked on ARIS (Scheer & Emminghaus, 1994) modeling software briefly while working for an ERP product company, breaking down every process of the value-chain and creating EEPCs (Extended Event Process Chains).

ARIS House – as it is called, relies on five distinct views of the enterprise business process architecture. Function view, organization view, data view, control view, and product/service view. As I recall, ARIS modeling software licenses were expensive, and while a product company could afford to buy the software, it was definitely overkill for an everyday CIO who likes to rely on implementing commercial off-the-shelf (COTS) software; something absolutely safe and non-controversial like SAP – which anyway ensures 100% compatibility as advocated by ARIS (Figure 8.5).

ARIS HOUSE

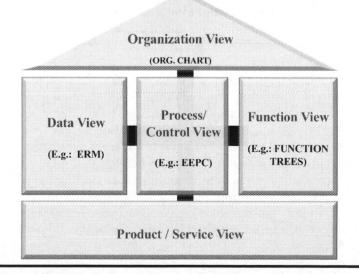

Figure 8.5 ARIS house.

However, the everyday CIO must ensure:

- SAP (or any other ERP) must cover the enterprise in entirety – all the products, geographies, legal entities, transactions, and reports with and needs to be a global single instance.
- If there has been an ill-advised best-of-breed approach with the usual mix of multiple locally developed applications in each geography, then ensure real-time integration, and master data compatibility between different applications at the enterprise level.

If there are still *manual processes* and manual *handoffs*, and most importantly if *data* is traveling between people and locations by the irreplaceable email, then keeping the applications in sync. manually is an impossible task. However, this is the reality many CIOs face in their organizations. Sometimes it is their own doing, but sometimes they inherit the islands-of-information architecture due to the confused and ill-informed decisions of their predecessors.

8.5 Data-Driven Application Portfolio Analysis and Rationalization

One of my erstwhile clients, a global top-10 pharma company, had thousands of applications across the world; most of them defunct, many with just a handful of users, and a sizable number with less than a handful of logins through the year. For reasons best known to them, they rejected the idea of implementing a global single instance ERP, while most of their competitors implemented SAP in the mid 1990s. So, in less than a decade, their total number of applications swelled to over 6000, while their IT budget swelled to be more than double of their competitors'. They fired and hired four different CTOs in as many years while I was working with them.

Once you create and release an application, no matter how small or big, it has to be maintained. As long as there is a budget and a mandate, the IT departments keep on updating applications; adding new functionality and new releases every few months, forever optimistic that the intended number of business users would actually use the application someday and actually derive intended value from the application.

The only catch is – no one ever goes back to audit if an application is actually being used by the intended-number of business users or if such application is actually delivering the dollar value it is supposed to deliver.

A fair few of my clients and consulting companies insist they have a time-tested methodology for application life cycle management (ALM). In my experience, the way the ALM typically gets defined in organizations is not very different from standard software development life cycle (SDLC): requirements, design, build, test, deploy, maintain/manage. The ALM definition in most organizations is based on an unshakable assumption – that the applications are built to last for eternity (Figure 8.6).

Application Lifecycle Management: The Missing Logic

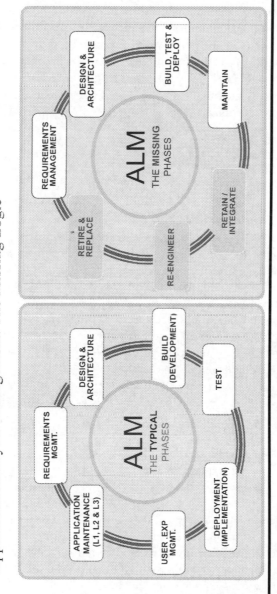

Figure 8.6 Application life cycle management – getting IT right!

In my experience, the reality is very different. Every application has a useful life; well-run IT organizations need to audit the status of each of the applications periodically and take a decision on whether to retain-reengineer or retire-replace for each of the applications. The exercise of taking a comprehensive look at complete application portfolio to cull the applications that need to be retired, reengineered, or replaced, is called application portfolio analysis, or application rationalization.

Application portfolio analysis refers to the exercise of *collecting and analyzing the data pertaining to IT applications* in use by plant, by location, by country and by legal entity. Application rationalization refers to the process of keeping the number of active-applications and instances – *relevant, useful, small and manageable.*

I was involved with organization-wide application portfolio analysis twice in my career.

INSTANCE 1

The first instance was for a global automobile component supplier, which was a resounding success. The CIO of the company was trying to understand if there was a way to prove to the management that *the right investments in information technology can have measurable impact on the financial performance.*

> The CIO was relatively new and the eleven IT directors who reported to her from across the world were old company men, people who enjoyed substantial freedom and influence within the territories they handled. Each of them was convinced what they had done in their territories (a group of countries) was beyond compare and the best.

In many ways it was a pioneering effort. This was the early 2000s, and the concept of application portfolio analysis was not very popular, much less the idea that we need to collect vital performance indicators for each country, along with a complete list of applications, their age, value-chain coverage and so on. While creating a questionnaire, it was not just to collect as much data as we could, but also to enable correlating the IT application data with the performance metrics for each of the sites. While there was ample budget, the time available was too short for traveling across the globe, hence we collected the data from 70+ countries in a record time by using a web-based questionnaire. We created what we called information technology maturity score based on the response to questionnaire by each of the sites (plants). The IT maturity score was based on a variety of factors including, but not limited to, transactions-coverage, visibility into supply chain, value-chain coverage, integration, single source of truth, stability, and maturity. The consolidated score from each plant was then co-related with key performance indicators such as inventory turns and asset turns for each of the sites (Figure 8.7).

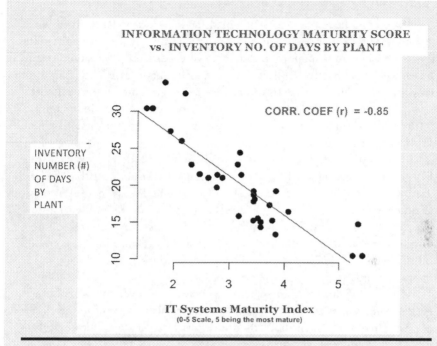

Figure 8.7 Information technology maturity influences on organizational efficiencies.

The results were astonishing: the plants with a high IT maturity score had the lowest inventory number of days (or the highest inventory turns). The data showed a very strong correlation between IT system maturity score and the financial performance of the plant. The coefficient of correlation was close to one if we removed the data from three to four mavericks, essentially plants where inventory turns were very high in spite of IT applications being primitive and score being poor.

INSTANCE 2

The second instance was for a multinational pharma company and like the earlier instance we proposed a web-based survey to collect the data. But the global CTO had very limited control and visibility in the 100+ countries they operated in, and we ended up collecting not-so-great quality data from a few better run plants from across the world during the pilot. The data was insufficient for any conclusive analysis. They had thousands of applications; a good number of them had just a handful of users, and many applications were not used for well over 12 preceding months.

As a part of the response to their global vendor selection RFP, we proposed an innovative method for application rationalization based on application-usage statistics and application-stability. Three different decisions: retain, reengineer, or retire the applications were to be made based on analysis of usage statistics and the analysis of remedy-tickets generated for each application. We proposed a VED analysis of applications prior to portfolio rationalization. (VED refers to the categorization of applications into: Vital, Essential, and Desirable) (Figure 8.8).

More importantly the proposal gave them a methodology for allocating IT (dollar) budgets rationally and save millions of dollars by retiring the least used, least desirable applications. The CTO could focus on the business-critical applications and allocate bigger budgets for integration and improving the service quality. If multiple applications exist for the same purpose in different countries or different divisions of the organizations, a common multi-tenant application can be built on the cloud, to replace the multitude of applications.

While the company I represented was selected as a vendor, we could not get the comprehensive application portfolio analysis kicked off in the couple of years I handled the client. Years later, I saw a paper on application rationalization from a well-known IT consulting firm pretty much using the same concept, a little more colorful and embellished version of my proposal. The paper does mention the client was a pharma company!

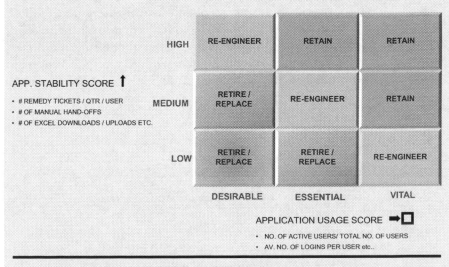

Figure 8.8 Application portfolio rationalization.

8.5.1 Playing Catch-Up

This is a popular story I used to hear about the IT Director of one of the largest construction equipment manufacturers based in Illinois: Pointing towards the cupboard behind his chair, he would say (and I quote):

> Name any software, and we have a huge number of licenses in this cupboard. We make sure we buy every piece of the latest software ever released in the market. Implementing what we buy is a different matter though…
>
> Sometimes, even before we get started on the last release of earth-shattering software that we bought as the final answer to all our troubles, there is newer and better software on the market. *Sadly, we never seem to catch up.*

So best-of-breed, tech superiority, industry benchmark, and being ahead of the competition among others, are all nice terms to talk about, but in practice it is like chasing a mirage, and there is always the danger of losing focus on the all-important net business value from information technology investments.

8.6 Summary: The Making of the Holy Grail!

To summarize, a comprehensive IT strategy document must cover the following. The third column indicates how frequently organizations cover the specific strategic area while creating their IT strategy documents (Table 8.7).

Table 8.7 Summary

Strategic Area	The Data that Drives Strategy	If Covered
Balanced Scorecard / Business integrated IT strategy	a. Strategy map: IT strategy derived from Business strategy b. Balanced scorecard for IT department	Rarely
Benchmarking	a. With industry and competition b. Internal benchmarks	Rarely
Application Portfolio Analysis and Application Rationalization	a. Instances, integration, cloud and collaboration b. Licenses and usage statistics by application c. Application portfolio: retain, reengineer and replace recommendations	Very rarely

(Continued)

Table 8.7 (Continued) Summary

Strategic Area	The Data that Drives Strategy	If Covered
Application-wise Business Value Score	a. Usage statistics (No. of users, logins, transactions by application b. Business value $ for each of the applications in the inventory	Never
Information Security Infrastructure Audit	a. SWOT analysis of current information security infrastructure b. ISO/IEC 27007 / 2020 standards compliance report	Rarely
Reports and Self-Service Analytics	a. No. of reports generated and usage statistics by report b. Usage statistics for self-service analytics	Rarely
People and Resources	a. Current and planned	Covered
IT Coverage for Each Stage of Enterprise Value-Chain	a. Enterprise-wide and by legal entity b. By geography and by product line c. Extended enterprise value-chain	Rarely
Constraints and Bottlenecks in Information Supply Chain	a. Breakpoints in information supply chain – incl. manual activities, Excel sheet downloads / uploads b. Application integration plans	Rarely
A Time-Bound Plan to Develop and Implement New Applications	a. Value-chain stages currently not covered by any application b. Application integration to avoid manual handoffs and Excel sheet uploads c. Collaborative cloud-based applications for audit trail	Usually Covered
IT Investments Planned, and In Progress	a. Investment appraisal with discounted cash flow (DCF) for investment > threshold value b. Measures of success, $ returns planned	Usually Covered
Social Media Strategy	a. LinkedIn, Facebook, Twitter, Wikipedia etc. b. Social media (SM) popularity index c. Analysis of SM data and action plans based on insights.	Rarely

(*Continued*)

Table 8.7 (Continued) Summary

Strategic Area	The Data that Drives Strategy	If Covered
New Technology Adoption	Cost-benefit analysis of adopting each of the emerging technologies, including: a. Mobile apps., automation and AI, Blockchain, IoT and connected devices etc. b. e-commerce engines – integrated with ERP c. Enabling remote working for employees and contactless delivery of goods	Rarely
Key Performance Measures	a. Periodic reports, b. Early warning systems, and alerts. c. Review and audit plans	Sometimes covered
Governance Report	a. Data governance board – No. of meetings, people and decisions taken b. IT governance board – No. of meetings, people and decisions taken, governance for future	Rarely
Value-Delivered Audit	A report on cumulative $ value-delivered through IT investments	Never
Data Strategy	A separate document	Rarely
Digital Strategy	A separate document	In vogue now

The IT strategy is never complete unless it is accompanied by the strategy map and balanced scorecard for the IT department, derived from/and compatible with the enterprise strategy map and the enterprise balanced scorecard. A typical example is shown below (Figure 8.9):

Finally, a stakeholder's wish list could be never ending, and it may not be possible to include everything listed on Gartner's hype cycle from IoT, Blockchain to Artificial Intelligence into an IT strategy document, but it makes sense to include a comprehensive evaluation cost-benefit for each of the new technologies.

Typical Stakeholder's Wish List:

a. Near 100% uptime for all systems
b. 100% audit trail for all transactions and handoffs
c. No manual handoffs / Excel uploads
d. Completely automated-assisted workflow
e. Self-service analytics accessible on mobile

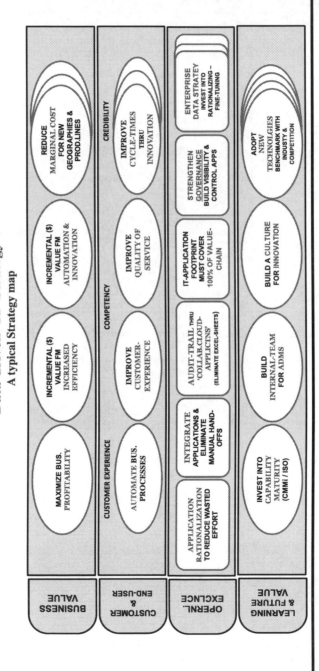

Figure 8.9 Data-driven IT strategy.

f. Best in the industry and ahead of the competition

g. 100% real-time data. Zero lag

h. Adoption of new technologies - Blockchain, IoT etc.

i. Urgently enabling remote working for employees, and contactless delivery of goods.

j. ……

As one can see, not everything on the stakeholder's wish list is an impossible ask. Sometimes, the requirements can be sudden and unforeseen; like enabling remote work and contactless delivery of goods – a requirement forced on the enterprises by the pandemic. Incrementally delivering on each of these items on the wish list influences the customer experience, both internal and (in turn) the external customers; the true purpose of IT strategy.

8.7 Does Information Technology Really Matter?

Is information technology a big differentiator? There are numerous research papers and Big 3 studies mentioning that companies with right investments in information technology do much better than their peer group companies; information technology here is an omnibus word that includes everything from the entire IT infrastructure to complete application portfolio, to the latest buzzwords like digital strategy, big data, and analytics, among others. The incremental profitability numbers quoted varies from 3 to 10% depending on the season and the survey.

While the exact numbers are debatable, that fact that right investments into information technology can improve business performance is an undeniable truth now. Yet, many companies fail to extract real business value from their investments and IT budget gets allocated to resolving the same business problem, year after year. Here is a historical perspective of growth of importance of information technology and why some companies could get IT right, while many fail.

Information technology was not central to what a company did for a long time; but it started becoming a serious differentiator since the 1990s. People started noticing that the organizations with the most well-oiled and connected IT systems seem to do better than those others with disjointed / isolated IT systems. The head of information technology typically reported to the CFO, but a good number of companies have created a position called Chief Technology Officer initially, and subsequently the post of the Chief information Officer. The CIO is usually a top management position and reported to the CEO. As the CIOs position kept gaining importance, the IT budgets as a percentage of the revenue has also shown a steady growth, now averaging between 2% in manufacturing to just under 8% in the banking sector (source: Deloitte Insights: 2018 Global CIO survey) (Kark et al., 2017).

From my personal experience working with some of the largest and globally spread Fortune-500 companies, those few who opted for a global single instance ERP (usually SAP), have a much stronger centralized control and visibility into their global operations. Over a period of time, as their ERP instances stabilized, their internal support requirements and delta requirements have come down to bare minimum; a fairly compact internal IT teams at their headquarters and at each country, and their IT budgets as a percentage of their revenue are among the smallest in comparison. Not surprisingly, their overall application inventory including CRM, SRM and so on is also the smallest.

And those others who strongly believed in *laissez-faire*, took pride in decentralized decision-making with the IT heads of each country deciding on what best-of-breed in their opinion is most suited for their country... paid a price. Not only they have no centralized visibility into global operations, but their IT budgets also ballooned year after year with little to show for it – in terms of incremental business benefits.

Bibliography

Anderson, M. C., Banker, R. D., & Ravindran, S. (2006). Value implications of investments in information technology. *Management Science*, 52(9), 1359–1376.

Costello, K., & Rimol, M. (2020). Gartner identifies five emerging trends that will drive technology innovation for the next decade, *Gartner Press Release*, Aug 18, 2020. https://tinyurl.com/y49j7y8w

Cuenca, L., Boza, A., & Ortiz, A. (2011). An enterprise engineering approach for the alignment of business and information technology strategy. *International Journal of Computer Integrated Manufacturing*, 24(11), 974–992.

Farooq, R. (2016, September). Does information technology really matter?. In *Proceedings of the International Conference on Changing Dynamics in Global Markets* (pp. 294–299).

Fleckenstein, M., Fellows, L., & Ferrante, K. (2018). *Modern Data Strategy*. Springer International Publishing.

High, P. A. (2009). *World Class IT: Why Businesses Succeed When IT Triumphs*. John Wiley & Sons.

High, P. (2014). Does IT strategy matter?. *Forbes*, Sept 22, 2014.

High, P. (2016). Five steps to a better IT strategy. *Forbes*, Nov 7, 2016.

Josey, A. (2016). TOGAF® Version 9.1 A Pocket Guide. The Open Group, Van Haren.

Kane, G. C., Palmer, D., Phillips, A. N., Kiron, D., & Buckley, N. (2015). *Strategy, not Technology, Drives Digital Transformation - Becoming a Digitally Mature Enterprise*. MIT Sloan Management Review – with Deloitte University Press, 2015.

Karimikia, H. (2012, February). Impact of it strategy on business strategy in small Malaysian enterprises. In *Proceedings of the International Conference on Economics, Business and Marketing Management, Singapore* (pp. 26–28), Singapore.

Kark, K., Shaikh, A., & Brown, C. (2017). *Technology Budgets: From Value Preservation to Value Creation*. Deloitte. CIO Insider (November 2017).

Mazzei, M. J., & Noble, D. (2017). Big data dreams: A framework for corporate strategy. *Business Horizons*, 60(3), 405–414.

McLaughlin, S. Using the IT-CMF as an enabler for transformational change. IVI White Paper Series – 2013.

Medeiros, M. M. D., Maçada, A. C. G., & Freitas Junior, J. C. D. S. (2020). The effect of data strategy on competitive advantage. *The Bottom Line*, 33(2), 201–216.

Michael, D., Aggarwal, N., et al. (2013). *Ahead of Curve – Lesson on Technology and Growth from Small Business Leaders. Boston Consulting Group* 2013.

Mithas, S., & Rust, R. T. (2016). How information technology strategy and investments influence firm performance. *Mis Quarterly*, 40(1), 223–246.

Parkins, D. (2017). The world's most valuable resource is no longer oil, but data. *The Economist*, 6.

Scheer, A. W., & Emminghaus, F. (1994). ARIS-toolset. IDS Prof. Scheer.

Schmuck, R. (2012). Key to a successful company: Operations strategies. *E-conm.*, 1. 47–56.

Shilling, M., Menzel, T., & Ehrenhalt, S., et al. Deloitte (2012). Financial services: Subledger accounting driving the finance function to a lower common denominator. *Deloitte White Paper: Appeared as an article in WSJ*, Dec. 18, 2014.

Smythe, E. (2012). IT Strategy – A Business driven perspective. *Gartner*, 2012.

Thorn, S. (2011). Developing an IT strategy: Aligning IT capabilities with business requirements. *The Open Group Blog*, 2011.

Chapter 9

Building a Data Strategy

Topics Covered in this Chapter

1. When data fails to deliver. • Water, water everywhere! • Legacy data: Data-lakes or data-warehouses? • The data conundrum	Why organizations find so little of enterprise-data relevant? and even less in normalized and readily-accessible form and format?
2. Enterprise data strategy • Defining data strategy • Who owns data strategy? • Recruiting a chief data officer • Skill set of a CDO • Who should be owning data strategy	• Why organizations need an enterprise data strategy? • Who exactly in the organization is qualified to build a data strategy? • Who owns data strategy?
3. A framework for building data strategy • Components of data strategy • Before building a data strategy: A time for organizational introspection • Case study	Components of data strategy, and a comprehensive framework for building enterprise-data-strategy, step-by-step.

DOI: 10.1201/9781003321347-10

4. The new dimensions of the data
  • How would you know you have big data in your organization that you need to handle differently?
  • Do organizations need a separate big data strategy?
  • Why most data is big data now: The big multiplying effect
	• How do you know if your organization has bigdata? Would you need a separate big data strategy?

5. Big data for big decisions: Towards a data-driven organization
  • Big data, AI, and the age of the robots
  • Transformational data-strategy for building a data-driven organization
	• Transformational data strategy for building a data driven organization… from data to decisions.

6. Integrated analytics strategy	Integrated Analytics strategy emphasizes the necessity for aligning the Corporate-vision & the IT Strategy, with the actual IT & data assets on the ground – all the way from data to decisions. Underscores the need for a data-preparation engine, in less-than-ideal situations.
Appendix 9.A A framework for Building Data strategy step by step	Detailed Framework for Building Data Strategy.

INTRODUCTION

All decisions, big and small, can be data-driven, assuming there is the right data to analyze and draw actionable insights from.

The "right data," however, cannot be produced instantaneously. One cannot go back in time to capture the right data if it was not designed to be captured in that instant. In case of multinationals, one cannot blackjack the IT systems of each country to produce the standardized-granular data if it was not part of their original design. In a nutshell, systems across organizations have to be designed to capture the right data.

Then comes the next big question! What constitutes the right data? How granular should it be? What are data standards? How exactly one goes about designing for capturing the right data? And what kind of data supports big decisions?

And most importantly: is all data equally important, or is it possible to identify the 10–20% of data that supports the big decisions – decisions which influence 90% of key business outcomes, and hence need to be treated differently?

Thanks to the internet, there is now an added complexity; there is plenty more data outside of the enterprise, that can be leveraged and combined with enterprise data to produce actionable insights with the kind of precision hitherto not possible.

The purpose of a comprehensive data strategy is for institutionalizing a process for capturing the right information (data + insights*) and distributing it to the right consumers of information, at the right time.*

9.1 When Data Fails to Deliver

In one of my offshoring assignments, I had a mandate to set up shared services for a fairly large multinational company. The transition for Phase 1 was relatively smooth and eventless, given that I was taking back and consolidating the IT services from a set of external vendors. The trouble started when we kicked off Phase 2, essentially focused on finance and accounting (F&A), risk and operations, and I was also asked to evaluate the feasibility of setting up a center of excellence for enterprise analytics. Naturally, there was substantial resistance from the managers of different countries, specifically from chief financial officers (CFOs) and HR heads.

While the CFOs were worried about loss of control, the HR heads were worried about loss of morale. As I have always advocated in such cases, I proposed a thorough and joint due diligence to establish a business case and a sign-off before we actually transitioned the work to the shared services organization (SSO) at offshore. The due diligence questionnaire prepared was thoroughly vetted with the help of a set of senior finance managers at the head office (HO); people with years of experience in different countries and respected within the organization. The plan was to analyze the data collected from due diligence to identify the best-case opportunities for transitioning to SSO, with maximum return and minimal impact on the efficiency of the workflow.

Among other things, the questionnaire tried to gain an understanding of:

1. What kind of jobs are not location / country specific; can be remote; backed by data?
2. The overheads:
    a. What kind of overheads are employee-related – (preceding three years data)
    b. What kind of overhead costs are controllable, and what overhead costs are non-controllable – (preceding three years data.)
    c. All the data to be broken up by product line, by legal entity, and by country.

I proposed using a web-based questionnaire, but I encountered a stronger than usual push-back; I was told the managers were most comfortable communicating via email and using Excel. I tried telling them a web-based questionnaire can ensure a better audit trail and greater security of data; but in the end, I gave in... in the interests of time.

To ensure ease of consolidation of data from different countries, a *standard format* and a *master list of overheads* (yes, in an Excel format) was sent across by mail to CFOs of different countries, from the mail-id of a senior executive and the sponsor of the SSO initiative. The sponsor assured me that the responses would be received within two weeks, maximum. My mobile number was given to the CFOs as a hotline that they could use if they had an unlikely odd question while filling in the questionnaire... and my phone never stopped ringing.

I was repeatedly asked if they could send the data "as-is", as they had it, and if there was a way I could cull what I wanted out of their Excel sheets. I had to get the sponsor to issue a clarification mentioning the Excel format is *sacrosanct* and *inviolable*. Then, three weeks passed, and then a month. I was nowhere near getting a response from any country. Once again there was a new directive from head office, a new inviolable deadline; and, once again, my phone did not stop ringing. I tried providing as much clarity as I could on how to extract the data from their SAP and legacy applications and fill in the format of the questionnaire. The tension was palpable as the deadline approached.

Finally, the CFO of one of the largest countries called up and broke down:

"We have never captured the data with this kind of granularity. It was not my fault... the IT systems were designed this way... They (the HO) should've implemented SAP right... Thank God, I still maintain a parallel system on Excel... What can I do? My team has been burning the midnight oil for over a month to gather *the data* as per the format of your bl#*ted questionnaire… They had to go back and collect *the data* from invoices and vouchers …. Can you believe it? …I don't have the manpower to do this kind of wret#*ed work… may you guys rot in …"

As he poured his heart out, it became clear none of the IT applications, neither the legacy accounting applications, nor the newly rolled out SAP had the kind of granularity to break up the data. It turns out, he still files his monthly reports to HO from his trusted Excel sheets, not directly from SAP.

It was instantaneously clear to me that the chart-of-accounts did not have the requisite granularity; as I dug further, I discovered each country had its own unique chart-of-accounts (some devoid of any logic). While they seem to have created as many accounts as they fancied, most were irrelevant, and some had not been in use for over three years. I realized I had ended up accidentally unearthing a bigger issue than the one I was trying to resolve.

Those of you with an enterprise resource planning (ERP) background will know that chart-of-accounts rationalization is a necessary first step while creating a global template for implementing SAP, which apparently had not been done. While the IT department claimed they had consulted a senior manager in corporate finance, the said manager confessed that he did not understand what chart-of-accounts meant. He was asked for a list of accounts, and he simply provided a copy from his legacy application at the HO. It became clear, each country instance simply *inherited* its chart-of-accounts from their respective legacy applications, and there were comments such as "Oh… we did look at the so-called chart-of-accounts from HO, but our country requirements are so unique."

Further, data governance was conspicuously absent: each country added, edited, deleted its own chart-of-accounts, at will… a professional and irreversible harakiri!

Fixing the issue prospectively for the countries where SAP was yet to be implemented was not much of an issue, as long as a new integrated global standard chart-of-accounts was prepared and available before the kick-off. However, fixing the issues retrospectively for the countries where SAP was already rolled out – and currently live – was a different matter altogether: practically like a new implementation and estimated to cost several millions of dollars… way beyond their existing budgets for SAP implementation.

I had a bigger shock when I looked into how the global consolidation of accounts was happening. The accounts from each country were being sent in Excel sheets by mail, and a battery of people from the accounting department at HO and at SSO, struggled 24/7 every month to pool together a meaningful consolidated statement of accounts. Reconciliation of accounts was an absolute nightmare. I was no longer sure if they were doing 100% reconciliation, or if they had an adjustment account that took care of any and all differences.

> The global consulting firm implementing SAP blamed the chief information officer (CIO), and the CIO in turn blamed the F&A team; in the end, they found a scapegoat in the poor expendable corporate finance manager, who was relatively new in the organization...

This story may sound familiar to most people; a tell-tale case of everything that can ever go wrong, going wrong, *and the effect of not having a cohesive data strategy.*

While there are no questions about how an investment into data analytics could work wonders in enhancing the business performance of a company, it is still an enigma as to what constitutes a right investment. God's "chosen few" companies get it right, but most seem to get very little out of their analytics and big data investments.

Reasons? Primarily four –

- **The Right Data** – organizations have huge amounts of data, but much of it is either not relevant or not accessible. The example related above is a classic case of data from 200+ legal entities in 90+ countries being available, but lack of consistency and granularity in defining chart-of-accounts makes the data not useful in its current form.
- **The Right Project** – poor choice on where to apply analytics for maximizing dollar returns (dollar benefit/investment in dollars, time, and effort).
- **Data Architecture** – data is stored in isolated silos. Absence of common data definitions, data standards, and absence of an MDM.
- **Leap from Data to Actionable Insights** – data needs to be coaxed and cajoled to tell a story. This is possible by amalgamation of abilities in mathematics, IT, and business. Very few analytics companies have been able to do that.

9.1.1 Water, Water Everywhere!

Many organizations swim in data, a huge amount of enterprise data, in state-of-art data centers, and yet, only a fraction of such data would be *relevant* for meaningful analysis. Of the relevant data, only a small fraction would be *indexed, formatted, and*

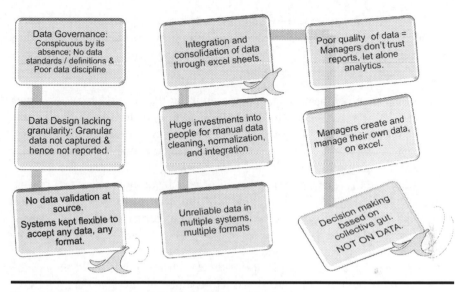

Figure 9.1   The Domino effect of poor quality data.

accessible. So, the *net relevant useful* data available for analytics may be a tiny fraction of the total data sitting inside the data center.

Reasons could be one or more of the following –

- Islands of disconnected IT applications in different locations that do not talk to each other.
- Absence of common data standards, or standard data definitions.
- Absence of Granularity for drill down at the required depth.
- Data capture process lacks consistency as organizations seldom have global standard processes.
- Poor Data Governance and Poor data quality. (Figure 9.1).

9.1.2 Legacy Data: Data Warehouses or Data Lakes?

Then there is the issue of legacy data; the data from systems of earlier era, some still being used, some dysfunctional. Legacy data is of two kinds:

1. The data residing in applications that are still live.
2. The data from now dysfunctional applications of yesteryears, still needed purely for the purpose of analytics.

The problem with legacy data is that it may not conform to the data definitions or data standards that are currently being followed in the organization, and hence will be difficult to normalize. Technically, the legacy data can be normalized and stored in a data warehouse (schema-on-write) or can be stored in its natural format in a data lake (schema-on-read) – to be retrieved and normalized at will, as and when required by a skilled Hadoop programmer or by a data scientist. Here is how reality works though:

a. Normalizing the legacy data is a bigger monster than most data lake salesmen would have you believe. That is because it is not just format of the data, the requisite granularity of the transactions may simply not exist in some applications. (For a simplified example: the legacy data at a used-car showroom may have a single product code for all Ford Taurus cars irrespective of their color, and hence the legacy transactions will never tell you how many cars of what color have been sold, while the new POS application effective 2012 may have a different product variant code for each color of Ford Taurus). So, it is immaterial if one uses a data warehouse or a data lake, the non-existent granularity of data can never be addressed.

b. A bigger issue is in identifying *useful data* from hundreds of application instances (both live and retired), structured and unstructured data, contracts, emails, social media data – all in their natural format from a multitude of sources being brought on to a now not-so-expensive data lake, with the innocent hope that everything that you are bringing in would be of use some day, and a super intelligent Hadoop algorithm would bring in brilliant actionable insights that would save millions for the organization.

Note: I met a gentleman from a reputed consulting firm at a Gartner's "Data and Analytics Summit" a few years back; He argued no rational logic needs to be used in deciding what goes into a data lake; the very purpose is to pour everything you have in the name of data into the lake and worry about its usefulness some other day.
   ...and, *with luck, it may not be your problem when the day comes!*

9.1.3 The Data Conundrum

"Not everything that counts can be counted, and not everything that can be counted counts." A popular quotation that is, perhaps wrongly, attributed to Albert Einstein. *Quote Investigator* credits W.B. Cameron (the sociologist, not the author of *A Dog's Purpose*). He is supposed to have said:

> "It would be nice if all of the data which sociologists require could be enumerated because then we could run them through IBM machines and draw charts as the economists do. However, *not everything that can be counted counts, and not everything that counts can be counted.*"

The above is one facet of data conundrum. The other facet is related to how one defines one's universe of data.
   Let me explain further.

The philosophy this book advocates is that one should always start from a decision – an important decision that can seriously influence the business outcomes – and then work backward to identify which data, when analyzed, can give insights that can make a material difference to the quality of decision!

Now the question is, where do we find the data that we need for a meaningful analysis? Is it all available within the enterprise applications, or in its data warehouses – all normalized and dressed up, just ready to be used? In the unstructured data stored in the data lakes? In social media, internet, and other external data sources? The answer more often than not, is a combination of all.

In Figure 9.2, the lighter blue middle circle represents the data you have within the enterprise, of which accessible formatted data is a small fraction, hence the smallest circle. The data that you need is the biggest circle in blue and includes both external and internal enterprise data (Figure 9.2).

The problem that data scientists and data analysts face is that *not all data that you need is within the enterprise*, and even if you do manage to identify all data, both external and internal, the accessible formatted data would still be a tiny fraction of the data that you need. Hence, the quality of analytics that they could produce using this insufficient data, may never be as good as stakeholders would like it to be. *Slicing and dicing your internal data may not necessarily provide earth-shattering insights.* This is a key reason, if not the crux, to explain why analytics investments fail in delivering real business value!

Further, the data scientists and data analysts can help analyze the data by running an algorithm to recognize hidden patterns, trends and so forth. However, when it comes to identifying what data could potentially support a particular decision, it is way outside their field of expertise. Identifying the data, or in other words connecting *the data to decisions*, requires substantial expertise and understanding of the domain, considerable expertise in the decision sciences, and along with expertise in data sciences; something most data scientists are not endowed with!

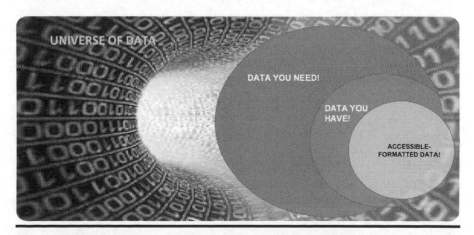

Figure 9.2   The data that you need vs. the data that you have!

So how does one resolve the data conundrum? Below are the steps to be followed:

1. In the first step, identify all the data that could potentially support a key decision – without worrying about where to source the data from.
2. Not all data you need is within the enterprise, so, one must explore both internal and external sources of data.
3. Not all data needs to be structured, so, explore both structured and unstructured data sources.
4. Finally, carefully cull useful relevant data from the redundant, and wasteful.
5. Work with the net remaining clean, concise, and relevant data.
6. *Time* is an important dimension to the data – dig into the useful relevant data deep enough into the past, to get the full perspective of changes through the years.
7. All analytics and all insights need to be accompanied with a caveat – the limitations of the model, and more importantly the limitations of the data

9.2 Enterprise Data Strategy

9.2.1 Defining Data Strategy

A SAS white paper (SAS, 2018) titled "The five essential components of a data strategy" insists defining a data strategy in the organization is key. The paper says traditionally the data strategy has always been about data storage, but it is important to address and plan for how the data is acquired, stored, managed, shared, and used. The five essential components include: Identify, Store, Provision, Process, and Govern, broadly referring to different phases of the data life cycle in the organization.

The Gartner glossary (Maguire, 2019) defines the data strategy as "a highly dynamic process employed to support the acquisition, organization, analysis, and delivery of data in support of business objectives."

In their *Harvard Business Review* (*HBR*) article, DalleMule and Davenport (2017) argue that the ideal data strategy requires a trade-off between defensive and offensive strategies; that is, a compromise between having a single-source-of-truth (SSOT) or multiple-versions-of-truth (MVOT). The authors explain through a series of case studies, why globally spread organizations may need to support MVOT. The paper specifically refers to how Guy Peri, the CDO of Proctor & Gamble realized that each of the BUs may have need for customized interpretations of data and allowed for "controlled data transformations" towards MVOT. While I personally believe this is a brilliantly authored paper, a *word of caution*: The MVOTs still need to come from a single source. One must understand the operative word in the phrase "controlled data transformations" is "controlled"… it is critically important to carefully control all data transformations so that *the truth is not lost in translation*.

In another, equally impressive *HBR* article (Davenport & Redman, 2020) titled "Your organization needs a proprietary data strategy", Thomas H. Davenport and Thomas C. Redman, argue that given the emergence of new technologies like AI and machine learning, and new sources of data like IoT and mobiles, there is a greater need for proprietary data strategies. There is an interesting reference in this article to alternative data sources – for example, one could analyze how the retail industry is performing by observing satellite photos of parking lots.

9.2.2 Do Organizations Need a Data Strategy?

One of my erstwhile colleagues, who moved out of IT consulting to become the chief technology officer (CTO) of a large appliances company, once confessed to me over a drink:

> "I am tired or trying… Yes, the ERP was implemented, but half the invoicing continues to be on legacy applications, and the Excel-culture refuses to die. Every report continues to be on Excel, including those few on SAP which get downloaded into Excel. Each guy has his own *private stash* of data, that he keeps in Excel. I tried getting budgets for a data lake and an analytics platform, but I have been shouted down. I've made several futile attempts at educating my boss about the importance of investing in e-commerce, supply chain visibility apps, social media, analytics… and integrating the application instances."

He went on:

> "None of the applications speak to each other, and there is no consistency in how data is defined; We have as many customer-masters and material-masters as the number of applications. The chart-of-accounts is a joke, over 80% of the accounts had no transactions reported in last three years… there is no consistency in how transactions are reported in accounts, sometimes in bulk, sometimes transaction-by-transaction. None of the managers believe in the IT systems or the reports we generate, they just trust their own Excel sheets… I have tried educating the top management and given them an estimate for finding a short-term fix and a long-term fix… I was not taken seriously… none of them think the data is important enough for their attention. Nothing ever really changes in this place… and the same old hint always."

Apparently, his colleagues would never lose an opportunity to remind him that he was new-and-expendable saying: "Hey new guy! We built this business from scratch. Why do you think you know better than us?" He reported to the CFO – an old school chartered accountant and a confidant of the family which owned the controlling stake in the now publicly traded company. He struggled for a few more months before giving up and finding a different job.

Years later, the same company was in the news for filing for insolvency. The company started losing out to the competition around 2010. The backward supply chain had completely changed in the appliances industry. Most of the competitors started importing completely knocked down (CKD) units from China, and hence could launch newer models every couple of months, while keeping their overheads small. The family-owned business, which had heavily invested in backward integration, could hardly keep pace. Further, while this company continued to bet on its age-old network of distributors and stockists, the consumers started buying more and more appliances online. The competitors with strong online presence could cross-sell and get repeat business from the same customers much better, while the family-run company just could not keep pace.

Both technology and business models are changing so fast these days that most businesses are struggling to keep up. Every company worth its name now understands they have to find a way to leverage the huge amount of data available within the enterprise, and outside the enterprise on social media and internet; so much so that the data is no longer just an enabler, but a distinct competitive advantage.

Those few companies which learn to capitalize and profit from the data are able:

- to make better products faster and cheaper.
- to know their customers' ever-changing preferences.
- to customize and deliver a product service bundle tailor-made for each customer, at their doorstep.

Those God's "chosen few" companies will not only survive but thrive! And those who fail in leveraging the data are unlikely to stay competitive, even if they do survive by some miracle.

Since capitalizing the data is a survival necessity, companies must find a way… to start with, by attempting to create a data strategy.

So let us settle this argument and conclude: *the organizations that intend to survive and thrive, do need a strong data strategy.*

I am resisting calling it a "big data strategy" right now, given most organizations do not have a plain-and-simple data strategy documented in black and white yet. However, technically every company with a large and diverse customer base, selling in a large geographical territory, or selling a large number of products and services needs to prepare itself to deal with big data and hence, would need to devise a big data strategy. The first step, however, is to get their enterprise data strategy right.

9.2.3 Who Owns a Data Strategy?

The next question is, who exactly in the organization is qualified to build a data strategy? Is it the CTO or CIO, or does it necessarily require a brand-new person with a unique expertise, and who must be given a hitherto non-existent but important-sounding designation: the Chief Data Officer (CDO)?

Not long ago, data was considered a by-product of business operations, but now there is near-complete acknowledgment among the global companies that the data is perhaps their biggest asset and hence deserves greater attention. Many companies believe a CDO can pay undivided attention to innovating and managing the all-important asset – the data – besides acting as a bridge between IT and operations.

In a 2017 survey (Kotwal et al., 2017), PWC predicted over 90% of all global companies will have a CDO by 2019. However, the survey acknowledged there was still substantial confusion about the role; only 39% of those organizations surveyed agreed that the CDO should own the data strategy, while 24% felt there was no single point accountability.

KPMG conducted a similar survey in 2020 (Marra et al., 2020). Of the 188 companies surveyed, 57% claimed they had a data strategy, while 43% admitted they had nothing like a data strategy.

Further, an even more interesting finding: Over 75% of the respondents mentioned they used Excel as their primary analytics tool, while 69% agreed they are too reliant on Excel. The good news is that 66% of the respondents believed the core purpose of data strategy is to enhance decision-making.

In an article published in *MIT Management* in Feb 2021 titled "Making the business case for a chief data officer" (Stackpole, 2021), author Beth Stackpole mentions that 65% of the companies had a CDO; the article also quotes IDC market researcher, Dan Vesset saying: "People spend 60% to 80% of their time trying to find data. It is a huge productivity loss."

In conclusion, it is an excellent idea to recruit a CDO and make the person unequivocally responsible to data strategy and for acting as the bridge between IT and operations. Most global companies are in the process of doing so.

9.2.4 Recruiting a CDO

Given the prevailing confusion in defining the role of the CDO, most companies do not know what kind of skill set would be most appropriate for the role. Companies which do not have strong internal information technology expertise find it difficult to understand the specific technical and operational skills the role demands. While some take help from consulting companies to define the role, others recruit someone with a fancy degree with the hope that the new guy will somehow miraculously set everything right. Given they have no internal expertise, the recruitment of the new guy is left to hapless HR heads and CFOs – who almost always end up getting some IT guy who worked for the same or similar industry, irrespective of his abilities to drive innovation.

To illustrate the point: I have seen people who have handled hardware – boxes, network, and telephony – being recruited as CTOs and CIOs purely because they have some domain expertise in the same industry. The hardware infrastructure CTOs, while being good at what they know, would have no expertise or experience in all-important enterprise application design and development, let alone any understanding of digital transformation or data-driven organization. So, in turn, they depend on external consultants, who, one hopes, know their jobs. They diligently attend every Gartner's summit so as to pick up the right jargon to throw at the clueless CEOs and CFOs they report to. The story of how so-called CDOs are being recruited is not very different.

HR folks are mere mortals, so one cannot blame them for not understanding the annoying tech jargon like "digital transformation" and "data-driven organization".

9.2.5 Skill Set of a CDO

The CDO owns the information supply chain of the organization. The primary goal of the CDO is to ensure the right information (data + insights) is captured and distributed to the right consumers of information, at the right time. A CDO is responsible for the quality of data, and the privacy of the data.

Given the CDO has to act as a bridge between IT and operations, it would be ideal if the person has actual hands-on experience in both functions. A CDO need not be data scientist; but he should understand the data through different stages of its life cycle, besides the organizational value-chain and its value-drivers. The data essentially describes the organizational entities and their interaction through time: the value-chain, the inputs, outputs, the actors, and the partners who play their roles as the organization strives to deliver on its goals. The CDO should understand what kind of analysis would help bring out the potential anomalies, inconsistencies, and constraints that might hamper the organization from maximizing its throughput. The CDO should understand what kind of analysis can help organization prevent adverse events. A CDO should understand what kind of analysis can help the organization improve its customer experience. A CDO should identify which vital-few big decisions need to be supported with data and insights.

In essence, a CDO should understand how to deliver value from analytics.

9.2.6 Who Should Be Owning a Data Strategy?

While there are not many organizations with a clearly defined and documented data strategy, even among those few who do, there are some common misconceptions:

1. Data strategy is a sub-component of IT strategy; hence it is the IT team's responsibility.
2. Data needs to be defined by IT teams, those qualified as data architects, people who understand creating relational database structures and entity relationship models.
3. There is no need for a formal data governance committee and there is no need to formally define data owners.
4. Master data changes can be ad hoc decisions taken by IT teams based on ad hoc requests from users and so on…

It stands to reason that both IT strategy and Data strategy need to be necessarily business aligned, emanating from business goals delineated in the organization's strategy map and balanced scorecard. IT strategy is indeed a sub-component of operations strategy, with clearly defined linkages to financial goals and customer goals.

The IT team can build the IT strategy completely independently and without consulting any other department, as long as they can convince the management of the business value of each initiative and ensure alignment with corporate business objectives. Data strategy, however, is more inter-disciplinary and would require collaboration between different departments and the IT department. As mentioned earlier, not all data resides inside IT applications; a good amount of useful data exists outside in IT applications; in Excel sheets, documents, contracts, and emails.

Ideally, the data strategy needs to be owned by a CDO, along with an inter-disciplinary, inter-departmental committee, which can be same as, or a part of the governance committee.

9.3 A Framework for Building a Data Strategy

9.3.1 Components of a Data Strategy

Back referencing to my argument about how every company runs multiple parallel supply chains in tandem, each supporting the other. We mentioned a services supply chain underneath every physical goods supply chain, supported by a cash supply chain, and an information (data) supply chain. The collective speed of these interdependent supply chains determines the speed of cash-to-cash cycle in a company; the inventory turns, the asset turns and the overall profitability.

The efficiency of the supply chain here indicates the optimal use of resources available, maximizing throughput and the service levels. The effectiveness indicates exceeding the expectations of all stakeholders – customers, employees, partners, shareholders, government, and society. The intent of a data strategy is to make sure the information (data) supply chain not only runs at optimal efficiency but is also effective in delivering the right data for the right end-user (Figure 9.3).

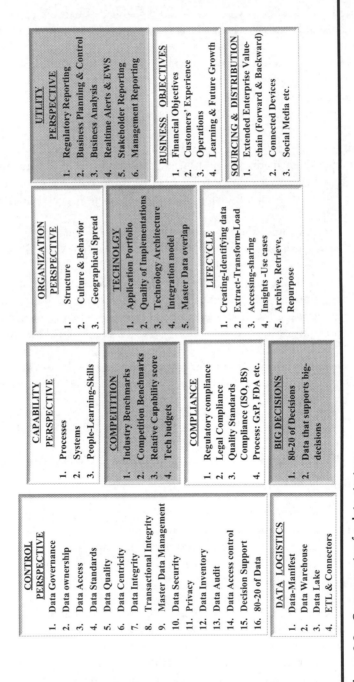

Figure 9.3 Components of a data strategy.

9.3.2 Before Building a Data Strategy: A Time for Organizational Introspection

I have read multiple articles and white papers on how to build a data strategy. What I have encountered are multiple definitions of data strategy; the most common being *how a company collects, stores, manages, shares, and uses the data*. There is one from the MIT CISR Data Research Advisory Board (2018), that every other white paper refers to: "A central, integrated concept that articulates how data will enable and inspire business strategy."

In my view, there are three critical questions to be answered before building a data strategy.

1. What is the state of data in the organization? And the maturity of data governance systems and protocols within the company?
2. Does the data strategy need to be an offensive one, or a defensive one?
3. Most importantly, what data supports the big decisions, and hence is business-critical?

Any organization, irrespective of its age and maturity, may choose to embark on a journey to become a data-driven organization. Hence, there is no one-size-fits-all data strategy. The data strategy needs to be customized for each company based on its industry sector, number of years in business, application inventory, integration, the efficiency/effectiveness of its IT assets, governance & internal control mechanism, and most importantly the competency of the people within.

The case study below describes a typical brick and mortar company aspiring to become a data-driven organization.

CASE STUDY

When organizations are set up, they are quite small, fewer than 10 people operations, typically run out of garages or small rented premises. The information supply chain can be completely informal. If we are talking about a company set up in the late 1980s or early 1990s, perhaps all data could reside in someone's computer; and if we are talking about a start-up set up in the last decade, all data could be on a Google drive.

Let us talk about a typical brick-and-mortar organization set up in late 1980s. As business grows, they add new employees, new offices, and new infrastructure. The promoters feel the need for strengthening the information supply chain to handle the incremental complexity and the incremental compliance requirements; they may not fully understand the dynamics of information supply chain but do feel frustrated with the bottlenecks in information flow. Not being tech-savvy, and because the immediate need is for hardware and telephony, they end up recruiting someone from an IT infrastructure background, and yes… from the same industry vertical. The new IT head, given his background understands very little of enterprise applications and even less about data engineering. So, he depends on external consultants for direction, while learning enough jargon to keep up appearances with the promoters.

The new IT head makes sure he is the single point of contact for all IT requirements, and nothing ever goes over his head. Over a period of time, the IT head becomes the insider. Even though the promoters start feeling uncomfortable with the never-ending problems with the information supply chain, they still hesitate to fire the IT head; he becomes like a bad habit that they cannot shake off.

Over the next 30 years, the IT head becomes the CTO of the company. In the 30 years journey, the company would have added hundreds of applications along with the all-important ERP; besides investing into a data warehouse, data lake and an analytics platform, and acquired licenses for a data visualization engine. There is a governance committee made up of departmental heads and the CTO, but it exists only on paper; they never formally met in the last couple of years. Company byelaws mention large investments have to be cleared by a finance committee – a sub-committee of governance committee – but the CTO meets each of the members individually to get their approval. The CTO is proud of fact that there is a series of demo projects running on Block-chain, IoT, AI and machine learning.

Meanwhile, the managers and employees (users) keep complaining how nothing ever works in IT. The management still does not understand why they keep allocating budgets for resolving the same issues year after year. In the midst of all this, an external consultant talks directly to the top management on the importance of digital transformation and data-driven organization. The external consultant not only successfully sells the concept, but also provides a business case with projected investments and monetized returns over the next five years. The CTO has been assigned to work with the external consultant to make it happen in a time-bound manner. Among other things, the management wants to recruit a new CDO; the task of defining the role and the job description has been assigned to the CTO and the new external consultant.

Across the table, the external consultant asks for the IT strategy and data strategy of the company. The CTO did share the IT strategy document, but there is no data strategy for the organization, yet.

As the case study above demonstrates; in a good number of organizations, there may be a substantial amount of reengineering of the applications, systems and processes *inherent* to building and executing a data strategy. A select few well-run, well-designed organizations may require relatively less effort, as they may require only bridging the few odd gaps in processes, systems and applications, followed by strengthening of the existing process framework.

> What we are trying to do here is to provide a flexible framework for building a data strategy customized for the unique requirements of any company, irrespective of its age, capability, or maturity.

A comprehensive framework and a step-by-step methodology to create a data strategy is covered in the annexure at the end of this chapter.

9.4 The New Dimensions of the Data

9.4.1 *How Would You Know If You Have Big Data in Your Organization That You Need to Handle Differently?*

What if the organization has big data that requires a separate strategy? And where does this big data come from? How does one distinguish between plain-vanilla data and the big data?

Most people credit John Mashey with popularizing the term "big data" while working for Silicon Graphics in the 1990s. It originally referred to a large volume of data that is generated very fast and has a lot of variety. A lot has been written about the original three Vs of big data – volume, variety, and velocity, which has since expanded to include veracity and value.

To my mind, big data essentially is something too large and too complex for someone to choose a representative sample from, and difficult to process using the computing power at one's disposal. However, the words "large" and "complex" are relative and can mean different things at different times, in different contexts. It was a big event for IBM when they first introduced a hard disk breaking the 1GB barrier in the early 1980s. I used to work for an aerospace company in the late 1980s and I still remember we had to choose between processing payroll vs. doing an MRP run on the Univac mainframe, as both could not be run simultaneously. Now, most basic cell phones can support and process more data than the mainframes of the 1980s.

Now that we are in 2021, I believe there is enough and more computing power at the disposal of most CIOs, when it comes to pure enterprise data, assuming they have all the right data, cleaned, formatted, normalized and accessible. The typical exceptions include R&D institutions, BFSI, and credit card companies –

where both the number of transactions and complexity can be very high, and the enterprise data can indeed qualify as big data. The internet brings in added complexity: the data available for analysis increases exponentially when one considers multiple platforms, websites, locations, and customer profiles among others, and more importantly the social media data. It is a different matter altogether at pure internet and e-commerce companies like Google and Amazon; both the number of transactions and the number of customers can be phenomenally high. A 2008 estimate records Google processes over 20 petabytes of data per day through an average of 100,000 MapReduce jobs spread across its massive computing clusters (Lakshmanan, 2019).

I have come across a variety of definitions of big data, and found a useful summary in an NIST (National Institute of Standards and Technology) publication of September 2015 (Chang & Grady, 2019). As per the article, TechTarget defines big data as data size exceeding one petabyte, but most agree it is not just about the volume; but more about volume along with variety and velocity put together that qualifies the data that you are handling as big data. Sometimes, the presence of a large volume of unstructured data also prompts people to classify the data as big data.

> In my view, definitions just do not matter. If you have large volume, complex data being produced with high velocity, and if you have a problem choosing a representative sample, or if the number of samples are becoming too many, then you need to treat the data as big data and use techniques like MapReduce to handle the data.

9.4.2 Do Organizations Need a Separate Big Data Strategy?

The answer is yes and no.

- Do you need separate tools, technology, and infrastructure to handle big data? Of course, yes!
- Do you need an altogether different strategy for handling big data? Absolutely no!

This is because any comprehensive data strategy devised must cover all types of data and all sizes of data that an organization might encounter. All data including but not limited to: Structured, unstructured, semi-structured, enterprise data, external data including social media data, and most importantly big data: all varieties and variations without exceptions. So, the framework laid down above is still valid, and would work even if the organization has large amounts of big data that need to be handled differently.

9.4.3 Why Most Data is Big Data Now: The Big Multiplying Effect

Life was relatively simple about 30 years ago. There were no mobile phones and no internet. A manufacturer distributed and sold their products through a fixed set of dealers, stockists, and stores. The advertising was even simpler; one engaged an Ogilvy or Wunderman Thompson to do the creative, negotiate, and release the ads in select print-media and the couple of popular television channels. Among the handful of channels everyone knew, which channel was more popular at prime time. There was little disruption in the market, hence very little need for complicated business intelligence. The odd exception was made, and a slightly more elaborate analysis is ordered, only on occasion, typically when an organization decides to launch new products for a new market.

Marketing managers and product managers could afford to work for 40 hours or less in a week, break for an early drink on most days, and yet knew exactly what was happening in their market, and knew most of the existing customers in their localized small market personally.

All was well, until the arrival of the internet. Suddenly one could view the entire world as one large market. While it opened the floodgates in terms or opportunity, it also brought in enormous amounts of complexity.

Here is how the internet has brought in a number of hitherto non-existent new dimensions of data, and hence a multiplying effect on the overall data size.

Assuming the organization has all the varieties of data in ample quantities; has multiple products, and operates in multiple geographies; the following would be different dimensions (attributes) of the data that could potentially have a multiplying effect on the overall size of the data.

Enterprise data: structured, unstructured, semi-structured – some of it over 1 petabyte per day.
External data: the internet, social media – Twitter, FB, LinkedIn, Reddit among others.

1. The organization has **C** customers – each of them may buy one or more of the **P** products ($P = 0 \sim n$)
   a. Each of the customers has profiles on different social media channels.
   b. Each of the customers has multiple connections who can be potential customers for the same product or service.
2. The organization operates in multiple countries, each country has a number of states, a number of districts, a number of counties:
   a. In essence the organization operates in thousands of geographies, and hundreds-of-thousands of micro-markets.
   b. Each micro-market, each geography has a different level of demand for each of the product variants.

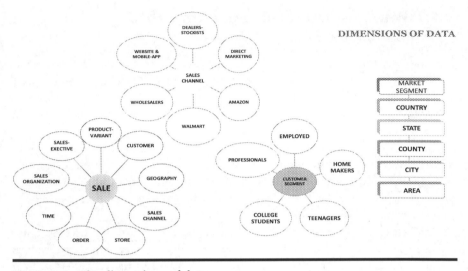

Figure 9.4   The dimensions of data.

3. The organization has **P** number of product variants.
4. Transactional channels: Physical, online-web and online-mobile.
5. Advertising channels: Print, television, online, mobile (each of them come with hundreds of options).
6. Time period: Years, months, weeks, days.

Each of these dimensions have a ***multiplier effect*** on the overall data size. For example, if the organization were to *analyze the market share* and the *demand vs. actual sales* in each of the micro-markets (i.e., villages) in India, for each of the product variants, we would be looking at data from 600,000 villages for each month of a year (Figure 9.4)

No. of records = (600,000 villages) × **P** (No. of product variants) × 12 months

Each micro-market may have "c" number of existing customers, and each of them with a social media presence, and each of them can influence other prospective customers. As external data (market data, social media data etc.) gets interfaced with enterprise transactional data, the overall data-size multiples multi-fold.

9.5 Big Data for Big Decisions

9.5.1 Big Data, AI, and the Age of the Robots…

The new CDOs came in and talked about how big data analytics is going to transform the way organization would function, and the importance of building a *data culture*. A few did talk about data governance and creating a data strategy. Yet on the ground, not much seems to be changing. It is true that a select set of companies are brilliantly executing analytics projects and reaping disproportionate rewards, while a much larger number of companies are still groping in the dark as far as a data analytics strategy is concerned.

The truth is, a number of CIOs including a sizable number of newly minted CDOs have invested in one of those promising advanced analytics platforms, sold to them as the very best in the market, and a panacea for everything that ever gets done in the name of analytics in organizations. Sadly, a vast majority of them overlooked the importance of ensuring the ***right data*** feeding into these well-intentioned advanced analytics platforms, and hence not surprisingly a vast majority of such projects have failed to deliver value.

Ever since buzzwords like big data, Hadoop, machine learning (ML), AI and so forth have become popular, people have started believing perhaps data may not be all that important anymore. After all, they have been hearing about those wonderful tools which can read through completely unstructured data and random transactional data to produce actionable insights for fraud detection. There are a number of NO-SQL databases in the market, RDBMS is passé. There are XML databases like MarkLogic, which one hears can enable searching for a keyword or phrase from thousands of ISBNs in seconds.

Many otherwise intelligent people in the industry actually think data is overrated; data formats and data standards are no longer important in the age of No-SQL databases. I heard a few argue given the sophisticated AI, ML, and deep-learning tools available in the market, nothing stops them from automatically creating data and actionable insights out of thin air if need be.

The age of AI is already here, the age of robots cannot be far behind...

I am reminded of Asimov's 1957 classic book *The Naked Sun* which portrays an utopian planet called Solaria, where all work is done by robots while humans pursue leisurely professions of their choice out of their 10,000 acre estates. Well, I am afraid there is a long way to go before we get there, and in the meanwhile, we have no option but to pay attention to data.

A good many otherwise intelligent CxOs, and a few not-so-hands-on CIOs have also fallen prey to the very same temptation and false hope. A magic platform to turn not-so-good data into wonderful actionable insights... If only wishes were horses...

For well over a decade, Gartner has been consistently predicting that anywhere between 60–85% of all big data projects fail to deliver any meaningful value to the company. In an article (Heudecker, 2014) titled "Big data challenges move from tech to the organization," Nick Heudecker – then a VP at Gartner – says:

> What became clear during the process of selecting and refining predictions is the focus has changed. Technology is no longer the interesting part of big data. What's interesting is how organizations deal with it. The hype is receding, and big data is no longer viewed as a simple technology problem.

He further adds:

> organizations have to focus on the building blocks of enterprise infor-
> mation management (EIM). So far, only the most rudimentary elements
> of enabling infrastructure have been considered. This is not sustainable;
> 60% of big data projects will fail to make it into production

The key phrase that needs attention here is "only rudimentary elements of enabling infrastructure have been considered" – meaning making analytics work and deliver value requires comprehensive engineering and creating of the enabling infrastructure, definitely a lot more than investing in some advanced analytics platform.

9.5.2 Transformational Data Strategy for Building a Data-Driven Organization

Building a data-driven organization, where all the key decisions – the 10% of the decisions that influence 90% of the business outcomes – are taken based on data, requires developing a comprehensive data strategy as explained in the earlier part of this chapter. Here is how different components of data strategy can be aligned towards building a data-driven organization.

Please do note the individual importance of each of the components and how they all need to be aligned together, and work in tandem to produce the actionable insights for those big decisions.

Data is often said to be the lifeblood of an organization. A well-designed organization is akin to a healthy body, with a healthy blood circulation system and with clean fresh blood being produced in the bone marrow in sufficient quantities, while the old existing blood is being cleaned and circulated to different parts of the body to ensure they run their respective functions effectively.

A well-designed data strategy has to make sure the right data is produced at the right time, and delivered to the right function, or right decision-maker. A well-designed data strategy should make it easy for data to flow from any part of the organization to any other part of the organization instantaneously. A well-designed data strategy should make it easier for data to be pooled/consolidated, easier for dissection at will, and ready for any deep-dive analysis business may demand. A well-designed data strategy should *enable decision-making based on data, at least for those decisions considered big decisions* (Figure 9.5).

While the framework provided earlier in the chapter describes how data is to be produced, cleaned, and circulated, the steps mentioned below connect the data to decisions.

1. **Infra**: The foundational layer of the strategy has to be setting up the enabling infrastructure; a combination standard, protocols, applications and so on, to cover the entire information life cycle. Information here refers to all data and all content – structured and unstructured.

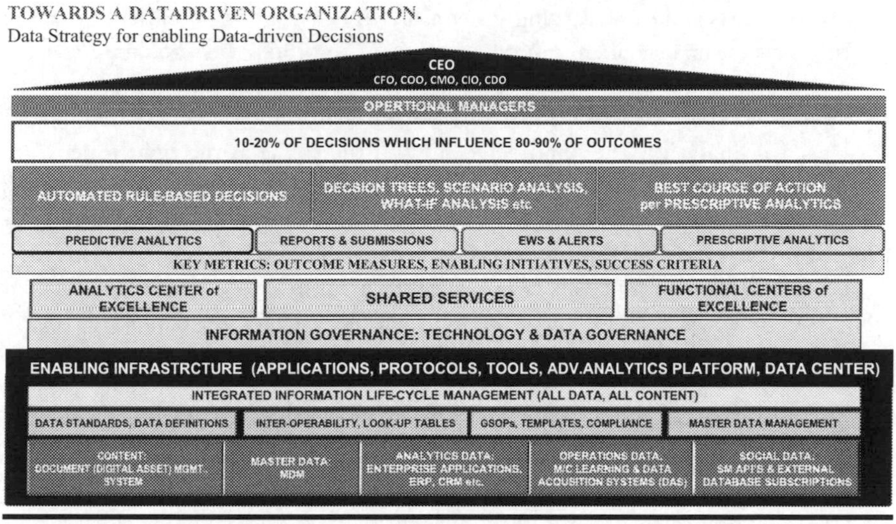

TOWARDS A DATADRIVEN ORGANIZATION.
Data Strategy for enabling Data-driven Decisions

Figure 9.5   The data strategy to enable data-driven decisions.

2. **Governance**: Once the foundational layer is in place, the next step would be to set up the governance mechanism; without a proper functioning governance, the carefully set up foundational layer can be run to ground in virtually no time.

3. **Shared services**: While the shared services can help consolidate IT and data operations into one integrated entity servicing the entire enterprise, the Centers of Excellence (CoEs) embedded into the shared services organization can help establish and roll out specialized functions like analytics across organization very quickly.

4. **CoEs**: There are multiple models for setting up Centers of Excellence, but I personally advocate CoEs piloting a *perfect scale model*; For example, each time a new analytics requirement comes in, the CoE would pilot an algorithm & a solution and perfect the solution, by subjecting it to thorough testing, followed by scaling of the solution across the enterprise using a standard template and methodology perfected during the pilot. Even those solutions involving machine learning and deep-learning algorithms need to go through the same phases, *except that the perfecting of the solution will keep happening as the algorithm continues to learn even after implementation and deployment.*

5. **Automation and AI**: An intelligent data strategy must segregate those decisions which can be *rule based* and can be automated from those which require managerial discretion and intervention. All such decisions should be completely automated saving the precious managerial time and effort.

6. **Analytics:** Developing customized predictive and prescriptive analytics for those decisions which require managerial discretion, will be the next step.

7. **Alerts**: Alerts and early warning systems are to be designed for either informing the decision-makers of an important event, or to propel them to take a specific action after the conclusion of a specific event or a specific period; meaning, the alerts can either be event-driven, or period-driven.
8. **Data for analytics**: The unhindered flow of right data at the right time, from different corners of the organization into the analytics Center of Excellence, is as important as the quality of analytics algorithms designed and deployed.
9. **CSFs**: The following aspects are absolutely critical for the success of data strategy:
    a. Availability of data: Ensuring the right data is available at the right time, at right location, accessible to the right people. Further, the data needs to:
        • Be relevant
        • Be granular
        • Be interoperable
        • Cover every aspect of the value-chain.
    b. Data governance: Even if data is extremely good to start with, it can quickly deteriorate and turn bad in the absence of an equally good data governance framework.

9.6 Integrated Analytics Strategy

While I have advocated a comprehensive grassroots transformation of the entire data-to-decisions value-chain, *not every organization has the capability to transform itself overnight*; it is important to recognize that the implementation takes time. Further there is a serious and not so easily breachable gap between, *the ideal state of one centralized data office controlling the entire data life cycle*, and *the actual reality in most enterprises with isolated islands-of-data and weak data governance*. So, in the interim, the actual IT infrastructure, the actual application stack, the governance models and so forth on the ground, may be very different from the ambitious plans on paper in the IT strategy or data strategy documents.

In the meantime, the data available for analytics will be a combination of good quality data and bad quality data. Hence the need for a *data preparation engine* that helps collate, integrate, and normalize the data from multiple sources into a form and format useful for analytics; while the grand data strategy that unifies, and integrates all enterprise data retrospectively is being implemented across enterprise in the medium-term (Figure 9.6).

It is also important to recognize, analytics strategy is different from data strategy. While data strategy is more comprehensive and has long-term perspective of fixing all the problems with data right from grassroots, the analytics strategy is about using the data as it exists today, and yet producing the best possible analytics to support the decision-making in the organization. The analytics strategy needs to be aligned with the corporate business strategy, IT strategy, and data strategy.

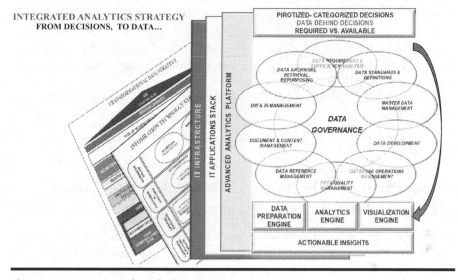

Figure 9.6   Integrated analytics strategy.

There are three important components of the analytics strategy:

1. **Data Preparation Engine**: the all-important component. Usually a combination of:
    a. Extract, transform, and load (ETL) tools like Spark, Talend, or if you can afford the price – ab initio, Informatica among others.
    b. Excel Macros.
    c. Data mining tools including MonkeyLearn, RapidMiner, H2O and others ... apart from IBM, Oracle, and SAS.
    d. There are a host of other tools like Trifacta, Microsoft PowerQuery, and Waterline Data which are self-service data discovery platforms.
    e. The Cloud computing platforms like Amazon AWS come with built-in ETL tools like AWS Glue.

Data preparation uses up over 70–90% of all analytics resources in terms of time, cost, and effort. If the data in the organization is of bad quality and the data standards and data definitions are non-existent, then this percentage can be as high as 95%.

2. **Analytics Engine**: Usually the advanced analytics and machine learning platform the organization may have invested in. The most popular include SAS, IBM, Tibco and MathWorks. Amazon AWS is steadily gaining ground.
3. **Visualization Engine**: While some advanced analytics platforms come with their own visualization engines, it is common to notice large companies investing in a separate visualization solution. The popular ones include Microsoft Power BI, Tableau, and QlikView.

Organizations are not static entities. There is always a change; new business or new geographies being added, new products being launched, new distribution channels introduced, or complete business models undergoing a transformation. Then, there are mergers and acquisitions which require integrating diverse and disconnected IT applications and data streams. The net result: the IT is always on a catch-up mode, and there will always be some amount of disconnected data or even bad quality data. So, it makes ample sense to invest in a data lake and a data preparation engine.

Appendix 9.A: A Framework for Building a Data Strategy – Step by Step (Figure 9.7)

More often than not, a "data strategy" is just a sub-component of the IT strategy; and hence, the activity is seen as something squarely in the domain of a CIO or a CDO if such a role exists. Unfortunately, such CDOs are usually outsiders; later-day-recruits with not-so-strong understanding of the value-chain and operations of the organization. In my opinion, a thorough understanding of the value-chain and the operations of the organization is essential for creating a viable and comprehensive data strategy (Figure 9.7).

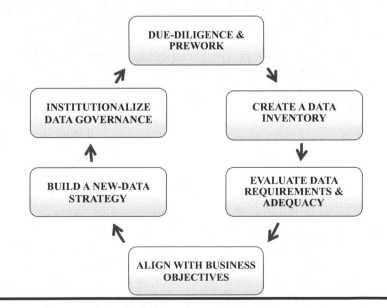

Figure 9.7   A framework for building a data strategy.

A. DUE DILIGENCE and PRE-WORK: Identifying the Sources of Data in Your Organization

I recommend a thorough due diligence prior to actually building a "data strategy". (*Note: This activity is different from creating a "data-inventory" where you simply catalogue existing data from different applications and documents.*) There are two core outcomes expected out of such due diligence:

1. Identifying all the sources of data in your organization;
   - Comprehensive list of functions, compliance requirements, people, resources, and processes.
   - Mapping the complete value chain – and data needed to run the value-chain
2. Identifying the big decisions in your organization, as one key purpose of data is to support decisions
   - Listing decisions, identifying the big decisions
   - Identifying the data behind "big" decisions –

The data requirements in a company emanate primarily from the following:

By Function and Purpose

For Supporting Decisions: Analytics
- Start from the decisions; prioritize decisions that needs to be supported with data
- List and prioritize the strategic opportunities for the company (for example: doubling its top-line and bottom-line by launching new brand-extensions of popular brands)
- List and prioritize the threats / risks (for example: Exxon faces a serious risk of the complete passenger-car market moving over to non-<u>fossil</u> fuels, especially electric cars)

For Statutory Reporting and Compliance
- Statutory and regulatory compliance requirements
- Quality and standards compliance requirements

For Management Reporting
- Performance reviews
- Business analysis

For Performance Measurement and Control
- Business process performance Metrics
- Score KRAs
- Revenues
- Costs

For People, Materials and Resources
- Measuring and managing the supply and consumption of people, materials, and other resources

For Capital and Assets
- Measuring and managing the availability, supply and utilization of capital and assets

Value Chain Coverage

Vendors and Backward Supply-Chain
- Vendor collaboration portal – SRM
- Raw materials, consumables, alterative materials
- Prospective suppliers, alternative suppliers
- Vendor contracts – rate/ running contracts
- Vendor performance evaluation
- Correspondence, collaterals
- Analytics – supply lead-times, costs, quality – comparison with benchmarks and targets

Operations and Internal Value-Chain
- Demand planning
- Goods-inward and inventory management
- Products
- Product planning and product mix
- Product collaterals and communications management
- Factory operations planning and workflow management
- Finished goods inventory and distribution management

Customers and Forward Supply-Chain
- Customer collaboration portal – CRM
- Prospects, opportunities
- Geographies, territories, market-potential by territory, by product
- Marketing budgets, advertising in each territory – marketing collateral
- Salespeople, sales quotas and performance management
- Inquiries, quotations, purchase orders, sales orders, invoicing and collection
- Communication and correspondence

Corporate Objectives as Sources of Data

(Corporate Vision, Strategy and Balanced Scorecard of the Organization)

1. Finance Perspective
   - Finance targets and corporate initiatives planned
   - New geographies, new products planned
2. Customer Perspective.
   - New customers and customer-segments targeted
   - Customer experience management initiatives planned
3. Operations Perspective
   - Operational transformation initiatives planned
4. Learning and Growth perspective
   - New Learning initiatives planned

Big Decisions as Sources of Data

1. Categorization of Decisions
   a. Rule-based automatable decisions
   b. Other including decisions requiring managerial discretion
2. Prioritization of Decisions
   a. Identifying the 10% of decisions which influence 90% of the business outcomes.
   b. Identifying the data behind decisions
   c. Data available vs data needed – gap analysis

B. Create a Data Inventory – (For Both Structured and Unstructured Data)

Before embarking on journey to understand the data that the organization needs, it is important to capture, inventorize, and catalogue the data that the organization has on its hand, right along with the current set of systems, applications, processes, and protocols. This phase is similar to "as-is analysis" in a typical business-process-reengineering assignment, except that the rigor required is substantially higher. The following are the sources for creating a data inventory (structured and unstructured data):

1. Applications inventory and application rationalization analysis
2. Applications footprint across global value-chain
3. Enterprise integration, point-to-point integration
4. Inventory of manual processes, manual controls
5. Data inventory – by application-instance, by system and process
6. Data glossary – capture data definitions as they exist in each application, system, and process
7. Inventory of dashboards, reports, alerts, and early warning systems

8. Inventory of Excel sheets – for control / for reports / for application-integration uploads
9. Inventory of documents
10. Inventory of contracts
11. Inventory of information assets including: product catalogues, marketing collaterals, financial reports and so on

C. Evaluate: Data Requirements and Data Adequacy Analysis

The next step is to create a comprehensive catalog of the data that the organization needs across the enterprise; followed by a "gap analysis" of the gap between the data that the organization needs and the data that it has. The current inventory of data and its sources may be inadequate in covering the business-value-chain in its entirety and its complexity. The purpose of this phase is to evaluate the gap and identify the missing data. Here is a checklist for evaluating data adequacy, the data that organization needs, but currently fails to collect and catalog.

1. **Enterprise Applications Data (Structured)**
   - Coverage of value-chain – gaps and data
   - Decisions support: business decisions by priority – 10% of decisions influencing 90% of outcomes, data behind the decisions, and data sufficiency
   - Reporting requirements – statutory, management, others, and data gaps
   - Regulatory reporting – income tax, RoC, GST, pollution control board, labor welfare office and so on
   - Global compliance standards – IFRS and others
   - Application data – integration models
   - Definitions, standards, and granularity
2. **Enterprise Data (Semi-structured) – Amenable to Data Mining Algorithms**
   - Documents (from document management system) – tagged PDFs, structured word documents.
   - Excel sheets
   - Contracts (contract management system)
   - XML documents (from XML data base)
   - Photos and videos (tagged, numbered)
   - Images (tagged, numbered) and drawings (tagged, numbered)
3. **Enterprise Data (Unstructured) – Amenable to Data Mining Algorithms**
   - Documents (untagged PDFs,) and contracts (untagged PDFs)
   - Photos and videos (untagged) and images (untagged)
   - Drawings (untagged) and scanned documents – OCR, tag, data mine
4. **External Data, Social Media, Internet – Pull through APIs, Data Scrape, Data Mine**

- Sourced and stored in data lake.
- Sourced real-time (such as Twitter feed)

5. **Data Requirements**
   - For regulatory, legal and tax compliance requirements
   - For other compliance requirements (IFRS, ISO, BS etc.)
   - By utility, purpose
   - By organization structure and by business objectives
   - Competition and industry benchmarks
   - Searchability, integration and look-up
6. **Big Decisions to Data**
   - Data required to support big decisions
   - Data available vs. data needed
7. **Big Opportunities and the data needed for analytics**
   - Identify 10% of big opportunities which could account for 90% of future growth
   - Identify data needed to analyze for each of the identified opportunities.
8. **Big Risks (threats) and the data needed for analytics**
   - Identify 10% of big risks which could potentially cripple the company
   - Identify data needed to analyze for each of the identified risks.

D. Set and Consolidate Corporate Business Objectives – For an Integrated Data Strategy

Building a future-proof data strategy requires capturing all the anticipated and planned requirements of enterprise as delineated in its strategy map and balanced scorecard. Here is a checklist for aligning the enterprise data strategy with the overall corporate strategy.

1. **Corporate Business Objectives** – financial, customer, operational, learning, and growth as per the strategy map and the balanced scorecard.
2. **Derive and Consolidate Goals of Data Strategy – DEFINE GOALS**.
   - **Data-definitions**: Organization-wide common data-definitions and data glossary
   - **Data Standards**: Organization-wide data standards.
   - **Data Interoperability**: Set-up and maintain look-up tables for interoperability
   - **DTD**: Document type definitions for XML
   - **MASTER DATA**: Master data management mechanism
   - **Metadata**: Organization-wide metadata standards
   - **Document Types**: categorize and catalog document types, keywords/tags
   - **Governance Mechanism: Comprehensive Governance Mechanism**
     a. Committee constitution, escalation model
     b. GSOPs and templates for data lifecycle management and information life-cycle management

E. Build a New and Comprehensive Enterprise Data Structure

1. **Delta-Data sourcing strategy for entities across enterprise**
2. **Extend information supply-chain to cover complete value-chain**
3. **Create applications assets and data elements to cover value-chain**
4. **Generate missing data**
   4a) **Create Data**
      - Missing data for decision support
      - Missing data for incremental granularity
      - Missing data for improving searchability (tags, codes etc.)
      - Parse and split columns for improving searchability.
      - Additional columns for standardizing data
      - Look-up tables and integration tables
   4b) **Update Data**
      - Source and update data and tags
      - Update missing units, missing definitions
      - Update missing standards
   4c) **Delete Data**
      - Delete / archive applications, tables, columns – surplus to requirements
      - Delete /archive unwanted data

F. IMPLEMENT and INSTITUTIONALIZE – The New Data Structure, Process, Protocols and Governance Model

1. Set-up MDM
2. Set-up PLM
3. Configure and set-up a DAM
4. Document Management System DMS
5. Set-up systems for tagging, archiving, retrieving
6. Set-up governance committee(s)
7. Set-up GSOPs and templates
8. Data standards, data definitions, interoperability, look-up tables, metadata, document types, keywords, tags etc.
9. Set-up cyber security protocols
10. Protocols for new data creation and updation
    - Master data
    - Transactional data
11. Set-up data quality audit protocols
12. Set-up application lifecycle management protocol
13. Set-up data / information lifecycle management protocols

Bibliography

Bowen, R., & Smith, A. R. (2014). Developing an enterprise-wide data strategy: data integrity is a critical concern for both the clinical and financial sides of the healthcare enterprise, ensuring both quality of care provided and accurate payment for services--and that also makes it a cr. *Healthcare Financial Management*, 68(4), 86–90.

Chang, W. L., & Grady, N. (2019). NIST big data interoperability framework: Volume 1, definitions.

Constantiou, I. D., & Kallinikos, J. (2015). New games, new rules: big data and the changing context of strategy. *Journal of Information Technology*, 30(1), 44–57.

DalleMule, L., & Davenport, T. H. (2017). What's your data strategy. *Harvard Business Review*, 95(3), 112–121.

Davenport, T. H., & Redman, T. C. (2020). Your organization needs a proprietary data strategy. *Harvard Business Review*, 2–6.

Heudecker, N. (2014). Big data challenges move from tech to the organization. Gartner Blogs Dec 2, 2014.

Kotwal, N., Wisnia, A. et al. (2017). Chief Data Officer Study. *Strategyandpwc.com*, 2022.

Lakshmanan, V., & Tigani, J. (2019). *Google BigQuery: The Definitive Guide: Data Warehousing, Analytics, and Machine Learning at Scale*. O'Reilly Media.

Maguire, J. (2019). Creating a data strategy. *Gartner Research*, Nov 26, 2019.

Marra, P., Wentz, R., et al. (2020), KPMG Data Strategy Survey. *Advisory.kpmg.us* 2020.

Mazzei, M. J., & Noble, D. (2017). Big data dreams: A framework for corporate strategy. *Business Horizons*, 60(3), 405–414.

McGroder, D., & Lashlee, J. (2011, April). An Emerging DoD M&S Enterprise Data Strategy. In *Proceedings of the Spring 2011 Simulation Interoperability Workshop*.

Nelson, G. S. (2017). *Developing Your Data Strategy: A Practical Guide*. Thotwave Technol. Chapel Hitt, NC, 1–15.

Redman, T. C. (1998). The impact of poor data quality on the typical enterprise. *Communications of the ACM*, 41(2), 79–82.

Reinking, J., Arnold, V., & Sutton, S. G. (2020). Synthesizing enterprise data to strategically align performance: The intentionality of strategy surrogation. *International Journal of Accounting Information Systems*, 36, 100444.

Rifaie, M., Alhajj, R., & Ridley, M. (2009, December). Data governance strategy: A key issue in building enterprise data warehouse. In *Proceedings of the 11th International Conference on Information Integration and Web-based Applications & Services* (pp. 587–591).

SAS (2018). The five essential components of a data strategy. *SAS White Paper*, 2018. https://www.sas.com/content/dam/SAS/en_au/doc/whitepaper1/five-essential-components-data-strategy.pdf

Stackpole, B. (2021). Making the business case for a chief data officer. *MIT Management Sloan School*, Feb 8, 2021.

The MIT CISR Data Research Advisory Board (2018). How to create a successful data strategy?. *MIT Center for Information Systems Research*, Nov 2018.

Chapter 10

Building a Data-Driven Marketing Strategy*

Topics Covered in this Chapter

1. What prevents the companies making data-driven marketing decisions	80% of the companies do not make data-driven marketing decisions, and those few who do are the leaders.
2. The data you need vs. the data you have	The most critical information needed for devising a market-strategy is the data available elsewhere, outside of the organization's ERP.
3. Should the FSE be collecting data or acting based on it?	Not many companies talk about enabling the field sales force with actionable information that helps them maximize sales, and personal productivity.
4. Marketing strategy: The anatomy of hitherto unresolved problems	Gist of hitherto never resolved issues in building a marketing-strategy.
5. Operating blind!	Marketing managers are forced to "operate blind" in the absence of real-time data and drill-down analytics for each micro-market.

* Part of this chapter was first published as an article in Data Science Central earlier (Jan. 2019).

DOI: 10.1201/9781003321347-11

6. And the blind leading the blind!	In the absence of data, marketing-decisions like where to locate new dealers / FSEs are purely gut-based decisions.
7. The importance of location data	'Location-data" is important because the "customer profiles and preferences" can be vastly different in different markets.
8. Sight to the blind: Building a data-driven marketing function	Estimating the market-size of each micro-market based on meta-data & Building a marketing strategy customized for each micro-market.
9. The big marketing decisions	Once the market-data and the internal-sales data, are geo-tagged and integrated into one consolidated data-base, building big-decision specific dashboards should be simple and easy.

INTRODUCTION

Organizations, often in their "me-too" hurry to adopt a new technology, just pour their old wine (data) into a new bottle. What was originally called a "sales information system" in the good old days underwent many avatars before it became BI (business intelligence for sales) and of late, it is time to switch again. In its latest avatar, it is called a "data visualization tool", and every CIO has a budget. Data visualization tools, undoubtedly offer a much better interface for sales and marketing teams to analyze data in their quest to do better, besides serving as a platform for "self-service analytics". The believers in data visualization (I am one of them) argue that plain metrics do not offer much of an insight, let alone actionable insights; while a well-constructed motion chart or a heat map could actually open the doors to insights that an old-fashioned marketing manager did not even dream of.

Data visualization is about cajoling the data to tell you a story; an interesting story with a lesson and insights that can transform the functioning of the marketing department. However, the purpose of this chapter is not to list ten best data visualization tools, or how wonderful they are in transforming the way the marketing manager devises his strategy. This is still about the data that resides inside the visualization tool that ultimately should provide actionable insights. The question is: do you have enough right data for your visualization tool? And there is lot more to data-driven marketing than just a visualization tool…

10.1 What Prevents the Companies Making Data-Driven Marketing Decisions?

A decade back, Prof. Mark Jeffrey of Kellogg School of Management, wrote about data-driven marketing (Jeffery, 2010) based on his research covering some 252 global companies with over $53 billion in marketing spend. His research indicated that 80% of the companies did not make data-driven marketing decisions, and those few who did were the leaders. As to why companies found data-driven marketing so difficult; a wide variety of reasons were listed, including:

- Not knowing how
- Too much data
- Too little time and limited resources
- Lack of analytics infrastructure to crunch the numbers

Prof. Jeffrey makes a perfectly valid argument: to get started you will never need 100% of data and multi-million dollar infrastructure. All you need is the "right data", and even if you do not have the data, you could use "proxy data" and customer surveys. The book also lists 15 important metrics everyone in the marketing should know: *the 15 metrics possibly represent the 15 "big" decisions to start from.*

I had a couple of other concerns as I was reading the book:

1. Customer surveys and other proxy data that Prof. Mark Jeffrey is referring to provide static data, meaning data "as of a date", or data pertaining to a period. Is this good enough for day-to-day ongoing marketing decisions? From my experience, market preferences and customer preferences, are always in flux; ever-changing moving targets.
2. Whether it is customer surveys, or other proxy data, it is bound to be *macro-level* data, meaning country-level average numbers for a customer segment, or for a product line. Does macro-data sans granularity really cover the singularly unique requirements for each of the micro-market segments the company operates in? Even if you do conduct a market survey every couple of months, you will still end up with indicative macro-market data. No company can afford to conduct market surveys in thousands of the market segments.

Considering this book was published in 2010, it is possible that a lot more companies could be making data-driven marketing decisions as of now, but I doubt if the type of data that is being used has substantially changed, especially considering most of the companies included in the research were not internet companies. While every surviving brick-and-mortar company has a digital strategy now, they still do not have the kind of granular, direct customer data that an internet company would take it for granted.

On the other hand, internet companies, specifically the Amazon kind of companies, have more granular data than they know what do with; every transaction can be tracked to a specific customer, and complete customer data could be found within the four walls of Amazon's data centers. As of 2021, while five of the global top 10 companies by market capitalization are internet companies, they still only account for two of the top 10 by revenue. The brick-and-mortar companies, retailers, banks, insurance companies and the like will never have the kind of granular customer data that an Amazon or Google can take for granted. The question is: what happens to them? Will they ever be able to do the kind of data-driven marketing that an Amazon or a Google can do with their eyes closed?

10.2 The Data that You Need vs. The Data that You Have

The spoiler, as usual, is "the data", or the lack of it.

Typical sales information system has limited value as it (essentially) slices and dices the same internal sales data. Last year vs. current year, or drill-down by product geography is the extent to which transactional data exists. Almost all of it is a post facto analysis, often used for forecasting based on historical data.

A typical marketing sales manager uses the sales information system for reporting requirements, usually when they need to submit a monthly report or make a PowerPoint for someone, but rarely ever as a tool to draw much needed insights for devising market strategy. For example: evaluation of a Dealer's performance or a field sales executive's performance gets done purely based on an internal target vs. actual, never on actual opportunity size vs. performance. Critical information like top 10 micro-markets by each state where majority of ad spend should be focused, or where exactly the market size justifies recruitment of more dealers or expansion of field sales force, among others, are all decisions based on collective gut feeling. The reasons are not difficult to see…

The critical information needed for devising a market strategy is the data available elsewhere, outside of the organization's enterprise resource planning (ERP). Namely – *the market opportunity size by product and the ever-changing customers' preferences by each micro-market, in each town and village, every year.*

Figure 10.1 depicts the data conundrum in the context of data-driven marketing. Only a small fraction of the actual data needed to make a data-driven marketing strategy will be available within the enterprise data. The larger market data that can be used to determine the opportunity size in each territory for each of the products will have to be sourced from outside of the enterprise (Figure 10.1).

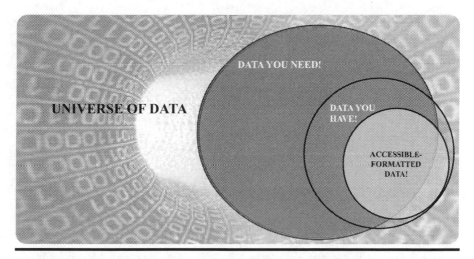

Figure 10.1 The data that you need vs. the data that you have.

Customers' profiles, their preferences, local factors and so on are very different in different micro-markets (small towns and villages) and hence determine the market size for a specific product or the relative market share of each brand, in each of the micro-markets. The marketing strategy (product, promotion, pricing, etc.) needs to be customized for each micro-market.

10.3 Should the FSE Be Collecting Data or Acting Based On It?

While every organization agrees a company's performance is usually just as good as its field sales force; the field sales executive (FSE), more often than not, is a low-paid, nameless, faceless guy who operates out of remote areas, never seen even at the regional headquarters except once-a-year during the budgeting season. The FSE is supposed to have his ear to the ground, know the local markets well, visit the key end-customers, and meet the dealers regularly. The FSE is at the bottom of the pyramid, where the rubber meets the road... hence, his mobile is tracked, he is asked to file status reports monthly, weekly, and in a few cases daily... in essence, a source for ground-level information.

A ship earns revenue when it is traveling from port to port, carrying goods on high seas, and it earns zero revenues while being moored at the docks. In fact, it has to pay berthing charges for each day it spends immobile and idle in a port. This analogy is absolutely true in case of the FSE too. The FSE should be on the field: meeting customers – both existing and prospective –, meeting dealers, resolving quality issues and logistics issues, striving for increasing the revenue, and meeting sales targets. The more time FSE spends on the field, the more productive FSE is. The more time FSE spends in the office, filing reports or collating and sending data to head office, the less productive FSE becomes.

However, it is not unusual to see organizations looking at the FSE as a key source of current market information, the daily happenings on the ground, reported through a "must-do" document called a "daily call report". The daily call report is supposed to be a proof of activity for the unsupervised FSE, besides being a source of useful information on what the customers and dealers are experiencing. The report is usually filed through a form on the CRM platform or just by an email or text, depending on the protocol and the comfort level between the FSE and his immediate manager.

The data from such daily call reports is to be collated and communicated upward right up to the marketing head on a daily basis. If the CRM if fully functional, technically any senior managers could log in and see a consolidated report either for an individual customer or for a territory. The sales executive typically is given access to their own customers at best... a consolidated report generated from their own data (Figure 10.2).

The sales information system – whatever may be the mode or the nomenclature, is almost always made for the higher management to review the performance of sales executives, and in most cases even the basic transaction level drill-down itself is never there, let alone a drill-down view of market intelligence by each village.

In my experience, *I have not seen any sales information reports being generated specifically to enable a field sales executive to do a better job.* Not many companies talk about enabling the field sales force with useful information – actually helping them maximize sales, and productively use their time.

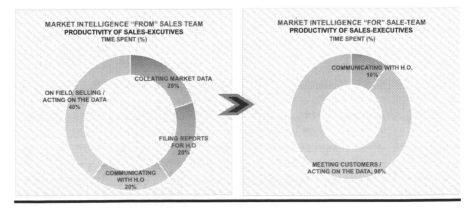

PRODUCITIVTY OF DATA-DRIVEN SALES TEAM

Figure 10.2   Productivity of data-driven sales team.

10.4 Marketing Strategy: The Anatomy of Hitherto Unresolved Problems

Most organizations devise a marketing strategy at a macro-aggregate level which seldom percolates down, customized for the specific needs of each micro-market. Geography-specific investments are rarely rational data-driven decisions.

Many organizations struggle to answer questions such as where to locate/recruit dealers, where to locate warehouses, ad spend, territory panning and so on. Metrics collection and reporting is almost always bottom up. The FSE (or the dealer, where rubber meets the road) is the chief source of market intelligence – which gets collated and supplied on a dashboard to the CxOs. While most companies have invested into CRMs, the source of market intelligence has not changed yet... it still continues to be the ever-reliable FSE.

As mentioned earlier, the typical sales information system has limited value as it essentially slices and dices the same internal sales data. Last year vs. current year, or drill-down by product geography the extent to which the transactional data exists. Nearly almost all of it tends to be post facto analysis, best used for forecasting based on historical data, or sometimes for root cause analysis; there is little that enables FSEs by providing actionable insights that help them to do a better job at bringing in incremental sales.

Why is enabling the FSEs with actionable insights important, assuming the organization believes in enabling FSEs rather than policing them?

1. To start with, the FSE is the person who can actually act based on certain field-level actionable insights. For example, in direct selling, it is important for the FSE to prioritize the specific customers who are most likely to close the orders in a particular month. In the case of mass-distributed products, the FSE has to prioritize and visit the territories (towns and villages) which account for relatively larger sales, for a specific season. *The managers, even if they do have such information will have to act through the FSE.*

2. Customer profiles and their preferences can be vastly different between different territories. The demographics and lifestyles could be vastly different between two neighboring counties, and the consumer behavior could be diagonally different. Most importantly the market size can be different in different territories. Even if the market size is comparable, it is possible there may be more early adapters in one territory compared to the neighboring one. For example, if a an agricultural district's primary crop is wheat, it is likely to have a bigger demand for the pesticide glyphosate, while a neighboring district's primary crop being corn, there could be larger demand for Atrazine. It is possible a close neighboring district might have gone *completely organic*, and hence may not have any demand for insecticides or pesticides.

   This essentially means, there is a strong need for analytics customized for each territory, for each micro-market; and for each FSE assigned to a specific territory.

3. In most organizations, marketing strategy is a macro-level document, usually an addendum to the business strategy and corporate balanced scorecard. It seldom percolates down to the bottommost layers, where the rubber meets the road. The FSEs usually live their lives one week at a time, or one month at a time, depending on how frequently they have a review call. The only strategy they know is a set of action items handed down by the immediate reporting manager.

10.5 Operating Blind

In a good many organizations, there is a lag between the date of transaction, and the date by which it is reflected in the central IT system, or the ERP of the company. The lag could be anywhere between a few days to few months.

- The reasons could be anything from using a separate disconnected point of sale (PoS) application where the actual invoicing happens, to pure indiscipline.
- The tell-tale signs that all is not well with the IT systems are visible when *the company takes enormously long time to declare the audited financials every quarter.*
- Multiple disconnected applications mean multiple hand-offs in the information chain, and, more disturbingly, multiple data standards which make tasks like the corporate consolidation of financials every quarter a nightmarishly difficult exercise.
- The tell-tale signs include hundreds of Excel sheets of floating around and sales and finance teams burning midnight oil each time the top management asks for a slightly different report.

Since there is a time-lag, the reports do not reflect the reality in real time; as a result, the marketing managers tend to develop a deep distrust of IT reports. Many resort to running a parallel system on Excel, as a private stash of data.

Marketing managers may fail to find the right expression, but instinctively know what they want. They prefer the field sales force to spend more time actually selling on the ground, rather than sitting in the branch office filing reports. They prefer the IT Department to be the source of information on demand for all reports and know the right information, aka actionable insights, delivered on demand can help the field sales force improve their performance by leaps and bounds.

But, more often than not, marketing managers operate at the mercy of the CIO. Given that they are not sufficiently tech-savvy, they blindly accept whatever system the CIOs push as the latest miraculous cure. Marketing managers fervently hope the new miracle solution would finally enable their team to act on the data, rather than continue to be suppliers of the data; enable them to *spend more time actually selling rather than hunting for data.*

CIOs on the other hand complain that systems are perfect, but the so-called marketing managers are like cave-dwellers, painfully slow to adopt and use such wonderful systems.

The truth in fact lies elsewhere.

Who exactly has responsibility for gathering market data? Marketing managers instinctively know the best actionable insights can only be generated when somehow internal sales data is combined with the market intelligence data; they also know all the market intelligence data that their teams have gathered essentially amounts to a set of word documents collated out of market grapevine… they know they would need *numbers* for analytics. While they have been hearing wonderful things about *social media data*, they are unsure how exactly it can be converted into actionable market intelligence.

While CIOs can take ownership of crunching the internal sales data and providing the best possible analytics to the marketing teams, they have no means or method to source the all-important market intelligence data, let alone combine the external market intelligence, and the internal sales data to provide those eye-opening actionable insights that marketing managers actually need (Figure 10.3).

Some CIOs have made excellent use of social media data, specifically in areas like understanding:

- Customer preferences, customer likes and dislikes.
- Brand health core issues with the products.
- The product's rating reflecting perceived value in the minds of customers.

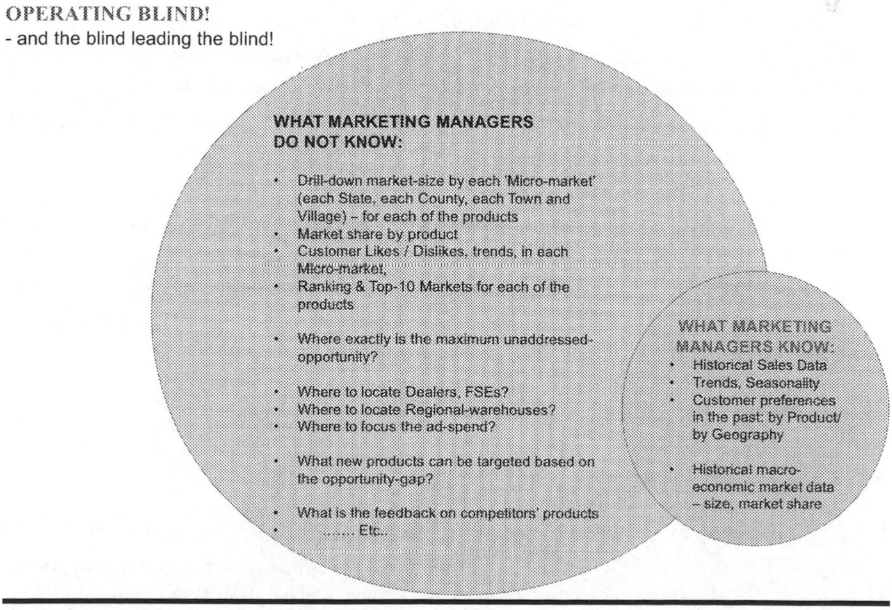

Figure 10.3   Operating blind!

In reality, most organizations *live in blissful ignorance*, and are unaware of the fact that data-driven marketing in the true sense is possible only by combining the market intelligence data and internal sales data and building analytics on top of it. Those few who do, are confused as to who should take responsibility for gathering the market intelligence data and how exactly this should be done.

10.6 And the Blind Leading the Blind

In my experience, marketing managers deeply distrust the data provided by internal IT departments. One often finds them developing a parallel information system on Excel sheets with data painstakingly collected from sales team or from dealers (we have covered this with reference to the theory of asymmetric information in Chapter 1).

A typical marketing manager uses the sales information system purely for reporting requirements, usually when needing to submit a monthly report, or when making a PowerPoint for someone, *but rarely as a tool to draw much needed insights for devising a market strategy*.

Most sales information systems do provide some useful data and insights, for example, the trend analysis of historical data, the impact of seasonality on specific products, or the projected forecast for each product based on the trends. While the data is definitely discussed during a budgeting session to fix the sales targets, the managers are more likely make important decisions based on the collective judgment of their teams.

For example, evaluation of a dealer's performance or a field sales executive's performance gets done purely based on an internal target vs. actual numbers; never on territory opportunity size vs. actual performance. Critical information like the top 10 micro-markets by each state, where the majority of ad spend should be focused, or where exactly the market size justifies recruitment of more dealers or expansion of field sales force are all decisions based on collective gut feeling.

The distrust between the marketing and the IT departments apart, the critical information needed for devising a market strategy is *the data available* outside of the organization's enterprise applications; specifically – the market opportunity size by product-geography and the ever-changing customer's preferences by *each micro-market, in each town and village, every year*. A good number of CIOs and a larger number of marketing managers are blind to this fact!

10.7 The Importance of Location Data

So far, the social media data available is largely macro-market data. This might change in future with 5G, if more comprehensive location data is made available along with the social media data. But as of now, we do not know if social media users would be willing to share their location data as freely, as it could mean losing their anonymity, and privacy. Most likely, they won't!

As mentioned before, location data is important because the customer profiles and preferences can be vastly different in different markets, and a majority of the marketing spend is allocated to different geographies. For example, the ad spend is typically allocated to different states and regions based on their size and population. However, further allocation within those states, is left to the discretion of the regional managers.

A granular nationwide micro-market data can help focusing the market spend on 10% of the micro-markets which account for 90% of the potential business, bringing in 10-fold returns for each dollar spent on marketing.

10.8 Sight to the Blind: Building a Data-Driven Marketing Function

10.8.1 Building Geospatial Analytics for Micro-Market Data

While there must be any number of approaches for gathering market intelligence, I prefer estimating the market size for each micro-market based on the metadata for each of the micro-markets; the metadata for geotagged micro-markets, which can be subjected to spatial analytics (Figure 10.4).

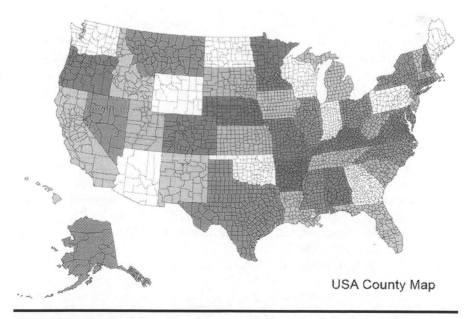

USA County Map

Figure 10.4   Selling in micro-markets.

The advantages of using metadata for micro-markets include:

- It need not be a frequent exercise.
- It can even be derived from census data; assuming the census data is complete, and error free.
- And most importantly, the same metadata can be used for estimating the market size for a variety of products.

For example, if we know the number of children below the age of five, we should be able to estimate the number of preschools required, how many are currently there, and the location specific gap that needs to be addressed. If we know the number of men between the ages of 17 and 70 in a set of micro-markets, we can estimate the approximate market size for shaving products. The same meta data can be used for a wide variety of applications from estimating the market size for different products to, making data-driven decisions like where to locate new retail stores and new gas stations, or where to recruit new dealers.

In my view, having the right data ready and accessible is a prerequisite for building a data-driven marketing function. Hence, defining the micro-markets, geotagging each one of them, and building comprehensive metadata are the necessary first steps before preparing the right data, which in this context is the complete market data for each of the micro-markets, for a set of products the organization in question wishes to market.

The step-by-step approach is explained below:

Step 1: Defining a Micro-market: There is no single definition of what constitutes a micro-market; it can be as granular as a marketing manager wants. For example, while a typical grocery retail chain like Walmart could define each village or a town as a micro-market, a unique lifestyle retailer like IKEA may not need to get so granular. IKEA perhaps could define each county as a micro-market.

Step 2: Geotagging the Micro-markets: It is best to define the micro-markets as per standard political divisions – like states, counties, towns and villages. An organization may choose one or more of towns/villages or counties as its micro-market. Census data websites in some countries like the USA come equipped with geo-coder tools (Morland & Shank, 2020). If not, the data can be geo-tagged using a paid geo-coding application like Google maps API (Hu & Dai, 2013).

From my personal experience: the process may look simple, but in practice, it is definitely not. Here is why:

- The census is mandated by US Constitution to take place every 10 years; the data is fairly accurate, and the processes seems to have been broadly standardized. (I did come across a couple of papers (O'Hare, 2019) questioning the quality). However, the quality and the completeness of census data is questionable in most countries. For example, in India nearly half the villages do not show up in most states, at least in publicly accessible websites. The numbers, names, and the sub-districts and districts they belong to, can all be wrong.

- The Geocoder applications are designed to fetch the geolocation (the lat-long value) based on the best match to the addresses provided in your data set. Usually, you may get a maximum of 50–60% geocodes in the first try. You are expected to correct your addresses, add/remove zip codes, and make multiple attempts to get the geocodes for 80–90% of the records.
- The rest will have to be done manually, or you have to segregate the records – correct the addresses and try again.
- Typically, a batch of records in CSV format are to be uploaded. For example, the US Census Geocoder allows 10,000 records per batch. Google used to allow some 2500 records per day for free, and a higher volume at a fee, currently being calculated on a pay-as-you-go model, subject to a quota of 50 QPS (queries per second).

Step 3: Creating the Metadata: While the US Census provides fairly comprehensive metadata for each of the states, counties, towns, and villages it is up to your organization's specific requirements as to what data sets you would like to choose for your metadata.

In countries like India, while the census data is not either complete or accurate, it does capture most of the demographic and economic data that forms the basis for calculating the potential market size for different products. While the 2011 census was a paper-based census, the 2024 census is expected to be a digital census (an e-survey) and hence more accurate.

The metadata however is not just downloaded census data. It has to be supplemented with other sources of data including:

A. Insights from your internal historical data and sample surveys:
- Typical customer profiles for each of your current products
- Expected customer profiles for your new products being launched
- Per capita consumption of the products – by geography / by gender etc.
- Seasonality of sales

B. Industry Surveys and Market Research firms (like A.C. Nielsen)
- Competition
- Market shares
- Per capita consumption
- Market share trends if any
- Brand equity
- Perception maps of different competing brands and changes over the years

Step 4: Building an Algorithm: Once the metadata by each micro-market is ready, juxtaposed with your product-wise data like per capita consumption, competition, and market share, an algorithm can be built to estimate the market size for each of your products. For example:

A. The overall market size for each of your products, in each micro-market. (This number represents the total market size for the product. For example:

the total market size for air-conditioners in a micro-market could be $10 million, while combined sales of all the brands put together could be $6 million... meaning there is an unaddressed opportunity of $4 million in the micro-market).

B. Actual combined sales of entire industry in each micro-market.

C. Unaddressed opportunity in each micro-market.

D. Your estimated market share in each micro-market, depending on your customer profile.

E. Your estimated revenue etc.

Step 5: Pouring the Market Data into a Visualization Platform: The geotagged market data needs to be uploaded into a visualization platform with geospatial analytics capability. The visualization platform can be any – it could be Power BI, Tableau, or QlikView; whichever platform your company has been using for sales analytics.

I personally used a natural language processing (NLP) based visualization platform called "Vizard" from Infruid Labs (now acquired by Pega Systems).

Step 6: Building Data-Driven Marketing Analytics: The market data juxtaposed to your sales data in each of the micro-markets can provide with insights hitherto not possible. Examples below:

- Compare sales opportunity size with actual sales in each micro-market (at village / zip code level).
- Identify high potential underserved markets.
- Focus on 20% of micro-markets, which account for over 80% of potential revenue.
- Deploy sales force closer to large, underserved markets.
- Place new dealers, retailers, or retail outlets closer to market opportunity.
- Improve territory planning while covering all major markets in each district and sub-district.
- Measure and reward sales performance on actual service levels in each market and on fulfillment of opportunity.
- Plan sales targets based on market opportunity at the granularity of a zip code/village.
- Eliminate blind spots and unlock insights with inside-out (from transactional data) and outside-in (from micro-market data) perspectives.
- Allocate 80% of marketing spend of 20% of micro-markets which account for 80% of the potential dollar revenue (Figure 10.7).

CASE STUDY

An agrochemicals manufacturing company based in India, has over 5000 FSEs located in 21 different states. Considering each FSE can cover a maximum of 18 villages, the total number of villages the sales team can cover will be 90,000, while India has over 600,000 villages. The FSE is expected to visit both the dealers as well as the farmers, to promote the brand and push the sales of specific products.

Further, the company sells through some 16000+ dealers on record, while they estimate no more than 60% of the dealers are active on the ground. The 5000 FSE and 16000+ dealers are being managed through a field sales management team of 500+ managers located in different districts and states.

Their IT infrastructure includes a fairly stable SAP instance along with a variety of smaller legacy applications. Considering the primary sales are all directly to the dealers – there is practically no lag in capturing the transactions in SAP. Most of the sales reports are being generated out of Excel, from data downloaded from SAP.

The "known questions" they were trying to answer included:

1. Considering we have enough FSEs to cover only a fraction of the total market, have we deployed our FSEs in the right locations?
2. Did we recruit the right dealers in the right locations?
3. What can we do to substantially increase our market share and revenue?

The solution proposed:

We proposed to do the project in two separate phases. In Phase 1, we proposed to create a market data base covering over 500,000 villages across 21 states. The idea was to collate the data from the census and other sources, geotag the villages, and load the data into a visualization platform, purely for the purpose of understanding where exactly the largest of the markets are located.

The "unknown questions" (the questions they were not asking) that we added as a part of the project deliverables included:

Phase 1

1. Which are the top 10 villages in terms of market opportunity size in each sub-district, each district, in each of the states? For each of the products?
2. Which 20% of the villages, sub-districts, districts account for 80% of the market?

Phase 2

3. What products have larger demand in each micro-market and what products are you actually selling?
4. What products are in demand in a particular season in each market and what products are you actually selling? (The crop patterns are different in different villages).

5. What is the opportunity size in each micro-market vs. the actual sales?
6. Which 20% of villages account for 80% of unaddressed opportunity?

Solution Delivery:

The most popular method for estimating the area covered by different crops and studying the cropping patterns is by creating a spatial database from remote sensing maps from ISRO in India, or from European Sentinel database (now called Copernicus Open Access Hub). While ISRO did not have a comprehensive Agri database then, it has a substantially improved version in the current Bhuvan initiative. But there were several issues with this method. While it could work for an overall macro-level calculation of the kind of crops being grown in a state, area in hectares covered by each crop, estimated total produce and so on based on NDVI data, it was very difficult to break up the estimates to micro-market level. Besides, the remote sensing maps did not show village boundaries then, while they do as of now. The remote sensing data is essentially for one-time use. Since our core purpose was to create metadata for each village, we had to look for alternative methods.

While researching for this book, I have also come across a 2020 article by Stanford students titled "Mapping Crop Types in Southeast India with Smartphone Crowdsourcing and Deep Learning" (Wang et al., 2020). While I am not sure of the efficacy of the method proposed in the paper, I believe crowd-sourcing the exact "crop patterns" from each of the villages in India – using a mobile-app with "geo-fencing" functionality… may definitely work (assuming you get a tech-savvy farmer from each village to use the mobile-app and do the needful).

We started off by downloading the census records. Since census data was incomplete, we had to collate and complete the data from some 19 other state and private databases. While the task was time-consuming and resource intensive, we did manage to complete it eventually.

The metadata for calculating the market size for agrochemicals included 30+ columns; the most important include (Figures 10.5 and 10.6).

- Net sown area in each village.
- Irrigation percentage (through borewells or otherwise).
- Top three crops (accounting for 70–80% of net sown area).
- Area under each of the crops in each micro-market (irrigated/not irrigated).
- No. of crops per year. In some villages it is three, and in some it is one, and so on.

There are several varieties of agrochemicals; insecticides, pesticides, herbicides, fungicides, etc.; and broadly we know how much of agrochemical products of

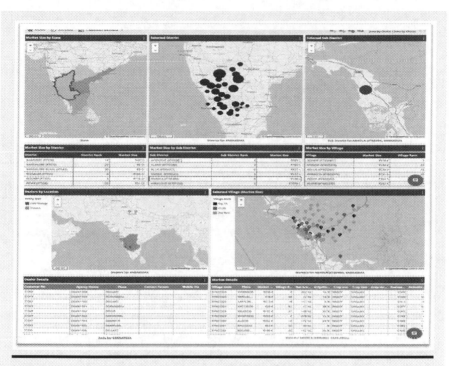

Figure 10.5 Geospatial analytics for micro-market data.

each type would be required for each variety of crop per acre. An algorithm was built to calculate the approximate market size for each of the product categories for each of the villages. The algorithm was validated in workshop session by comparing the actual numbers with the estimated numbers for a fairly large sample.

Complete geotagged data along with the estimates was uploaded into a visualization platform (Figure 10.6). I used Infruid Lab's Vizard (Now part of Pega Systems) as the software of choice for the first implementation. Any sales executive could access the feature-rich interactive dashboard to slice and dice and analyze the markets right up to village level, for each crop, and for each product. Vizard also had an NLP feature – a query-builder with English-like syntax; Any business user can frame & ask questions as per a standard English-like syntax, and the query is automatically built and executed.

Phase 2 was a bigger challenge; as we needed to upload the complete customer-dealer master, and product masters into Vizard. We mapped each dealer to a set of micro-markets, but we further needed to map each transaction to a precise village. Since such granular break up was not possible with the way SAP was configured, an algorithm had to be developed to allocate dealer sales to each village. Once again this algorithm had to be validated with the actual numbers from a fairly large, and diverse sample. Both the

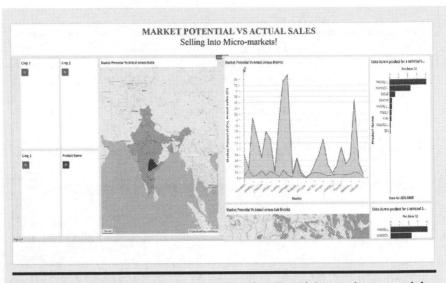

Figure 10.6   The actual sales are usually a fraction of the market potential.

customer-master and material-master in SAP had to be revamped with additional data.

A protocol with a built-in script for data validation, had to be established for automatically uploading the SAP transactions of the day into Vizard, every night on a batch-mode. Once again, a set of user-specific dashboards were built to provide analytics on demand.

Our idea was to become a value-added reseller of a data visualization tool like Tableau or QlikView, sell the products preloaded with the complete market data for each of the 650,000 villages in India. All you have to do is upload your sales data and viola, you have micro-market insights (Figure 10.6) that you have only dreamed of, but never seen before.

Post implementation of Phase 2, I started asking the users (sales managers) if they use the Vizard on a regular basis. As I talked to them, I realized that while sales managers had definitely felt empowered to make data-driven decisions, I had not exactly enabled the ground-level FSE. My client was not in a position to buy an additional 5000 user licenses to cover every one of those FSEs. While the area managers and above do spend time in the office accessing Vizard to make decisions, the FSE is always in the field, and there is little in terms of analytics percolating down to the FSE to do a better job.

I am currently working on developing the complete functionality on a mobile application to be made accessible to every FSE in the field. The mobile application, besides providing prescriptive analytics on the go for the FSE, would also track their location and activity for eight working hours a day (time spent with dealer, farmers or elsewhere), bringing in a 24/7 visibility for the managers to track the FSEs, their sales routes and so on to analyze if they are productively using their time. The mobile-app also comes with a twitter like interface that can be used by FSEs to record their interaction with the customers & dealers in 140 characters; each message gets geo-tagged to the specific customer/micro-market, and the managers can respond back in 140 characters too.

10.9 The Big Marketing Decisions

Once the complete market data and the internal sales data, all geotagged is available in one consolidated data base on a visualization tool, building big-decision specific dashboards should be simple and easy to handle.

As we have discussed in Chapters 5, and 6, identifying the "big" marketing decisions from the master list of marketing decisions will have to be a separate exercise; and these "big" decisions can be very different for different companies.

For example, for an Amazon kind of company with all sales happening online, improving the click-rate or click-through-rate (CTR) is a very important requirement that can substantially affect the top-line. While a Walmart-type company, which has both online and off-line models, with the online sales accounting for only 8–9% of the total sales, the CTR may, or may not be among the "big" decisions. But improving the customer-life-time value is bound to be among the "big" decisions

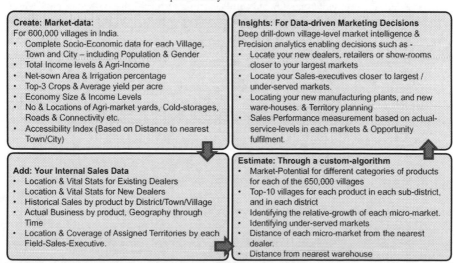

DATA-DRIVEN MARKETING STRATEGY
Geo-spatial Analytics of Micro-market Data

Create: Market-data:
For 600,000 villages in India.
- Complete Socio-Economic data for each Village, Town and City – including Population & Gender
- Total Income levels & Agri-Income
- Net-sown Area & Irrigation percentage
- Top-3 Crops & Average yield per acre
- Economy Size & Income Levels
- No & Locations of Agri-market yards, Cold-storages, Roads & Connectivity etc.
- Accessibility Index (Based on Distance to nearest Town/City)

Insights: For Data-driven Marketing Decisions
Deep drill-down village-level market intelligence & Precision analytics enabling decisions such as -
- Locate your new dealers, retailers or show-rooms closer to your largest markets
- Locate your Sales-executives closer to largest / under-served markets.
- Locating your new manufacturing plants, and new ware-houses. & Territory planning
- Sales Performance measurement based on actual-service-levels in each markets & Opportunity fulfilment.

Add: Your Internal Sales Data
- Location & Vital Stats for Existing Dealers
- Location & Vital Stats for New Dealers
- Historical Sales by product by District/Town/Village
- Actual Business by product, Geography through Time
- Location & Coverage of Assigned Territories by each Field-Sales-Executive.

Estimate: Through a custom-algorithm
- Market-Potential for different categories of products for each of the 650,000 villages
- Top-10 villages for each product in each sub-district, and in each district
- Identifying the relative-growth of each micro-market.
- Identifying under-served markets
- Distance of each micro-market from the nearest dealer.
- Distance from nearest warehouse

Figure 10.7   Building a data-driven marketing strategy.

for both Walmart and Amazon. It is important to go through the comprehensive exercise for identifying the "big" decisions, as relying on the experiences of other companies can be misleading.

Bibliography

Ambika, A. K., Wardlow, B., & Mishra, V. (2016). Remotely sensed high resolution irrigated area mapping in India for 2000 to 2015. *Scientific Data*, 3(1), 1–14.

Braverman, S. (2015). Global review of data-driven marketing and advertising. *Journal of Direct, Data and Digital Marketing Practice*, 16(3), 181–183.

Chavez, T., O'Hara, C., & Vaidya, V. (2018). *Data Driven*. McGraw-Hill Education.

Copernicus, E. U. (n.d.). Access to Copernicus Data.

Hu, S., & Dai, T. (2013). Online map application development using Google Maps API, SQL database, and ASP.NET. *International Journal of Information and Communication Technology Research*, 3(3).

Jeffery, M. (2010). *Data-Driven Marketing: The 15 Metrics Everyone in Marketing Should Know*. John Wiley & Sons.

Kenett, R. S., & Redman, T. C. (2019). *The Real Work of Data Science: Turning Data into Information, Better Decisions, and Stronger Organizations*. John Wiley & Sons.

Morland, M., & Shank, P. (2020). *Explore Census Data–An Introduction and Demonstration*.

O'Hare, W. P. (2019). The Importance of Census Accuracy: Uses of Census Data. In Differential Undercounts in the US Census (pp. 13–24). Springer, Cham.

Redman, Thomas C. (2015). Data-driven marketing: How to engage your customers. HBR, Jan 8, 2015.

Sheth, J., & Kellstadt, C. H. (2021). Next frontiers of research in data driven marketing: Will techniques keep up with data tsunami?. *Journal of Business Research*, 125, 780–784.

Sundsøy, P., Bjelland, J., Iqbal, A. M., Pentland, A., & Montjoye, Y. A. D. (2014, April). Big data-driven marketing: how machine learning outperforms marketers' gut-feeling. In *International Conference on Social Computing, Behavioral-Cultural Modeling, and Prediction* (pp. 367–374). Springer, Cham.

Wang, S., Di Tommaso, S., Faulkner, J., Friedel, T., Kennepohl, A., Strey, R., & Lobell, D. B. (2020). Mapping crop types in southeast India with smartphone crowdsourcing and deep learning. *Remote Sensing*, 12(18), 2957.

Chapter 11

Integrated Data Governance

Topics Covered in this Chapter

Establishing Value from Data Governance	
1. The need for data governance	The data to decisions value-chain however well designed, is not foolproof. The framework can progressively deteriorate in the absence of a robust data governance model.
2. Need for data governance in global organizations: Addressing the stakeholders concerns	A CIO embarking on a transformational journey towards centralized global "data governance" needs to identify and address the concerns of key stakeholders, besides his own. The transformational journey becomes extra-complex when it comes to multinationals with global value-chains, and multiple stakeholders with competing demands.
3. Recognizing poor data governance: The markers	All is not well with the data-quality of a company is easily recognizable, from its symptoms…

DOI: 10.1201/9781003321347-12

4. The cost of poor data governance: Overshooting overheads	Poor data-quality, a result of poor data-governance, leads to a large number of people employed in the completely "avoidable activity" of data reconciliation, besides a far higher process lead-time, higher inventories etc. Further the managers are forced to take decisions purely based on their "gut", as they lose "trust" in data.
Transformational Roadmap for Institutionalizing Data Governance	
5. Transformational roadmap for designing & institutionalizing data governance: An overview	Data governance essentially is about "deciding" how to decide, the bedrock of all digital transformation initiatives in an organization. Organizations necessarily need to get their Data-governance right, if they ever hope to get their data "right".
6. Step 1: Discovery The importance of "data catalog"	The purpose of a "discovery phase" prior to implementing data governance is to map the data from across the enterprise and assess the "current state" of data quality through different stages of data-lifecycle.

7. Step 2: Value definition
 	
  i. Prioritizing the data for governance
  ii. Creating a business-case for data governance
	i. Since we know all data is not equally important, it makes sense to categorize and prioritize the data that absolutely needs governance, rather than spreading the resources thin and wide. The data-governance needs to be focused on *the data that matters*.
	ii. While defining the scope and estimating the investment required is a relatively straight forward exercise, estimating the revenue (cash inflows) is the tricky part. One has to identify the data that can be monetized, before estimating the potential revenue from "monetizing" of such data.

8. Step 3: Plan & build
 	
  i. Components of data governance
  ii. Designing enterprise data governance framework
	i. Not all organizational data is structured, and a good part of it may reside outside of the IT systems, and consequently outside the "purview" of the IT governance.
	ii. Designing the new enterprise data governance framework will become a guided process if it is combined with implementing an "enterprise data governance platform".

9. Step 4: Grow & consolidate institutionalizing data governance	Institutionalizing data governance is best achieved through implementing a data governance software. For ex: an MDM module can help restrict the access to master-data to select individuals.

10. Data governance for big data: The emerging Trends
 	
  i. The importance of data governance for AI economy
  ii. The concept of data lakehouse
	i. Since the effectiveness of AI essentially depends on the quality and richness of the data that organization produces, institutionalizing data governance will be the key to managing the data quality and preparing the organization for the AI economy.
	ii. A data lake-house is a new emerging concept that combines the best of both, data warehouse and a data lake. The idea is to provide a structure and schema even for the "unstructured data".

11. The evolving role of a CDO	More and more organizations are recruiting a dedicated CDO as an investment into managing all "important" asset, the data.

INTRODUCTION

Even if the organizations do get everything right and manage to set up a data-driven organization, the success may not last. The data to decisions value-chain may still fail if the enterprise data governance as a process is not institutionalized through different stages of data life cycle. Data governance is the key to improving the quality of data, and a data-driven organization is meaningless unless the decision-makers have complete trust in the quality of data.

Institutionalizing data governance is an enormous change-management exercise, that requires the change agent investing in addressing the concerns of all the key stakeholders.

While there are hundreds of books and articles on data governance on the market, I believe they do not adequately cover the critical concerns of stakeholders, or that of a chief information officer (CIO) embarking on a transformational journey toward a centralized global data governance set-up.

The biggest gap in my opinion is that they do not emphasize the importance of focusing the data governance effort on the 20% of data that accounts for 80% of all business value (the data that matters). In the absence of such a distinction, the organization would attempt managing all data, both structured and unstructured, irrespective of its importance, spreading its resources thin and wide… and in the end, <u>not</u> managing any data at all.

Answering the questions below will be the core objective of this chapter:

Justifying the need for data governance

1. How does one justify the need for investing in data governance? Is there a greater need for data governance in global companies?
2. How to assess the quality of data and the effectiveness of data governance in an organization?

Building a business case for investing into data governance

3. Is there a correlation between the quality of data, and the operational efficiency? How does one quantify the benefits from improved quality of data?
4. How does one build a business case for investing in data governance? What are the sources of savings? Is monetizing data possible?

Designing and implementing integrated data governance

5. Given not all data is equally important, how does one identify and prioritize the "right" data for governance?
6. What are the key steps in designing and implementing enterprise data governance?

11.1 The Need for Data Governance

Let us assume for a moment an organization manages to get everything right with its IT strategy and data strategy:

- Defines its databases after carefully examining the data requirements across different departments for the purposes of internal and external reporting, business analytics, and statutory compliance.

- Makes sure the data definitions and data standards are clearly laid out. It further makes sure the data granularity is above and beyond its requirements for reporting and analytics. It ensures the master data is clearly defined once, and the same is replicated across different applications.
- Implements a global single instance enterprise resource planning (ERP) and ensures real-time integration of all upstream and downstream applications into the ERP using a state-of-the-art enterprise application integration solution; ensures the data is validated before and after the transactions are replicated in upstream and downstream applications.
- The ERP and connected applications together cover the entire value-chain of the company, and all enterprise data resides within these applications.
- Ensures all transactions (procure-to-pay to order-to-cash) are run within the ERP. No transaction is done outside of the ERP, unless it is in an application fully integrated real time with the centralized ERP.
- The key 10% of the decisions that influence 90% of the business outcomes have been identified. The data to decisions workflow has been reengineered to perfection.
- All data (integrated and normalized) gets captured in real time into a data lake. A state-of-the-art self-service analytics platform sits on top of the data lake. The analytics support the 10% of the decisions that influence 90% of the business outcomes.
- Where possible, decisions are automated; driven by data without any human intervention. In other cases, the executives take decisions purely based on data, and the system creates an audit trail.
- An IT governance board is in place, set up as per COBIT five principles.

By all standards, the organization qualifies to be called a data-driven organization. The question is: Is the system now foolproof … unlikely to ever fail?

My take: The honeymoon may last from a few weeks to few months, while everything works to perfection. However, sooner or later, the organization is likely face moderate-to-serious issues related to master data inconsistency, failing transactions, data upload errors, besides incremental internal customer complaints about not getting the data that they want when they want it.

The reasons are simple to deduce: An organization is always in flux; constant change in the business functions, operational protocols, product portfolio, geographies covered and so on, and such changes need to be accommodated in the configuration of the ERP and master data of different applications, as well as in integration protocols. In the absence of an integrated and institutionalized "governance", it will not take long for everything to fall apart with an ever-widening gap between the organizational reality as reflected by data in the systems, and what exists on the ground for the decision-makers. Further, if nearly all decisions are to be made purely based on insights generated from data, then such insights not only need to reach the right person (decision-maker) at the right time; but also need to reflect the truth on the ground.

Hence, a true data-driven organization cannot exist without an enabling infrastructure and institutionalized and integrated governance...something that goes beyond what COBIT and ITIL frameworks currently prescribe.

One of the European pharma companies I know had a near-perfect IT strategy. They had a global single-instance SAP implementation that covered practically all the business transactions across the world in real time; technically, they could consolidate and close their books of accounts any time. But even there, the R&D teams had a separate set of homegrown applications, with each application an isolated instance with its own database, most of them developed and managed by the scientists themselves. There was an enormous amount of duplication of data, and duplication of effort; the same set of algorithms were being built by different scientists with different degrees of efficacy. They had an outdated LIMS (Laboratory Information Management System), and one of our consulting assignments was to create a business case for investing in an LDAS (Laboratory Data Acquisition System) that could potentially cut down their cycle time and cost by more than 60%.

The need for data governance has a very strong correlation with the three Vs (volume, velocity, and variety) of data. The three Vs are typically very high in multinational B2C companies; given the number of legal entities, countries, and product lines of business (LoBs) that need to be covered are higher than a typical one country-one location companies (Figure 11.1).

The three Vs are far higher and grow exponentially in companies with a strong digital presence. In all my experience, I have never seen an organization that gets everything right. Even if there is such an organization – with a perfect IT strategy, a

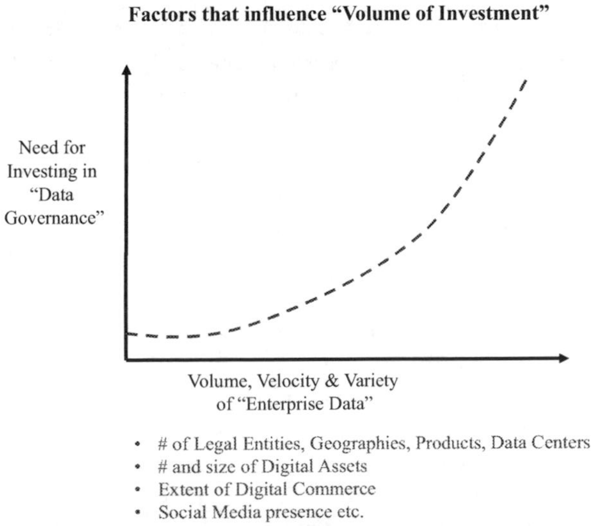

Factors that influence "Volume of Investment"

Need for Investing in "Data Governance"

Volume, Velocity & Variety of "Enterprise Data"

- # of Legal Entities, Geographies, Products, Data Centers
- # and size of Digital Assets
- Extent of Digital Commerce
- Social Media presence etc.

Figure 11.1 Need for investing in data governance.

perfect data strategy, and an IT footprint that covers entire breadth and width of the organization – it *can still fail* in the absence of a perfect governance model.

11.2 Need for Data Governance in Global Organizations: Addressing the Stakeholders' Concerns

A CIO embarking on a transformational journey toward centralized global data governance needs to identify and address the concerns of the stakeholders, besides his own. The transformational journey becomes extra-complex when it comes to multinationals with global value-chains, and multiple stakeholders with competing demands.

11.2.1 What Is so Different about Global Organizations?

Some businesses are simple by nature, all encompassed into a single legal entity and within one country's jurisdiction. Assuming such a business implements a single-instance ERP to cover near 100% of its business transactions and covers its value-chain end-to-end, the data governance in such a business is a fairly simple affair. As long as the master data is meticulously managed, and the ERP gets continuously reconfigured to keep pace with the changes in the value-chain, product portfolio, compliance requirements and so on, the integrity and quality of data can be sustained even without institutionalizing an elaborate IT/data governance model.

However, most businesses are far from simple. Apart from the product and value-chain complexity, the business structure can be complex with multiple legal entities operating in multiple country jurisdictions and tax regimes. Given the compliance requirements in each country could be different, the business processes and value-chains need to be adopted for unique requirements of each of such countries. And such businesses are always in flux – a competitive and dynamic market dictates and necessitates changes in the product portfolios, geographies covered, and business processes, besides continuously changing information demands from the operating managers. More often than not, the multinationals tend to have islands of disconnected applications spread across the landscape with a global IT strategy that is always in a catch-up mode with changing business requirements (Figure 11.2).

In my experience, over 90% of the multinationals suffer from a poorly executed IT strategy and IT service management models. Global consolidation is almost always an exercise handled by a group of overworked accountants manually collating and consolidating data from Excel sheets. Poor data quality and reliability results in managers (consumers of information) circumventing the IT department and running parallel information systems with their own private stash of data. Even

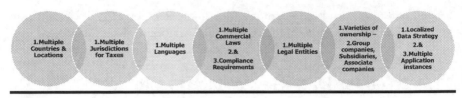

Figure 11.2   The source of data complexity in multinationals.

among the select few multinationals who get their IT strategy mostly right, with a reasonably well-designed set of applications, continuously deteriorating data quality and trust deficit among the consumers of data is common. Each year such multinationals dutifully sink millions of dollars into band-aid applications that aim at resolving the same set of issues, over and over, again and again, while the root cause of problem can always be traced back to data governance or the lack of it.

To conclude, assuming a few select CIOs do plan and execute their IT strategy right, institutionalizing data governance would be the key for ensuring proper data quality and gain the trust of internal consumers of data… and such a data governance should necessarily be integrated and centralized to make it really work.

11.2.2 Local vs. Global: The Need for Integrated and Centralized Data Governance

Many multinationals emphasize the importance of localized decision-making; the importance of taking decisions on the ground and closer to the markets they operate in. While there is nothing wrong with this premise per se, unfortunately the same logic is also applied in areas like design and deployment of IT systems, laying down operating procedures among others, in a mistaken belief that each country would have unique requirements, which get precedence over global corporate requirements (for example, chart-of-accounts standardization at global level to ensure ease of consolidation, operational visibility and control at corporate headquarters). Typically, a local IT Director (or a country CIO) gets to take all decisions on the IT strategy, and the data strategy for the country… hence they would end up with a unique set of isolated application instances, unique data structures, unique data definitions, data standards and so on.

The result is often most visible in the complete chaos at the time of accounts consolidation at global headquarters each quarter; or in the surprising amount of time and manual effort it takes to collate information from each country for consolidating at global level… just about for any information.

On the other hand, a globally centralized data governance, along with global data standards and data definitions, can mean substantial ease in global consolidation of accounts, automated instant portability of data, and a true real-time drill-down visibility into global operations for the top management of the company. However, implementing a centralized global data governance framework could mean an enormous change-management exercise that requires substantial investment in managerial time and effort, besides allocating sizable IT budgets into areas like MDM, global application consolidation, data lakes among others.

CASE STUDY

ACON Group is a conglomerate operating in more than 90 countries, with interests in manufacturing, metals, mining, global trading, shipping among others. ACON started off as a small regional metal scrap trading company in 1930s and grew into the multi-billion conglomerate that it is today, mostly through well-timed acquisitions and mergers. The original promoters are currently minority stakeholders, with the majority of stock being held by a well-known sovereign wealth fund. The company is currently run by professional managers. The corporate HQ in Europe is an essentially a holding company for the 200+ subsidiaries and associate companies (legal entities) operating in different countries across the world; but all global trading transactions go via HQ. The subsidiaries and associate companies do a substantial amount of business between themselves.

ACON believes in decentralized leadership. Hence, the local CEOs are given a free hand to run their companies as they see fit. The local CEOs report to a president (of the respective "lines of business" – LoBs) at the corporate HQ. The top management at the corporate HQ comprises the group CEO, with a set of group presidents responsible or different LoBs reporting to him, apart from global heads of different functions like finance, HR, and IT. The local chief financial officers (CFOs) and CTOs in different countries have a dotted line reporting relationship with the global functional heads. Given the country CTOs had absolute autonomy on what technology they chose, ACON as a group ended up with multiple ERPs, multiple application instances, multiple data centers, and besides, a very diverse set of data standards, and data definitions at each location.

Not surprisingly the corporate financial consolidation of accounts each month, each quarter is a gigantic battle – an exercise in sourcing, validating, and consolidating Excel sheets, with a battery of CPAs and CAs crunching the numbers, fighting against the odds to somehow close the books and declare the results within a deadline. ACON typically takes about seven to eight weeks (after the quarter ends) to declare the audited financials of the company, while some of its competitors manage to do so within two to three weeks. Whenever the ACON corporate asks for any information in a new format, the local CFOs are forced to burn midnight oil, given the difficulties in sourcing the specific information out of (what they call) unyielding, inflexible IT applications. The finance department is forced to add more and more people to its rolls every year, insisting they do need the brute power to coax such unyielding IT applications to produce the financial reports on time to ensure statutory compliance. On average, ACON's overheads grow much faster than its revenue, affecting the profitability.

Vexed with crippling data quality issues and overhead costs, ACON corporate engaged a well-known consulting company to understand the reasons, and possible solutions. The consulting entity listed the following as the key reasons affecting the data quality:

- Master data mismatch between the applications in different countries, coupled with variations in data standards and data definitions is making it impossible to automate the data consolidation at the corporate headquarters. The manual cleaning and reconciliation of data from different source systems is consuming enormous resources in time and effort.
- Data design in each country being different, there is not only a mismatch in what data is being captured and reported in each country, but also the granularity with which data is being captured.
- Corporate consolidation is mostly an exercise in collating data in excel sheets, and often the data that gets captured at corporate level are just consolidated numbers – (For example: Total sales and total changes in the inventory in a month in each country) consolidated numbers that cannot be drilled down into transaction level.

The corporate created the new role of global CIO fairly recently and the CDO of a similar sized rival organization was headhunted and brought in to fill the role. The CIO's brief on joining was succinct: Transform the company into a data-driven organization. As a first step, the new global CIO attempted to bring in some level of data standardization in chart-of-accounts, as a test case across the countries and legal entities. As expected there has been tremendous resistance from the local CTOs, each of them insisting their systems and practices are indeed the best.

The CIO knew he needed to centralize and integrate data governance as expeditiously as possible, and cautiously progress toward data standards, and data definitions before attempting something bigger like a global application rationalization and consolidation. As he embarked on the journey toward a globally integrated and centralized governance, the CIO realized he needs to *address the key concerns* (listed below) of different stakeholders, besides his own, in order to succeed:

Country management and CTOs

1. Minimal disruption of business with any new initiative.
2. Cannot compromise on time-tested local data standards, local work-flows, local IT policy among others and what it considers unique functional requirements of local management.
3. The country CTOs are also worried about losing independence.

Corporate top management

1. Would like to become the much talked about data-driven organi-zation at the earliest (the utopia they have been hearing about – insights backed by data to support every corporate decision they make – instant information on demand, real-time drill-down visibil-ity into the global operations of company for the top management, and automated statutory compliance, among others).
2. Smooth and eventless transition from localized governance to glob-ally integrated and centralized governance. Would prefer not to have a revolt by managements of different countries.
3. Expect the CIO to present a detailed roadmap and a business case as a must before kick-off.

CIO's personal concerns

1. Not easy to transition data governance from different countries to cor-porate headquarters. Expect stiff resistance from local management.
2. Quantifying the intangible benefits of investing into data gover-nance and creating a business case. There is no proven time-tested methodology.

The CIO is faced with the unenviable task of bringing in the much-needed uniformity in data standards, data definitions across the geographies, LoBs, and legal entities, so that data can be consolidated at the corporate level fairly quickly. The CIO is also expected to bring in a self-service analytics solution; a dashboard of corporate consolidated numbers, which can be drilled down right up to the transaction level. After much thought, and discussion with the country IT heads, the CIO formulated an action plan; the key initiatives listed below:

a) A global due diligence to identify, collate, and consolidate the master data, the metadata, data definitions among others (as they exist) from different locations across the enterprise.

b) Create comprehensive global data definitions and data standards covering the extended enterprise. Create Lookup tables linking global standards with local, where possible. Recognize the fact that varying degrees of granularity in data definitions may come in the way of covering all of master data, and all of metadata. Make compliance to global data standards mandatory.

c) Time-bound migration of entire portfolio of enterprise applications to the new global data standards and definitions. Use Lookup tables and Workarounds for data portability/inter-operability during the transition period.

d) Institute a centralized global data governance team that manages the enterprise metadata and master data. Invest in Master Data Management (MDM) and other data governance tools, and technologies.

e) Lay down an IT Policy, which among other things, should make it mandatory that any new application that gets developed must conform to global data standards.

f) Create a long-term IT strategy and plan for:

   • Global application rationalization and application consolidation.

   • Migrating myriad enterprise applications to a global single-instance ERP aligned with the long-term strategy of the enterprise.

   • Setting up a data-driven organization focusing on 10% of decision that drive 90% of business outcomes.

   • Create an enterprise data lake and implement an advanced analytics solution, complete with a self-service analytics platform.

While the top management appreciates the thought process behind the overall IT strategy, it insists there has to be a budget along with a business case, complete with internal rate of return (IRR) and net present value (NPV) estimates for the investment. The global CIO is now stuck with the task of estimating the dollar value returns, if any, from the proposed investment. The central question is how does one quantify the dollar value of returns from investing into data governance; the dollar value returns from incremental quality of data?

11.3 Recognizing Poor Data Governance: The Markers

Most CIOs claim they have a wonderful IT governance in place. To validate their claim, they either quote the best-in-class tools and technologies deployed in their companies, or the number of ITIL/COBIT certified people on their team. I have learned from experience not to question any claim made by CIOs, if I still intend to consult and get paid by them. So instead, I usually talk to their internal customers, especially people in their finance and accounts department. The finance teams are usually a bunch of CAs and CPAs; while not many understand the importance of IT and data governance, they sure can recount the issues they are facing in consolidating accounts, and the number of people employed, the time and effort it takes every month and every quarter for data reconciliation… a set of tell-tale indicators of poor data governance.

As a matter of fact, all is not well with the data quality of a company is easily recognizable from its symptoms. For example:

1. Substantially longer time to declare audited financial results at the end of the quarter.
   a. While the leading firms take two weeks or less, the companies suffering from poor data quality take anywhere between four and six weeks.
2. Cost of finance function as a percentage of revenue
   a. While the industry leading firms keep this number well below 1%, companies suffering from poor data quality are likely to record 3–4%, or even more.
   b. A 2015 Hackett Group survey mentions finance costs of world-class firms can be a mere 0.6% of revenue, while this number for organizations suffering from low data standards can be 1.64% of revenues… about 2.7 times the number of employees in the finance department… the incremental number employed just to make up for poor data quality.
3. A McKinsey white paper (Petzold et al., 2020) estimates that companies that suffer from poor data quality are likely to spend 30% of their time on non-value-added activities.

The table below provides a list of typical markers that indicate the state of data governance in the company (Table 11.1).

Similarly, there are some markers of reasonable-to-good data governance:

1. Globally centralized data governance with audit trail.
2. Global single instance ERP/centralized data lake.
3. Best in the market – data governance tools and technologies (assuming the quality of implementations are equally good).
4. Continuous and significant reduction in number of incidents/change requests reported per month.

Table 11.1 Data Governance: Markers of Good Governance vs. Poor Governance

Markers	"Good"	"Poor"
Time to audited financials every quarter end	<2 weeks	>4 weeks
Overheads as a percentage of revenue (overhead percentage)	Lowest in peer group	Highest in peer group
Administrative overheads as a percentage of revenue		
Finance function cost as percentage of revenue	<2%	>5%
Av. time to collate ad hoc global consolidated reports	<24 hours	>7 days
Excel sheet-based reports as percentage of total reports	<5%	>50%
# of people in accounts reconciliation in finance as percentage of total employees in finance function	2–5%	>20%
# of people in support functions building ad hoc reports as percentage of total	2–5%	> 20%
Av. percentage of employee time invested in non-value-added activities like data chasing and data reconciliation	<5%	>20%
IT – # of employees working in manual data cleaning and reconciliation as percentage of total	2–5%	>20%
Yearly IT budgets allocated for overhaul of older applications – as percentage of total budget	5–10%	>20%
Percentage of global transactions captured into IT applications in real time	>95%	<80%

In my experience, an organization could have all of the above and more, and yet may have serious gaps in governance protocols. It is better to institute a periodic audit and ensure constant vigilance.

11.3.1 Measuring Data Quality

Data quality is the measure of how accurately the data in the enterprise systems represents the true status of the organization; a single version of truth, complete in all respects, consistent, and up-to-date, and well-suited to serve its intended purpose.

Data quality refers to the quality of both enterprise master data, as well as the transactional data, that is, the data that gets posted into tables only through transactions: for example – sales orders, delivery challans, invoices get posted only when the relevant transactions are run on the enterprise applications like SAP. Master data on the other hand, can be directly added into the tables either through bulk uploads, or record-by-record, manually; for example – adding new customers into customer master, or adding new materials into material master. Given the multitude of enterprise applications that run in any large organization, any inconsistency in master data between different applications can be a serious source of repetitive errors.

It is largely true that if the quality of enterprise master data is managed well, the transactional data does automatically take care of itself; assuming all transactional data is posted into tables only through rule-driven transactions. However, even if all enterprise master data is completely in sync., it is still possible that manual errors do slip through into transactional data, especially if they do not get automatically detected through the set data validation rules.

11.3.2 Dimensions of Data Quality

Before we define metrics for measuring data quality, we must define the dimensions of data quality. Here is a list:

- **Completeness**: If the data that is provided is complete? Are there null values in a good percentage of table rows and fields?
- **Uniqueness/single version of truth**: If there is duplication of data that comes from multiple sources. If yes, do they match? And are such sources of data in sync with each other in real time?
- **Accuracy**: Does the data match the "reality" in the organization? How accurately does the data reflect the "reality of status" in the organization?
- **Timeliness**: Does the data reflect the current reality of the organization. Is there a time-lag between an event and the relevant data being captured into the organizational systems?
- **Validity**: Does the data confirm the validation standards defined in the systems and applications?
- **Compliance**: Is the data fully compliant with data standards, data definitions and other criteria defined as a part of data governance?

How exactly does one verify if the quality of the data within their company is poor? If it is poor, exactly how poor? While there are no measures for absolute value of data quality, a few metrics are popular when it comes to measuring the relative quality of data in different dimensions (Table 11.2).

Historically, there have been several attempts at creating global data standards, or industry data standards that are mandated to be followed by everyone

Table 11.2 Measuring Data Quality Sample Metrics

Sample Metrics	Measure
a) **Error percentage:** The percentage of errors measured in a sample data set.	Number of errors/Total number of records in the sample data set.
b) **Missing data percentage:** The percentage of number of records with null values in a sample data set.	Number of records with null values/Total number of records in the sample data set.
c) **Data Portability Error Percentage:** The percentage of records that fail the data validation tests in bulk uploads.	Number of records that failed data-validation rules/Total number of records in the sample data set.
d) **Data Replication Error Percentage***: The percentage of transactions that fail in batch-uploads.	Number of transactions that failed in batch-upload /Total number of transactions in the sample flat file.

*__Data Replication Error Percentage__ *usually refers to batch-upload of transactions being replicated from one or more downstream/upstream source applications to the centralized ERP such as SAP. For example, sales transactions from isolated point-of-sale applications get batch-uploaded into ERP – usually as flat files.*

within the jurisdiction, or everyone from the specific industry. These are usually aimed at ensuring easy portability of data across applications, and automated reporting of data into statutory data repositories, as mandated by the law. Examples include HIPAA standards aimed at automated portability of healthcare information from across providers, payers, and regulatory agencies. The IFRS (International Financial Reporting Standards) are global accounting standards and are mandated in over 140 jurisdictions across the world. The XBRL (extensible business reporting language) is a global XML taxonomy mandated for reporting financials. XBRL is machine readable and enables automated porting of data. ISO 8000 (Benson, 2008) is an emerging global standard for data quality, specifically for enterprise master data. It describes the standards and best practices to ensure data portability across systems and across locations. The standards are still evolving.

It takes time for data standards to take root, be accepted and adopted by organizations, even within an industry; and ensuring ongoing compliance is an even bigger issue. As of now, a good majority of Fortune 500 companies are struggling with their poorly implemented MDM solutions, ensuring that compliance to a set of master data standards itself is hard-fought battle every day.

11.4 The Cost of Poor Data Governance: Overshooting Overheads

Two similar sized, competing companies operating in the same market, but having a wide-ranging difference in profitability and revenue-per-employee is not uncommon, and at the outset it may appear quite normal given different companies operate at different productivity levels, besides being subject to other influencing factors such as relative pricing, manufacturing, and inventory policies.

However, if one digs a little deeper, tracing the difference in the profitability to *the significant* among different cost heads, one of the two companies is likely to have a larger number of employees, and consequently much larger employee overheads, more specifically, for supporting functions like finance, HR, payroll, and IT, among others. If one were to persevere and dig even deeper, one would notice the majority of such additional employees on rolls, are on rolls, essentially to handle just one activity – *data reconciliation*.

Poor data quality, almost always a result of poor data governance, leads to a large number of people employed in the completely avoidable activity of data reconciliation, as well as resulting in a far higher process lead time, and higher inventories, among others. Further, the managers are forced to take decisions purely based on their gut feeling, as they lose trust in data.

Instinctively, one may understand how poor data quality leads to a higher number of people employed just to handle reconciliations and to produce trustworthy data and reports through pure brute force. However, building a business case requires a foolproof methodology to estimate the dollar value of cost savings from investment in data governance (Figure 11.3).

I spent over two decades setting up and scaling shared services, and captives for multinationals. The two core reasons as to what originally triggered their interest and prompted these companies to consider setting up shared services were:

1. Spiraling overhead costs
2. Need for visibility (and control) into global operations

(A couple of decades ago, savings from offshoring also used to be a core reason, but not anymore. Most multinational companies have already outsourced the bulk of their transactional work to offshore vendors, so incremental dollar savings if any, are not significant).

The administrative overhead costs directly affect the bottom-line of the company, besides making any incremental expansion of the multinational into adjacencies (new products or new geographies) prohibitively expensive. Figure 11.4 below explains how

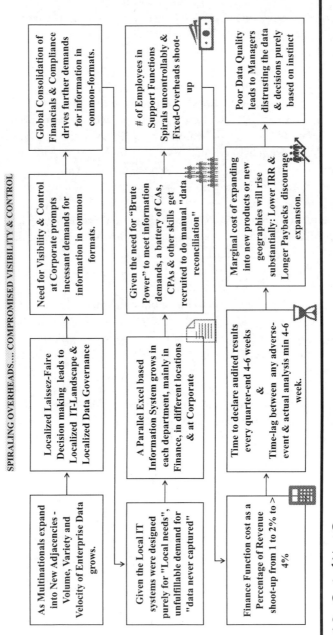

Figure 11.3 Cost of Non-Governance.

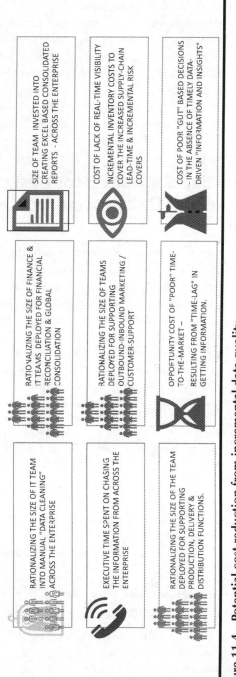

Figure 11.4   Potential cost reduction from incremental data quality.

spiraling overhead costs in multinationals, is essentially the result of decentralized and poorly designed data governance mechanisms.

I learned from experience that most CIOs are super-sensitive when it comes to any criticism on their governance model. While some told me: "Oh, we have a perfect governance mechanism in place, thank you" (meaning… mind your own business), a few others told me they used the best governance platform that money could buy, as if that closed all arguments on quality of governance in that organization (Figure 11.4).

While incremental data quality can definitely bring in productivity improvements and reduction in overheads, estimating such gains and assigning a dollar value is as difficult as accurately measuring absolute data quality.

11.5 Transformational Roadmap for Designing and Institutionalizing Data Governance: An Overview

Data governance essentially is about *deciding how to decide*: the bedrock of all decision-making in an organization. Organizations necessarily need to get their data governance right if they ever hope to get their decision-making right.

There are multiple approaches to designing and implementing an enterprise data governance program. A sizable number of experts advocate starting from developing a value statement and creating a business case and roadmap; others advocate starting with a discovery phase, followed by a "plan-and-build" phase, and finally a "grow-and-consolidate" phase. Institutionalizing data governance is usually a part of this phase.

Here is the sequence I personally recommend:

Step 1- Discovery Phase: Taking stock of existing investments in data governance has to be the first step. The outputs from this phase to include:

    a. "As-is" data catalog/data manifest/data dictionary.
    b. "As-is" status of data traceability and data lineage.
    c. "As-is" status of data standards, data definitions, data privacy, ownership, access among others.
    d. "As-is" status of data governance, existing investments into data governance.

Step 2- Value Definition Phase: Establishing a business case and broad roadmap – The data generated from discovery phase should help in assessment of the scope and the investment. The outputs expected from this phase include:

    e. Current state of data governance and value expected from investing into data governance.
    f. Gap analysis and scope of work ("to-be" analysis and defining future state of data governance in the organization).

g. Roadmap and business case for data governance.
h. Application priority and data priority assessment:
   - Identify the 20% of applications that account for 80% of business activities and business value.
   - The identity of the 20% of data that accounts for 80% of the enterprise business value.

Step 3- Plan-and-Build Phase: Create a detailed plan for implementing new data governance across the organization. The detailed project plan to follow the roadmap created in the earlier phase. The outputs expected from this phase include:

i. Project plan and implementation roadmap
   - List of initiatives, resources, investment
   - Prioritization, long-term vs. short-term
j. Interim data governance.
k. Reengineering the enterprise information architecture
   - The new data standards, data definitions among others
   - The new enterprise data manifest, data catalog and data dictionary
l. During build phase
   - Building status reports: periodic reports of plan vs. actual
   - Testing and acceptance report of the new enterprise data governance model.

Step 4- Grow-and-Consolidate Phase: In many organizations, the new global data governance gets implemented in central office and a few select regional offices to start with. The final solution is rolled out to the rest of the global offices in a phased manner. It is important to institutionalize data governance across the enterprise as a part of this phase.

11.6 Step 1: Discovery

The purpose of a discovery phase (or an "as-is" analysis) prior to designing and implementing data governance, is to map the data from across the enterprise and assess the current state of data quality through different stages of data life cycle.

Further, most organizations would have some pre-existing teams and technologies deployed in data governance, either as disconnected and isolated local teams in each geography, or in rare cases as one centralized global team. So, it is important to understand the existing data governance investments in terms of scope, functionality, successes/failures, and customer experiences before designing for enterprise-wide data governance initiatives. It is also equally important to understand the framework and tools available given the near unmanageable volume, velocity, and variety of data one has to deal with these days.

Creating a data catalog has to be the very first step in the discovery phase.

11.6.1 Data Catalog and Data Dictionary

Creating a data catalog and data dictionary has to be the very first step as a part of discovery phase, before implementing any data governance solution.

A data catalog is just another popular name for the enterprise data inventory. Many of the new age data quality management solutions, or data governance solutions have a feature for automatically creating a data catalog. For example: AWS Glue uses a crawler to discover, profile, and automatically create a data catalog; essentially an inventory of all metadata elements from the data lake as a separate table that can be edited and tagged for improved searchability. SAP Data Intelligence has a similar crawler functionality to create a data catalog. There are several other popular products like Atlan, Ataccama-ONE, Azure Purview, and Collibra, among others, which help create a consolidated data catalog from a data lake. The data catalog needs to be tagged, indexed, and fine-tuned further before creating a data dictionary. While a data crawler can help quickly create a data catalog from a complex data lake, it will still take substantial manual intelligence and effort to clean, correct, and tag the entire enterprise metadata inventory.

While many business intelligence (BI) solutions and big data platforms like Collibra provide interactive visualization of data lineage diagrams, I was particularly impressed by the functionality of SAP Information Steward, part of the SAP data governance solution. SAP's Information Steward promises a powerful search and drill-down of any data element in its data lineage, the tables and so on – a true 360 degrees view of any data element. The interactive visualization provided to navigate back and forth across the data lineage, right up to its source is particularly impressive.

11.6.2 Data Lineage and Data Traceability

Data lineage is a visual roadmap of each data element as it traverses through its data life cycle. Most of the popular data intelligence platforms provide data lineage diagrams – interactive visualizations of data, instant drill-down views, as data traverses through the enterprise landscape.

We defined the concept of a data manifest in chapter 1 of this book, as a data catalog along with the "from and to addresses" for each of the data elements, as data traverses through different stages of data life cycle. While the crawlers can be used to automatically detect data lineage as it exists – to get an "as-is" view – a comprehensive data manifest can help design a new improved "to-be" process. I have personally used a data manifest as an effective tool in a variety of assignments such as MDM implementations, and enterprise application-rationalization projects.

Here are two examples to explain what exactly *data traceability* is, and why it is important:

1. The US Government passed the Drug Supply Chain Security Act (DSCSA) in 2013 (Bernstein, 2013) a federal legislation unifying similar laws enacted by different states. The core purpose of the act is to ensure that any drug distributed in the USA and each of its ingredients can be traced back to its sources:

the manufacturers and specific batch numbers. The information is particularly useful for ensuring patient safety, specifically in cases where adverse events are reported, and to prevent counterfeit drugs being distributed on the market. The DSCSA act necessitated a complete overhaul of IT systems and data design in pharmaceutical companies, pharma distributors, pharmacies, hospitals and so on: the entire set of people involved in pharma supply chain. Each of the drugs batches being distributed needed to carry complete pedigree information, right from the origin of each of its components. There are similar compliance requirements imposed on food product companies as well.

2. The Big 4 accounting firms like Deloitte, PWC, Ernst & Young, and KPMG are the external auditors for a variety of multinationals, each of them listed in multiple countries. The external auditors are subject to substantial audit risk, given they need to verify millions of transactions every year, deal with difficult-to-check inventories held in upcountry (often inaccessible) locations, apart from the continuously evolving complexity of the business models. The more complex the business, the more the risk. The only method available to them to reduce the risk, is to collect as much *audit evidence* (see ISA 500 of the International Federation of Accounts (IFAC)) as they can. While it sounds simple, auditors work under tremendous time pressure, apart from the fact that collecting evidence is a time-consuming, manpower intensive exercise currently. Data traceability, a method to drill down the consolidated numbers on financial statements, to their origins and right up to individual transactions, can help external auditors to collect evidence quickly and without visiting each of the far flung locations. I came across a few recent academic papers advocating using of blockchain technology (Cheng & Huang, 2020) for auditing, to ensure not just data traceability, but also to reduce audit cost and improve the audit quality. ERP companies like SAP and Oracle have blockchain products, though it is unclear if they can help provide transparency in external legacy/cloud applications that exchange data with the ERPs.

In my experience, data traceability is possible only if such comprehensive and granular data has been captured, parsed-cleaned, indexed, and available in one's systems. While designing enterprise information architecture, providing for *end-to-end data traceability* as data traverses through different applications across the enterprise landscape is a difficult but unavoidable step, given the stringent compliance requirements in industry sectors such as food and pharmaceuticals.

11.7 Step 2: Value Definition

11.7.1 Prioritizing Data for Governance

Data governance costs money, besides substantial time, and effort from the key managers. Given there is a data explosion in most organizations, and since we know all data is not equally important, it makes sense to categorize and prioritize the data that absolutely needs governance, rather than spreading the resources thin and wide. The data governance needs to be focused on *the data that matters*.

How does one identify and prioritize the specific data that matters for governance? Here is a quick and easy method, that I employ:

1. Focus on the metadata and the master data that pertains to the 10% of applications that account for 90% of business transactions, and 90% of revenues of the company (I usually insist on an application-rationalization exercise prior to any enterprise-wide business transformation initiative).
2. Focus on the data and applications instrumental for statutory reporting and compliance.
3. Focus on the data that is accessed by employees from more than one location, more than one department, or more than a threshold number of employees.

The above method presupposes that the companies have the data from a detailed pareto analysis for their entire application portfolio; not just based on the number of transactions in the current year, but also on a variety of other parameters like:

- If management categorizes the applications as "vital, essential, or desirable".
- Number of employees accessing the applications.
- Revenues/geographical coverage of the applications...and so on.

If an organization has the necessary time and resources, it may attempt estimating the business value of data from across the enterprise landscape, and further identify the 20% of data that accounts for 80% of all business value as the core target for data governance. We have been hearing from everyone; from Gartner to people on the street tell us that data is the "new oil", but as of now most organizations consider data as a largely intangible and difficult to measure asset. While the problem is still not completely solved, there have been several notable attempts to create a framework for measuring the value of incremental data quality (if not the absolute economic value of data per se). I am limiting myself to the two popular approaches mentioned below:

> Gartner analysts, Ted Friedman and Michael Smith, in their article titled "Measuring the business value of data quality" (Friedman & Smith, 2011) posit that over 40% of business initiatives fail to achieve the intended objectives primarily because of poor data quality. They further estimate that poor data quality brings down the labor productivity by around 20%, besides seriously limiting the possibility of process automation. While the paper does not provide a method to estimate absolute value of data, they suggest using the Gartner Business Value Model (GBVM) to estimate the business value of incremental data quality.
>
> (Smith et al., 2006)

I was particularly impressed by the approach proposed in a recent article by David Nguyen– an economist in the OECD's Public Governance Directorate (Nguyen & Paczos, 2020). While a good part of the paper is devoted to cross-border dataflows, the article has a fresh perspective on measuring the economic value of data. Key pointers:

1. Distinguish between "data enhanced business" and "data enabled business". Identify the data that can be monetized, that can be used for launching new products or services, as different from the data that can be used for improving the profitability of the existing business, products, or services.
2. Identify the intended purpose of data to generate additional revenues either now or in future. Estimate the business value from selling raw-data or by launching new products or services leveraging such raw-data.
3. Four different approaches for financial/economic valuation of data as listed below: I believe each of the approaches mentioned are definitely doable, assuming the organization has the time and resources to take up such an elaborate exercise.
   • Market price of similar data, or
   • Cost of producing and distributing such data
   • Based on *value-added* or *value-generated* as data flows through data value-chain. The article estimates the value of data in Amazon Marketplace at US \$125 bn, or 16% of market value of Amazon back in 2020
   • *Comparing and correlating data flows* across organization value-chain with *significant addition of incremental business value*, such as incremental productivity or incremental new business.

The article also recommends analyzing the source and destination of the data from *data center to data center*, as different from *data center to actual-user*.

11.7.2 Creating a Business Case for Data Governance

Implementing and institutionalizing an enterprise-wide integrated data governance will always be a pathbreaking business-transformation exercise, involving reengineering of the entire enterprise data structure, the application portfolio, data standards, and data definitions. The initiative may also involve implementing data governance tools and technologies; MDM products like SAP, Tibco, or Informatica, and specialized enterprise data management platforms like Atlan, Enlighten, Miovantage, or Syniti (a few products rated highly by Gartner).

More often than not, implementing data governance is a part of a much larger enterprise business process transformation initiative, such as building a data-driven organization. There are no standard templates for creating a business case. An extended version of the approach used in chapter 6 is given in Figure 11.5.

While defining the scope and estimating the investment required is a relatively straightforward exercise, estimating the revenue (cash inflows) is the tricky part.

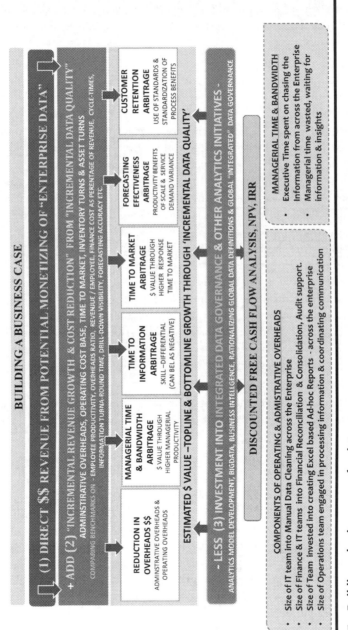

Figure 11.5 Building a business case for data governance.

One has to identify the data that can be monetized, before estimating the potential revenue from monetizing of such data. Incremental revenue growth and cost reduction from improved data quality, can only be "empirical estimates" at best. I have successfully estimated savings in procurement costs and reduction in inventory levels with improved data quality by comparing procurement lead time of different geographies with internal and external benchmarks.

In my experience, *the biggest and most visible cost-saving from incremental data quality comes from reduction in administrative and manufacturing overheads*; it is fairly simple to estimate the cost of people deployed for data reconciliation, data cleaning, and other such non-value-added activities. Further, the "incremental data quality" can mean a "material improvement" in the operating efficiency & the competitive advantage of the company, leading to "incremental profitability". Technically, it should be possible to correlate and measure the impact.

11.8 Step 3: Plan and Build

11.8.1 Components of Data Governance

The way most organizations are currently structured, "data governance" is a part of the larger IT governance framework. However, we may need to remember not all organizational data is structured, and a good part of it may reside outside of the IT systems, and consequently outside the purview of the IT governance. IT governance usually ignores any data that resides outside of the enterprise IT applications. Data governance, on the other hand, is about managing *all of the enterprise data, including the data that resides outside of the enterprise IT applications*; a good reason why organizations need a separate Chief Data Officer (CDO) (Figure 11.6).

It is also important to note that any attempt at localized data governance at legal entity level or at geography (country) level *is scripted for failure*. Extremely important is to make sure "data governance framework" covers the complete global organizational value-chain from the global head-quarters to right up to the branch offices of smallest region in the smallest country. In a nutshell, the data governance should encompass all data, both structured and unstructured, from every part of the organization.

Unstructured Data: The unstructured data is the tricky part, for two reasons:

1. The volume and the variety of the data can be extraordinarily large, depending on how many different data sources organization deems important, and how far into the past (time-line) the organization would consider analyzing.
2. There is no master data that needs to be carefully monitored in unstructured data. Instead, the governance should encompass:
   a. Picking and choosing what part of unstructured data is important for analysis.
   b. Given near 100% of unstructured data analysis will be processed through automated tools, picking-up the "right data" that needs to be mined depending on the context and purpose of analysis.

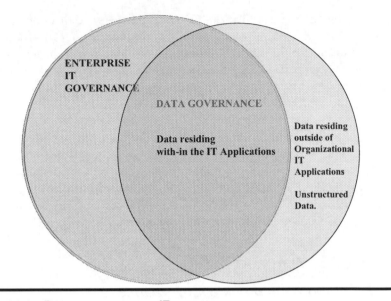

Figure 11.6 Data governance vs. IT governance.

(Note: There have been attempts to use AI and deep learning to identify the context-specific data and some claim such capability (Tskivin, 2021). But I believe even the best designed AI application may need to be monitored constantly to check if the training data being used continues to represent the actual contemporary business-context on the ground.)

Data on Cloud: Further, a typical multinational organization will have thousands of applications, some of the core applications on premises hosted on company-owned data centers, while a vast majority of them on the Cloud, the most preferable these days being AWS. The applications themselves are a veritable mix, from the standard ERP supply chain applications to thousands of web and mobile applications, some home-grown and a much larger number off-the-shelf, customized, and implemented.

These days a good number of applications are software as a service (SaaS) instances, hosted and managed by the SaaS application vendor. While a select few applications, like ERP, cover the entire enterprise, all geographic locations and product LoBs, a vast majority of them would have a limited footprint. limited to a specific country, legal entity, or product LoB (Table 11.3). So, the data governance should take cognizance of the following:

- Not all data is on premises; a good part of it may exist on SaaS applications on the Cloud.
- If there is a data lake (or warehouse) that stores the data from all applications on the Cloud including the SAS applications and social media.

Table 11.3 Components of Data Governance

Foot-Print Across Value-Chain	Type(s) of Data

1. All geographies:
 	
  a. Countries,
  b. Regions,
  c. Branch offices
 	
2. All legal entities:
 	
  a. Headquarters,
  b. Holding companies,
  c. Subsidiaries.
 	
3. All products in the portfolio
4. All lines of business
5. All departments
	All data (both structured and unstructured) residing in:
	
	1. All IT systems: IT applications, emails, websites, and so on.
	2. All documents – including physical documents.
	3. All social media platforms.
	4. Connected mobile applications.
	5. Connected devices.
	
	Any other internal or external data that organization deems necessary to collect and catalog, for any purpose including – reporting and analytics.

Sieve and funnel for:
Data that matters: look for 20% of data that accounts for 80% of business outcomes.

Prioritize data from:

- Applications that are used by multiple businesses, geographies.
- Applications that are used by more than (>) a threshold number of users.
- Applications that are current; avoid applications that are out of use.
- Applications that are vital to business, vital for compliance

Prioritize and select data elements that transcend multiple businesses, locations:

1. Master data from IT applications.
2. Metadata from across the organization.
3. Data standards, data definitions, data lineage.
4. Data creators, data owners, data consumers through the data life cycle.
5. Rights to the data – CRUD.
6. Mode and frequency of consolidation of transactional data.
7. Archiving, search and retrieve model – tags for keyword search.

(*Continued*)

Table 11.3 (Continued) Components of Data Governance

Foot-Print Across Value-Chain	*Type(s) of Data*
Data Governance Through Data Life Cycle	

I. Data Design: Master Data and Metadata
 	
 • Data definitions
 • Data standards
 • Data granularity
 • Data quality
 • Data validation rules
 • Data integration and interoperability
 • Data sovereignty
 • Data security (encryption standards)
    o In transit
    o At rest.
 • Data privacy
 • Data access management
 • Data lineage
 • Data manifest
 • Data traceability
	II. Data Creation
	
	   o Through upload of master data
	   o Through running transactions
	   o Through direct posting into tables
	
	 III. Data Propagation/Transfer
	
	   o Replication (extract-transform-load)
	   o Batch-upload (manual/automated period-driven)
	   o Realtime (event-driven)
	
	 IV. Data processing (run procedures – for e.g., MRP run)
	 V. Data storage (Data warehouse/data lake)
	 VI Data usage (reporting/analytics)
	 VII Data archiving (tag/replicate/archive)
	 VIII Data retrieval (search and retrieval)
	 IX Data repurposing
	 X Data destruction

Periodic Governance Audit	
• Compliance to laid-down governance policies of the enterprise. • A legal and statutory compliance audit, to cover areas such as compliance with privacy laws regarding personal information of customers, or employees posting confidential information on social media, or communicating information that could lead to insider-trading.	

11.8.2 Designing a New Enterprise Data Governance Framework

Designing and implementing a new enterprise data governance framework works like a typical BPR (business process reengineering) initiative. Key steps are listed below:

1. Complete enterprise information architecture: specifically, data models, master data, and metadata, will have to be rationalized and reengineered while simultaneously developing and documenting enterprise-wide data standards, and data definitions.

2. The global data standards may imply making changes to the data models of every legacy application-instance across the enterprise. Apart from ensuring commonality in data granularity, privacy, and access rights, it will be important to ensure standard data validation-rules apply across all applications.
3. It may mean implementing new software tools for:
    a. MDM and metadata management
    b. Document management
    c. Data/Information Life Cycle management (ILM)
    d. Digital Asset Management (DAM)
    e. Data lakes
    f. Data governance tools
    g. Governance, Risk, and Compliance (Enterprise GRC)

A typical model for designing and implementing enterprise data governance is given in Figure 11.7 the key is to identify 20% of the data that accounts for 80% of business transactions and business value, so that the entire governance effort can be focused on the "data that matters", rather than spreading the time and effort, thin and wide. Designing the new enterprise data governance framework will become a guided process if it is combined with implementing one of the popular enterprise data governance platforms like.

Most of the data governance software vendors in the market cover near-complete functionality mentioned above. Examples include SAP, IBM, Erwin, Informatica, and Atlan. Now it is possible to manage the enterprise structured data with zero incidents, assuming the right software is implemented, (and implemented well), and assuming all the legacy application data has been curated, tagged, and migrated into the new enterprise data model.

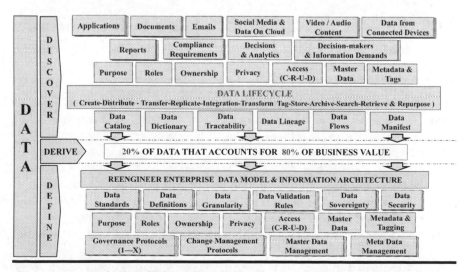

Figure 11.7 Designing data governance.

However, *managing unstructured data is still an evolving area.* One key reason being, while documents/files can be tagged, and it is possible to search and retrieve a particular document, it is not always possible to search for specific content within a document. For example, a large publisher having thousands of books (ISBNs) can search across ISBNs but searching within an ISBN for specific content is possible only if the book is available in the form of an XML file conforming to a standard DTD, and if such XML files are loaded and available on an XML database like MarkLogic. However, most of the legacy content that exists in corporates, exists in the form of Word documents or untagged PDFs at best. Migrating petabytes of legacy content into a standard XML format is not exactly feasible or economical. Similarly, most of the enterprise video/audio files cover and pertain to multiple subject areas, and with each file running into hours, it would be impossible to specifically tag sections of video file, and assign owners, privacy, and access rights for each section. There are a few new promising tools hitting the market, like Aprigo Ninja, claiming capabilities to provide automated visibility and governance for unstructured data assets on Cloud like Google-docs. Even if there are newer tools for automated segmentation and tagging of unstructured data, I would assume substantial human effort would still be required for testing and correction, and for assigning ownership, privacy, and access rights.

One perhaps needs to assume that a good percentage of the 20% of data that accounts for 80% of the business value is *structured*, unless one could clearly identify *unstructured data assets* with proven financial value; and such *unstructured data assets* are tagged and made available on a DMS (document management system) like Documentum, or in a data lake. Meanwhile, it will be prudent to focus the data governance effort on *the enterprise data that can be governed.*

11.9 Step 4: Grow and Consolidate – Institutionalizing Data Governance

11.9.1 Pilot and Roll Outs

As in the case of any other enterprise-wide transformational initiative, it would be prudent to set up a pilot to test run the new enterprise governance framework before rolling out across the global locations. The typical process for rolling out the enterprise data governance is given below:

1. Build a global template for institutionalizing data governance.
2. Implement at a pilot site:
   - Important to cover end-to-end value-chain as a part of the pilot.
   - So, the pilot site has to include the global headquarters + one or more geographies, as needed.
   - Centralized enterprise data governance team operating out of headquarters.

3. Test and fine tune the global template. The test cases will have to be custom-developed for each company. A few examples below:
   - Quality tests for random samples of data (both master data and transaction data).
   - Count of errors in integrations, transaction replications, data uploads, accounts consolidation, and so on that can be traced to master data mismatch.
   - Search and retrieve efficiency for specific data.
   - Marked reduction in the need for accounts reconciliations, or data reconciliations between the pilot geographies and headquarters.
   - The measures like *time to declare audited financial results* after the end of the quarter indicate marked improvement in the quality of data.
4. Roll out across global locations:
   - Important to accommodate geography specific increments in master data and metadata.
   - Important to accommodate geography-specific differences in areas such as statutory compliance requirements.

11.9.2 Institutionalizing Data Governance

Institutionalizing data governance is best achieved through implementing data governance software. For example: an MDM module can help restrict the access to master data to select individuals.

Institutionalizing data governance requires three essentials:

1. Clearly laid down, documented policies, accessible to all stakeholders:
   - Data standards, definitions, ownership, and access rights.
   - Integrated and centralized governance mechanism for defining the metadata and master data.
   - Centrally located full-time GCs (Governance Committees) with global jurisdiction.
   - Issue resolution mechanism (incident management and escalation protocols) and so on.
2. A mandatory workflow that should be used for making any changes to the enterprise metadata or master data.
3. A mechanism for monitoring and reporting the compliance to policy framework laid down, in real time.
   - Reporting and red-flagging any non-compliance.
   - Reporting the data quality errors that are systemic, stemming out of governance failure.

Most of the data management software from SAP, IBM, and Oracle stables, or the ones from new age vendors like Ataccama, or Collibra come with a full set of features for institutionalizing data governance. But, in my experience, *any software is only as good as how it is implemented.* Engaging a set of techno-functional consultants with a deep understanding of data flows through different stages of the extended enterprise value-chain, key decision points, compliance requirements and so on, is a must.

11.10 Data Governance for Big Data: Emerging Trends

11.10.1 *The Growing Importance of Data Governance for the AI Economy*

The McKinsey Institute believes AI (artificial intelligence) has the potential to add about $13 trillion to the global economy by 2030 through improvements in productivity, products, and customer experiences (Bughin et al., 2018). While the number is debatable, no one disputes the value and the potential of AI. I believe AI/ML (machine learning) has the potential to transform the way organizations function in the future; those few organizations which adopt AI/ML well and early will be able to improve their productivity multifold, while reducing their staffing costs and overheads to a fraction of what they currently operate at.

Since 2030 is almost here, the transformational journey toward becoming data-driven organizations is not just a source of competitive advantage anymore; it is a survival necessity, if the organizations intend to prepare themselves for the AI economy. And, since the effectiveness of AI essentially depends on data – the quality and richness of the data that organizations produce – institutionalizing data governance will be the key to managing and maintaining the data quality and preparing the organization for the AI economy.

On the other hand, *AI can help drive data governance*, specifically for unwieldy and the unstructured big data. Deep learning technology can be very effective for automation of clustering and classification of big data, automatically assigning the metadata tags, assessing ownership, privacy, risk, and so on.

11.10.2 *Data Lakehouse*

As mentioned earlier, while a data warehouse is essentially used to store structured enterprise data, a data lake is used for storing all data, both structured and unstructured: the big data. There is supposed to be a treasure trove of information and insights in hitherto rarely analyzed data formats – for example, pictures, videos, documents, emails, social media data, and so on. In theory, a properly implemented advanced analytics solution sitting on top of a data lake, can access and analyze the raw unstructured data to produce valuable insights. But in reality, most data lakes end up becoming data dump-yards… a place where all data from across the organization gets dumped, with the hope that someday someone will find a use for it.

A data lakehouse is a new, emerging concept that combines the best of both data warehouse and data lake. The idea is to provide a structure and schema even for the unstructured data being stored in the data lakehouse, a layered architecture with a data warehouse layer on top of the data lake. Obviously, this would involve classification and clustering of the data using AI/ML algorithms, and automatically creating one or more metadata layer(s) to help the speed and efficacy of the search and retrieval process. As I understand it, a few data lake vendors offer this architecture (including AWS and data bricks). While popular business authors like Bernard Marr (Marr, 2022) are quite excited about the prospects of this new architecture, a few are skeptical.

While I do agree with Bernard Marr, I believe **the real solution would lie in creating a standard structure for all digital assets right at the source**. For example:

- All emails could conform to a standard XML format and the same could be stored in a data lakehouse. Right now, organizations use NLP algorithms or parser-engines (like Zapier) to automatically detect patterns in emails.
- All documents could be created on a Collaborative enterprise-authoring platform that automatically creates and stores an XML in the data lakehouse. A few years back, I mentored a start-up working on a "collaborative-authoring-platform" on cloud, that automatically creates an XML file in the backend conforming to a predefined DTD & tags and stores the file in an XML database like MarkLogic. (Contract-management platforms create and store an XML in the backend).
- Video-audio files could be segmented and tagged while being produced, or while being edited. (RSS feeds are a common an example of segmentation and tagging of unstructured data.)

I would think a good part of data governance of future organizations would involve managing the XML engines and the metadata.

11.11 The Evolving Role of a CDO

Is there an absolute need to recruit a dedicated Chief Data Officer? Here are the key reasons why I think it is a must:

1) Most organizations are now talking about monetizing the data, a step beyond using the data as an enabler of higher productivity and competitive advantage in the market. High availability of relevant and quality data is a survival necessity for organizations. More and more organizations are recruiting a dedicated CDO as an investment into managing the all important asset, the data.
2) Like I mentioned earlier in this chapter, not all organizational data is structured, and a good part of it does reside outside of the IT systems, and

consequently outside the purview of the IT governance. Since data governance is about managing all of the relevant data, including the much larger unstructured data that resides outside of the enterprise IT applications, i.e. the data hitherto unexploited for analytics, many organizations feel a dedicated CDO needs to be brought on board to take the responsibility for all data; not just the enterprise data residing in IT applications. The unstructured data outside of the enterprise IT systems may account for 80–90% of all data for many organizations.

3) Sheer size of the data. Not just the volume, but also the variety, and velocity. From video-audio files to billions of emails, social media data … the variety and volume is not just unmanageable, but also beyond the bandwidth of the regular IT team, trained and deployed to take care of enterprise data alone.

4) Artificial Intelligence and data-driven decision-making, are going to be the key sources of competitive advantage for organizations of future; and the efficacy of AI and data-driven decision-making will be dependent on the availability of quality data.

Many books and articles that I have referred to strongly recommend setting up the office of a CDO, as if it is a mantra for institutionalizing data governance in the organization. While the recruitment of a CDO does definitely mark the increasing importance given to data, lack of role-clarity between a CDO and CIO could be disastrous. Some organizations also have the role of a Chief Digital Officer complicating the matters even further. I personally believe a CDO can deliver on data governance, if and only if, there is sufficient enabling investment in the process, the tools, and the compliance mechanism, as well as stakeholders buy-in.

Bibliography

Addagada, T. (2021). Five data governance trends for digital-driven business outcomes in 2021. Datavarsity.net, Jan 14, 2021.

Azcoitia, S. A., Paraschiv, M., & Laoutaris, N. (2020). Computing the relative value of spatio-temporal data in wholesale and retail data marketplaces. arXiv preprint arXiv:2002.11193.

Benson, P. (2008). NATO codification system as the foundation for ISO 8000, the international standard for data quality. Oil IT Journal.

Bernstein, I. B. (2013). Drug supply chain security act. (Eds.): "Book Drug Supply Chain Security Act" (2017, edn.).

Biery, M-E., Sageworks Stats (2014). A sure-fire way to boost the bottom line. Forbes.com, Jan 2014.

Bughin, J., Seong, J., Manyika, J., Chui, M., & Joshi, R. (2018). Notes from the AI frontier: Modeling the impact of AI on the world economy. McKinsey Global Institute.

Cheng, C., & Huang, Q. (2020, January). Exploration on the application of blockchain audit. In *5th International Conference on Economics, Management, Law, and Education (emle 2019)* (pp. 63–68). Atlantis Press.

Coyle, D., Diepeveen, S., & Wdowin, J. (2020). *The Value of Data Summary Report.* The Bennett Institute, Cambridge.

Friedman, T. & Smith, M. (2011). Measuring the business value of data quality. Gartner Research, Oct 10, 2011.

Galer, S. (2019). SAP tackles food safety with blockchain breakthrough. news.sap.com, Oct 2019.

Glue-Reply.com (n.d.) The valuation of data as an asset: a consumption-based approach.

Hagiu, A., & Wright, J. (2020). When data creates competitive advantage. *Harvard Business Review*, 98(1), 94–101.

Hubbard, D. W. (2014). *How to Measure Anything: Finding the Value of Intangibles in Business.* John Wiley & Sons.

Kim, O. K., Park, J., Park, C. W., & Cho, W. S. (2021). Data asset valuation model review. *The Journal of Bigdata*, 6(1), 153–160.

Knight, M. (2021a). Managing data governance throughout the data lifecycle. *Data Varsity*, April 20, 2021.

Knight, M. (2021b). Top nine data governance trends in 2021. *Datafloq.com*, June 16, 2021.

Lawton, G. (2019). How Bumble Bee is using SAP blockchain for food traceability. TechTarget, March 2019.

Leatherberry, T. & Mears, R. (2010). Data as an asset: Balancing the data ecosystem. The Fourth MIT Information Quality Industry Symposium. Jun 14–16, 2010.

Loshin, D. (2011). *Understanding the Financial Value of Data Quality Improvement.* Whitepaper sponsored by for Informatica Inc., January 2011.

Marr, B. (2022). What is a data lakehouse? A Super-Simple Explanation For Anyone. Bernardmarr.com, Jan 31, 2022.

Nguyen, D., & Paczos, M. (2020). Measuring the economic value of data and cross-border data flows: A business perspective. *OECD Digital Economy Papers*, No. 297, OECD Publishing, Paris, https://doi.org/10.1787/6345995e-en.

Open Data Science (2019). Data Valuation - What is your data worth and how do you value it?. *Medium.com* available at: https://odsc.medium.com/data-valuation-what-is-your-data-worth-and-how-do-you-value-it-b0a15c64e516

Petzold, B., Roggendorf, M., Rowshankish, K., & Sporleder, C. (2020). Designing data governance that delivers value. McKinsey Digital. Available at: https://www.mckinsey.com/business-functions/mckinsey-digital/our-insights/designing-data-governance-that-delivers-value

Saxena, A. (2019). What is data value, and should it be viewed as a corporate asset?. Datavarsity.net, Mar 18, 2019.

Smith, M., Audrey, A., & Mitchell, R. (2006). The Gartner Business Value Model: A Framework for Measuring Business Performance–mayo ID Research Number: G00139413 USA.

Sharpe, W. (1964). Capital asset prices: A theory of market equilibrium under conditions of risk. Journal of Finance, 19(3), 425–442.

Stedman, C., & Vaughan, J. (2020). What is data governance and why does it matter?. Techtarget.com, Feb 2020.

The Handbook of International Standard on Auditing 500 on Audit Evidence. IFAC.org, 2009. International Auditing and Assurance Standards Board (IAASB) – part of IFAC. https://www.iaasb.org/consultations-projects/audit-evidence

Tskivin, B. (2021). AI transforming unstructured data governance. The Data Administration Newsletter, Jul 7, 2021. Available at: https://tdan.com/author/btsivkin001

Index

Pages in *italics* refer figures and **bold** refer tables.

Printed in the United States
by Baker & Taylor Publisher Services